Spirit of Nobility

Sermons on the Weekly Torah Portion

Leviticus, Numbers, and Deuteronomy

Michael Scharf
Publication Trust
Yeshiva University Press
RIETS

מגיד
MAGGID

Rabbi Aaron Levine

SPIRIT OF NOBILITY

SERMONS ON THE WEEKLY TORAH PORTION

LEVITICUS, NUMBERS, AND DEUTERONOMY

The RIETS Hashkafah Series
Rabbi Daniel Z. Feldman, Series Editor

The Michael Scharf Publication Trust of
Yeshiva University Press

Maggid Books

Spirit of Nobility
Sermons on the Weekly Torah Portion
Leviticus, Numbers, and Deuteronomy

First Edition, 2020

Maggid Books
An imprint of Koren Publishers Jerusalem Ltd.

POB 8531, New Milford, CT 06776-8531, USA
& POB 4044, Jerusalem 9104001, Israel
www.maggidbooks.com

The publication of this book was made possible through the generous support of *The Jewish Book Trust.*

ISBN 978-1-59264-560-2, *hardcover*

A CIP catalogue record for this title is available from the British Library

Printed and bound in the United States

In loving memory of
Sarah Levine

Contents

Foreword xiii

Preface xv

LEVITICUS

VA-YIKRA

The Source of the Error in Judgment 5

Paternalism in Jewish Law 10

SHEMINI

I Will Be Sanctified through Those Who Are Close to Me 16

Torah from Heaven 21

Subversion of the Dietary Laws 25

Yom Ha-Atzma'ut 28

The Test of the Strength of One's Kevod ha-Torah 32

Moral Vegetarianism and Halakhah 36

TAZRI'A

The Birth and Development of a Nation 42

He Will Know that There Is a Prophet in Israel 47

METZORA

Death and Life Are in the Hands of the Tongue 54

The Moral Climate of Society 59

Mayor Koch's Dilemma 62

AḤAREI MOT–KEDOSHIM

The Building Blocks of the Good Society 68

Love Your Fellow as Yourself – This Is the Entire Torah 73

Plant Closings 77

The Ḥok Test for the Gentile Society 81

Rights or Duties? 84

His Mercies Are on All His Works 87

EMOR

Hallel on Yom Ha-Atzma'ut 92

Kindness in Truth, and Truth in Kindness 97

The National Holocaust Museum 101

BE-HAR

The Double Standard of Morality 108

The Relevance of Shemittah Today 113

BE-ḤUKKOTAI

The Value of Human Life 118

NUMBERS

BE-MIDBAR

Retirement in Jewish Law 126

Achieving Optimality in the Service of the Levites 131

The Two Desert Trips 135
The Hypothetical Acceptance of the Torah 138

NASO

From the Strong Came Forth Sweetness 142
The Limits of the Instrument of Truth: Polygraphs 146
Prohibition of Profiting from Crime 150
Fulfilling a Fantasy 154

BE-HA'ALOT'KHA

Why Should We Be Diminished? 160
The Ideal Community of Public Servants 163
Humility 167

SHELAḤ LEKHA

A Land That Devours Its Inhabitants 174
The Hysterical Personality 178
The Devastation of an Evil Report 181

KORAḤ

The Sons of Korach Did Not Die 186
Peace for the Sake of Heaven 191
Merciful in Judgment 195
Blossoms before Leaves 198

ḤUKKAT

Because You Did Not Believe in Me to Sanctify Me 202
Let Them Hatch Plots 207

BALAK

How Goodly Are Your Tents, O Jacob 212

PINḤAS

One Nation under God 218

The Two Temidim 221

MATOT

According to Whatever Comes from His Mouth Shall He Do 226

DEUTERONOMY

EKEV

What Is One Born of a Woman Doing among Us? 234

Reb Meir's One Hundred Club 238

RE'EH

Charity 244

SHOFTIM

Social Outrage 250

KI TETZE

I Have Strayed Like a Lost Sheep; Seek Out Your Servant 256

One Mitzvah Leads to Another 260

The Work of Amalek Today 264

KI TAVO

The Three Keys 270

The Reproof 274

NITZAVIM–VA-YELEKH

Producing Fear of Heaven in Public 278

HA'AZINU

Full Containers and Leaking Buckets 284

EPILOGUE

Kaddish Gadol 288

Glossary 291

Bibliography 307

Name Index 317

Subject Index 327

Foreword

Rabbi Dr. Aaron Levine was a quintessential gentleman and scholar, embodying the values of Torah virtue and ethical behavior that he taught in his classes and writings. He was a world-renowned economist who served as the Samson and Halina Bitensky Professor of Economics at Yeshiva University, and as the editor of *The Oxford Handbook of Judaism and Economics*. His published works, including *Free Enterprise and Jewish Law*, and *Case Studies in Jewish Business Ethics*, are considered classics in the domain of Jewish business ethics and law.

In addition, Rabbi Levine served as the Rabbi of a synagogue in Brooklyn for many years, during which time he inspired his congregation with homilies on the Torah portion of the week and on the Festivals, providing timely commentary on the topics of our times. As the grandson and namesake of the Reisher Rav, a preeminent Polish scholar who was the author of *Ha-Derash ve-ha-Iyyun*, a masterful collection of insights into the Torah, Rabbi Levine adroitly continued his family tradition of extracting penetrating ideas and lessons from the weekly Torah portions.

This book, edited with love by his family, is a compilation of Rabbi Levine's sermons on the weekly Torah portion that he delivered in his synagogue. Each essay is a self-standing gem, offering timeless wisdom in both scholarly and succinct fashion. Rabbi Levine's penchant for academic precision, combined with his reverence for the word of God, enabled him to convey an authentic Torah Weltanschauung for the complex political and socioeconomic challenges of the modern age. We are now all able to be beneficiaries of these pithy pearls of perspicacity.

The Talmud (*Ḥagigah* 15b) teaches us: אם דומה הרב למלאך ה' צבקות יבקשו תורה מפיהו ואם לאו אל יבקשו תורה מפיהו, "if the Rabbi resembles an angel of God, then learn Torah from his lips, but otherwise do not learn Torah from his lips." One only had to gaze at Rabbi Levine's countenance to recognize the face and demeanor of an angel. Those of us who were privileged to be his students can attest that he was a man who occupied a special plane of holiness. This book, endowed with the beauty of the words that once emerged from Rabbi Levine's lips, is similarly blessed with the sanctity of his spirit.

It is thus with great pleasure that we present this important volume in homiletics as the latest installment in the RIETS Press series. We are of course indebted to our indefatigable executive editor, Rabbi Daniel Feldman, as well as to the past and present visionaries and architects of the RIETS Press, former Presidents Rabbi Dr. Norman Lamm and Richard M. Joel, President Rabbi Dr. Ari Berman, Rabbi Zevulun Charlop, and RIETS Dean Rabbi Menachem Penner. It is through their herculean efforts on behalf of the Yeshiva that we continue to imbibe the fruits of YU and RIETS scholarship.

Rabbi Yona Reiss
Director, RIETS Press

Preface

With deep gratitude to Hashem, we present this volume of sermons of our dear father, Rabbi Dr. Aaron Levine, *zt"l.*

A renowned authority on Jewish business ethics, Rabbi Dr. Levine was the Samson and Halina Professor of Economics at Yeshiva University. A paragon of *Torah u-madda,* he published widely on the interface between economics and Jewish law, particularly as it relates to public policy and modern business practices.

Rabbi Dr. Levine was also a distinguished pulpit rabbi, toiling tirelessly in the rabbinate for nearly thirty years. In his sermons, he would urge his congregants to seize nobility, to leap toward greater achievement in religious observance and refinement of character. In his personal conduct, he was the very embodiment of those ideals.

This volume is a selection of Rabbi Dr. Levine's sermons on the weekly Torah portion, transcribed from his manuscripts dating from 1982 to 2011.

We extend our heartfelt gratitude to Rabbi Yona Reiss for including this volume in the works published under the auspices of the Rabbi Isaac Elchanan Theological Seminary of Yeshiva University, and for his eloquent and meaningful Foreword. To Rabbi Daniel Z. Feldman, we express our sincere appreciation for his enthusiasm toward this work and his steadfast devotion in shepherding it though the publication process.

To Matthew Miller, Rabbi Reuven Ziegler, Ashirah Firszt, Tomi Mager, Ita Olesker, Shira Finson, and Caryn Meltz of Maggid Books, we extend a special note of thanks for their thoughtfulness, dedication, and professionalism in bringing this book to publication.

Rabbi Dr. Levine was born on the second day of Passover and passed away on the first day of Passover. On Passover, we observe the mitzvah of *haggadah,* the telling of the story of the Exodus, so that we can feel as if we ourselves had gone out of Egypt. As Rabbi Dr. Levine noted, "We are bidden to somehow leap the generations and touch the lives of our ancestors, to make the biblical figures come alive and vicariously feel their pain and triumph, to feel the birth pangs of a nation of Hashem."

May the recounting of these sermons strengthen our Jewish identity and commitment to the Torah, connecting us not only with our father, the author of this work, but with the previous generations, back to Abraham, Isaac, and Jacob.

Family of Rabbi Dr. Aaron Levine, *zt"l*

Leviticus

Va-Yikra

The Source of the Error in Judgment

March 10, 1984

In our scale of values, a transgression committed by the entire nation certainly evokes a deeper feeling of shock and dismay than when the same transgression is committed by a single person. Yet with regard to the most serious of transgressions, one that if committed intentionally invokes the penalty of *karet,* the Torah equates the atonement process for the nation with that of an individual. Accordingly, if the highest Jewish court of seventy-one errs in judgment in such a matter, and the majority of the nation follows the ruling and sins, each of the Twelve Tribes must offer a *par*. The blood of the offering is sprinkled in a unique and peculiar manner. The exact procedure is prescribed for the High Priest. If he errs in judgment and follows his own ruling and sins, he must bring the sin-offering of the bull of the anointed Priest.[1]

1. Leviticus 4:3–12.

More disturbing is that the transgressions are not at all comparable. The High Priest follows his own error and commits a misdeed. He is therefore at fault. Now, if the Supreme Court of the Jewish people issues a ruling, what fault is it of the people who follow the ruling? While the Sanhedrin is the one that brings the sacrifice, why does the financing of the sacrifice fall on the shoulders of each individual of the Twelve Tribes rather than the national treasury?

Perhaps the first question helps answer the second. By focusing on the life of an individual, whose role in life is very defined, the nexus between the intellectual error of the Sanhedrin and the culpability of the nation can be understood.

The High Priest is the highest representative of the Jewish nation. His mission is clearly to exude a profound love for his fellow Jew, fostering the most idyllic interpersonal relationships.[2] He is the man whose death returns the unintentional manslayer from the city of refuge,[3] so as to say that he, the High Priest, is held responsible in some very indirect way for even the most contemptible attitude towards human life.[4] If he would have been a little more zealous and enthusiastic in carrying out his mission of being an *ohev ha-bri'ot*, the moral climate of society would have been different and the contemptible attitude of the manslayer would not have been the reality.

The High Priest affects the moral climate of society. He is the man who carries the Ineffable Name on his forehead, the name of Hashem that protrudes in a visible manner,[5] and also carries the Ineffable Name in the folds of the Breastplate,[6] recessed, invisible to the eye, personifying perfection in action and in motive. If this man made an error in judgment and sinned following his erroneous concept of the law, the

---

2. See Mishnah, *Avot* 1:12.
3. Numbers 35:25.
4. See R. Solomon b. Isaac (*Rashi*, France, 1040–1105), *Rashi* ad loc., s.v. "*ad mot Kohen Gadol*"; *Makkot* 11a.
5. Exodus 28:36 (specifying that the words "*koshesh la-Hashem*" (holy to Hashem) are to be inscribed on the golden headplate of the High Priest); *Shabbat* 63b.
6. *Rashi* to Exodus 28:30; Nahmanides to Exodus 28:30; R. Yom Tov Ishbili (*Ritva*, Spain, ca. 1250–1330), *Ḥiddushei ha-Ritva*, *Yoma* 73b.

genesis of his error must have been his failure in fulfilling his role of "loving people and bringing them closer to the Torah."[7]

To drive home to him his failure, he is told to carry the blood of the sin offering deep into the Sanctuary, bypassing the *mizbe'aḥ ha-ḥitzon,* where the blood of all sacrifices was usually sprinkled.[8] First the blood is sprinkled seven times facing the *parokhet,* the dividing curtain between the Holy and the Holy of Holies, between the Staves of the Ark.[9]

What does this symbolize? What sentiment is thereby evoked? Two symbols of the Torah reside in the Tabernacle. One is the Menorah. The Menorah symbolizes the seven branches of wisdom, all turned toward the center, the *ner ha-ma'aravi,*[10] signifying the supremacy of the Torah as wisdom.[11] But one who has the love of Torah to realize its supremacy as wisdom is asked to produce an even deeper love for the Torah and direct his mind toward the Ark in the Holy of Holies, where the Torah stands completely alone, with no other appurtenances. And even with regard to the Staves of the Ark, it is said that the Ark carried its bearers.[12] The High Priest fixates on the singularity of the Torah in life, a higher level of love for the Torah.

---

7. Mishnah, *Avot* 1:12.
8. Leviticus 4:5.
9. Leviticus 4:6.
10. Lit., "the western lamp." The middle lamp is called the western lamp because its lip, upon which the wick rested, faced west, toward the Curtain of Testimony and the Holy of Holies. *Rashi* to *Shabbat* 22b, s.v. "*ner ma'aravi*" (second opinion); *Rashi, Kitvei Yad, Menaḥot* 86b, s.v. "*ner ma'aravi.*" This explanation follows the opinion that the lamps of the Menorah were lined up from north to south. Another opinion is that the lamps of the Menorah ran from east to west, and the "*ner ma'aravi*" was the second lamp to the east. According to that opinion, the second lamp was called the "western lamp" because it was to the west of the most eastern lamp. *Rashi* to *Shabbat* 22b, s.v. "*ner ma'aravi*" (first opinion); *Rashi* to *Menaḥot* 86b, s.v. "*hayah madlik.*"
11. R. Bahya b. Asher (*Rabbeinu Beḥaye,* Saragossa, 1255–1340), *Rabbeinu Beḥaye al ha-Torah,* Exodus 25:31; R. Isaac b. Judah Abrabanel (Portugal, 1437–1508), Exodus 25:31; R. Meir Loeb b. Jehiel Michel Weisser (*Malbim,* Poland, Romania, and Russia, 1809–1879), *Terumah, Rimzei ha-Mishkan;* R. Naphtali Tzvi Yehudah Berlin (*Netziv,* Russia, 1816–1893), *Ha'amek Davar,* Exodus 37:19.
12. *Sotah* 35a; *Rashi* to II Samuel 6:7.

The genesis of the High Priest's sin is not his intellectual drive. It is that something is missing in the love of Torah, the little extra awe and reverence and love that derive from the belief in the singularity of the Torah in our lives. One source of his error in judgment is a failure in the love of Torah.

But then he turns with the blood toward the Golden Altar and sprinkles the blood on the four corners of the Altar. Apart from this instance, the Golden Altar is never used for sprinkling blood. It is used for bringing the *ketoret.*[13] The Golden Altar represents the perfect harmony of all the various elements of the Jewish people, including the *ḥelbbenah,* which was a putrid-smelling herb.[14] All the elements amalgamated and produced a *re'ah niho'aḥ* (pleasing fragrance), rising straight up as a stick, not scattered in all directions.[15] The High Priest, whose robe carried the *pa'amonim* (bells), which effected atonement for *lashon ha-ra,* sprinkles blood on the Golden Altar, which also effected atonement for *lashon ha-ra* with the bringing of the *ketoret.*[16]

Now, why is there a need for two atonements for *lashon ha-ra*? The answer is that there are two different types of *lashon ha-ra*. One is the matter that has a *kol,* for which the *pa'amonim* provide atonement.[17] This is the *lashon ha-ra* that has a very discernable voice. It is the maligning of our fellow Jew when the motive is hatred.

But the man who exudes human warmth to such an extent with his *pa'amonim* is asked to go a bit deeper and display an even more profound love. This is the force against *lashon ha-ra she-be-ḥashai* of the *ketoret.*[18] It is the maligning of a fellow Jew that we feel is justified. The Children of Israel said to Moses and Aaron after the 250 followers of Korach were killed with the test of *ketoret,* "You have killed the people of Hashem" (Numbers 17:6). They thought that they were justified. It is the deeper love that we expect of the High Priest.

---

13. Exodus 40:26–27.
14. Exodus 30:34; *Rashi* ad loc., s.v. "*ve-ḥelbbenah.*"
15. *Yoma* 53a. See also *Yoma* 38a.
16. *Zevaḥim* 88b.
17. *Yoma* 44a; *Zevaḥim* 88b; *Arakhin* 16a.
18. The *ketoret* is referred to as a *davar she-be-ḥashai,* "something in private," because it was offered by the designated Priest in private. *Yoma* 44a; *Zevaḥim* 88b; *Arakhin* 16a.

Now, what is judgment? It is the decision to reject one idea and assimilate another idea in the analysis. It is the process of the integration and alienation of ideas. If an error was made on an intellectual plane, ideas that should have been assimilated were regarded as irrelevant and other ideas that should have been rejected were given prominence. This happened only because the moral climate of *bein adam le-ḥavero* was decadent.

This allows us to understand why the nation is culpable when the Supreme Court issues an erroneous judgment. It is the climate of discord in society that has the effect of causing an incorrect analysis, an assimilation of what should have been alienated and an alienation of what should have been assimilated. Because society is not in harmony, the intellectual process is distorted.

We are now living in a society in which people look at cosmic forces as part of a system that they cannot control, including issues such as war and peace, the nuclear armaments race, and national priorities. But the Torah's aim is that the intellectual life of society, the direction of its technological advances, and the character of its institutions be formed directly by the quality of interpersonal relations. If man would only imagine that he is the High Priest, carrying the Ineffable Name on his forehead openly and in the recesses of the Breastplate, the *ketoret* would be produced. The *re'ah niho'aḥ* would then foster the vibrant, healthy intellectual development of the nation, with its judgments clear and undistorted.

Paternalism in Jewish Law

April 4, 1987

We are living in a society that cherishes freedom. The Reagan presidency has promoted the notion that government itself is a threat to our freedom.[1] We are told that government has no business interfering in our personal lives, regulating the marketplace. And with respect to the needs of the weak, the disadvantaged, and the elderly, we would be best off relying on a system of voluntarism.[2]

If paternalism has been dealt a lethal blow with respect to the domestic economy, paradoxically, the concept has been stretched to its very outer limits when it comes to national security and foreign affairs. Reagan has always pushed for increased military expenditures.[3]

---

1. Andrew E. Busch, *Ronald Reagan and the Politics of Freedom* (Lanham, MD: Rowman & Littlefield, 2001), 78–79.
2. Ibid., 162–165; Herbert H. Denton, "Reagan Urges More Church Aid for Needy," *Washington Post*, April 14, 1982, A3.
3. See Leslie H. Gelb, "Reagan's Military Budget Puts Emphasis on a Buildup of U.S. Global Power," *New York Times*, February 7, 1982, 28; Bill Keller, "Surge in Spending

The shockwaves of the Iran-Contra Affair have demonstrated that the government, nay a very small part of the government, knows better than the private citizen where our best interests lie in the realm of foreign affairs.

While coercion is anathema to our secular society, we are quite comfortable with it in Jewish society. In the realm of mitzvot, any time that we have a definite obligation, the principle of coercion applies.[4] In fact, the main source of this is from today's portion with respect to the sacrifices. In connection with the burnt offering, "*kofin oto ad she-yomar 'rotzeh ani,'*" "they force him [to bring it] until he says 'I am willing.'"[5]

How do we rationalize this law? It is by means of the paternalism principle. We suppose that the Jew really wants to be God-fearing and discharge his obligations as set forth in the Torah. It is only the Evil Inclination that interferes. There is an intrinsic will to perform the dictates of the Torah.[6]

And we, too, have a paradox. The area of *tzedakah* apparently does not fit into the rule of coercion because it is a positive commandment for which the Torah specifies a reward.[7] Nevertheless, all ingenuity is

---

on Space Weapons Sought by Reagan," *New York Times*, February 2, 1985, 1.1; Robert Pear, "Reagan Sends $1 Trillion Budget to Congress, and Battle Is Joined," *New York Times*, January 6, 1987, A1.

4. *Ketubbot* 86a–b.
5. *Rashi* to Leviticus 1:3, s.v. "*yakriv oto*"; *Torat Kohanim, Va-Yikra, parashah* 1, 3:15.
6. *Berakhot* 17a; *Rashi* ad loc., s.v. "*se'or she-ba-issah*"; Maimonides (*Rambam*, Egypt, 1135–1204), *Mishneh Torah, Gerushin* 2:20; R. Elijah Mizrahi (*Re'em*, Constantinople, ca. 1450–1526), *Sefer ha-Mizraḥi*, Leviticus 1:3, s.v. "*yakriv oto*"; R. Judah Loew b. Bezalel (*Maharal*, Prague, ca. 1525–1609), *Gur Aryeh*, Leviticus 1:3, s.v. "*ad she-yomar rotzeh ani.*"
7. *Ḥullin* 110b. *Beit din* generally may not coerce an individual to perform a positive commandment for which the Torah specifies a reward. This type of commandment is referred to as a *mitzvat aseh she-matan sekharah be-tziddah* (lit., "a positive commandment whose reward is found by its side"). In the case of the positive commandment to give charity, the Torah states, "You shall open your hand to him… for in return for this matter, Hashem, your God, will bless you in all your deeds and in your every undertaking" (Deuteronomy 15:8–10).

used by our Sages to effect coercion, even coercion of the majority by the minority.[8] And this is codified in the *Shulḥan Arukh*.[9]

Now, when it comes to national defense, we start with the clear-cut statement that the minority can coerce the majority.[10] But this is extenuated considerably because the actual exercise of military power is limited by an intricate system of checks and balances. Both the Sanhedrin of seventy-one and the *Urim ve-Thummim* must be consulted.[11]

The challenge to every society is how it will build up the south-east corner of the Altar. The Altar, which symbolizes coming closer to Hashem[12] and our fellow man,[13] was built on a base. But the south-east corner had no base.[14] Why? We are told that a desperate struggle ensued between Judah and Benjamin. A strip of land extended from Judah's lot into Benjamin's territory, and on this strip, the Temple was built. The entire western portion of the Temple, including the Holy of Holies, was in the portion of Benjamin, and the eastern approach was in the portion of Judah. "The righteous Benjamin longed to swallow it every day."[15] He did not want to share.

---

8. One explanation given for the inapplicability of the prohibition of coercion to *tzedakah* is that the mitzvah of *tzedakah* also includes a negative prohibition, "you shall not harden your heart or close your hand against your destitute brother" (Deuteronomy 15:7). See *Tosafot* to *Bava Batra* 8b, s.v. "*akhpeh le-Rav Natan*." For other explanations, see R. David b. Solomon ibn Abi Zimra (*Radbaz*, Egypt, 1479–1573), *Yekar Tiferet* to *Mishneh Torah, Matanot Aniyyim* 7:10 (distinguishing *tzedakah* from other positive commandments in that the welfare of the poor depends upon it and analogizing coercion to give *tzedakah* to enforcement by a creditor of its right to take legal action to collect payment from the debtor).
9. *Shulḥan Arukh, Ḥoshen Mishpat* 163:1; *Rema* to *Shulḥan Arukh, Ḥoshen Mishpat* ad loc.
10. *Shulḥan Arukh, Ḥoshen Misphat* 163:1.
11. *Berakhot* 3b. The Talmud derives the principle of consulting with the Sanhedrin and the *Urim ve-Thummim* from II Samuel 16:23 ("Now the counsel of Ahitophel that he advised in those days was as if someone would inquire of the word of God; such was all the counsel of Ahitophel both to David and to Absalom.").
12. A *korban* (offering), which is brought on the Altar, is from the root word *karev*, to come close. See Nahmanides to Leviticus 1:9; *Maharal, Gur Aryeh, Mishpatim*, Exodus 21:1; R. Samson Raphael Hirsch, Leviticus 1:2, s.v. "*yakriv*."
13. See R. Hayyim Joseph David Azulai (*Ḥida*, Jerusalem, 1724–1806), *Tzavvarei Shalal: Perush al ha-Haftarot, Ki Tissa* 1.
14. *Zevaḥim* 53b.
15. *Yoma* 12a.

Is this the same fellow we encounter in the Book of Genesis, the great sentimentalist?[16]

The answer, I submit, is that the sentimentalist is never comfortable with the man of power. It is how society mediates the force of power and sentimentality that determines its character and how it builds up the southeast corner.

16. Benjamin named his ten sons after Joseph. Genesis Rabbah 94:8. See also Genesis 45:14 (recording that Benjamin wept upon Joseph's neck).

Shemini

I Will Be Sanctified through Those Who Are Close to Me

March 24, 1984

An event that deeply shocked an entire nation was fully anticipated by the great leader of the generation. When the eighth day of the dedication ceremony for the Tabernacle arrived, it was a day of unparalleled joy, equivalent, according to our Sages, to the joy that the Al-Mighty felt when he created heaven and earth.[1] It was a day that was crowned with ten exalted events.[2] It marked the long-awaited resting of the Divine Presence on the Jewish people.

1. See Genesis Rabbah 3:9.
2. *Shabbat* 87b; Genesis Rabbah 3:9. The ten special events that occurred on the day of the dedication of the Tabernacle are: (1) the dedication occurred on the first day of the week, the same day as the creation of the universe; (2) the Princes offered their consecration sacrifices; (3) the Priests performed their service in the Tabernacle for the first time; (4) communal sacrifices were brought for the first time; (5) the

On that selfsame day, tragedy struck. Nadab and Abihu offered a strange fire, which they were not commanded to offer, and were killed.[3] When everyone was in a state of turmoil and shock, Moses turned to Aaron, the bereaved father, and said, "I knew this would happen, but I thought that the Tabernacle would be sanctified either through me or through you. Now I see that your children, Nadab and Abihu, are indeed greater than we."[4]

When God visits judgment on the righteous, on the purest and most faithful element of his people, the fear of God spreads to everyone. People reflect: If divine punishment falls upon the righteous with such severity for relatively minor sins, how much more so do we, ordinary people, have to fear retribution.

But what gave Moses the inclination that this tragedy would happen? Why was it necessary? The answer, I submit, is that Moses knew Jewish history all too well. In the whole history of our people, as R. Samson Raphael Hirsch points out, a divine revelation never occurred that generated only a euphoric emotion.[5] It was always accompanied by a message and an awesome mission. Before Abraham experienced the vision of the Covenant between the Parts, the Torah tells us, "Behold, a dread! Great darkness fell upon him" (Genesis 15:12). The vision gave him a glimpse into Jewish history, and he viewed the Revelation as only a possibility of what might happen. He knew that he must make it a reality. He regarded the vision as only a dream to aspire to. So, too,

---

Heavenly fire descended and consumed the offerings; (6) the sacrifices were eaten for the first time only within a specific sacred area, whereas previously the offerings were permitted to be eaten anywhere; (7) the Divine Presence settled in the Tabernacle; (8) the Priests blessed the Children of Israel with the Priestly Blessing (*birkhat kohanim*); (9) for the first time, private altars (*bamot*) were prohibited; and (10) Nisan became the first of the months.

3. Leviticus 10:1.
4. Leviticus Rabbah 12:2; *Rashi* to Leviticus 10:3, s.v. "*Hu asher dibber.*" Hashem had previously alluded to Moses at Mount Sinai that the Tabernacle would be sanctified through those who are close to Hashem by stating "I shall meet there with the Children of Israel, and it shall be sanctified through My honor (*be-khevodi*)" (Exodus 29:43). The word *be-khevodi* should be understood as *be-khevudai*, "My honored ones." *Zevaḥim* 115b; *Rashi* to Leviticus 10:3.
5. See R. Samson Raphael Hirsch (Germany, 1808–1888), Genesis 15:1.

Jacob in his vision at Beit El.[6] And the Patriarchs were obsessed with *shema yigrom ha-ḥet*, that perhaps sin would cause Hashem's promise not to be fulfilled.[7]

After witnessing that the entire nation experienced the Divine Presence – "The people saw and sang glad song and fell upon their faces" (Leviticus 9:24) – Moses knew that there was room for error on the part of the people. Would they be misled into thinking that spiritual euphoria is the ultimate end? There is reward only in the World to Come. "The righteous sit with their crowns on their heads enjoying the brightness of the Divine Presence."[8] Here, in This World, divine inspiration must be accompanied by a great sense of urgency to action, a sense of restlessness. The ideal is that two opposing emotions should reside in man at the same time: on the one hand, the feeling of Transcendence – the feeling that a divine spark resides in oneself – and at the same time, the keen awareness of the transient nature of human life, its shortness, and its futility. This combination produces nothing less than an energizing feeling, a grave sense of urgency to sanctify the mundane.

Our Sages tell us that the joy that the Al-Mighty felt, in a manner of speaking, on the eighth day of the consecration of the Tabernacle was equivalent to the joy that He felt, in a manner of speaking, on the first day of creation.[9] This imparts to us, in our view, that the Jewish people achieved the highest potential as a creator on the day of the consecration of the Tabernacle. Just as Hashem created on the first day two opposites, light and darkness, and everything else, and it was only left for everything to find its place on the subsequent days of creation,[10] man, too, would be a creator of the highest order. Man had the potential to create heaven and earth. Moses brought the heavens down to earth,[11]

6. Genesis 28:12–22; *Rashi* to Genesis 28:20–21.
7. See *Berakhot* 4a; Nahmanides to Genesis 15:2; *Keli Yakar* to Genesis 32:8.
8. *Berakhot* 17a.
9. *Megillah* 10b.
10. Nahmanides and R. Hayyim b. Moses ibn Attar (*Or ha-Ḥayyim*, Morocco, 1696–1743), *Or ha-Ḥayyim* to Genesis 1:1.
11. Moses brought the Torah down from the heavens. Moses is thus referred to in *Kabbalah* as the "*shushvina de-Malka*," the "escort of the King." *Zohar* 3:53b. See also

and Aaron elevated the earth up to the heavens.[12] And it was these two paragons, the two great bridge makers, who served in the consecration ceremony. The tragedy therefore became necessary to demonstrate that man as a creator could achieve his highest heights only when the two opposing emotions of the sublime and the transience of human life would blend perfectly within himself.

To give Aaron a vote of confidence that his role of creator could be accomplished in its highest form when two opposing emotions resided within him, the commandment to refrain from drinking wine when coming to the Tent of the Meeting was given to him alone.[13] As the *Netziv* points out, the purpose of this teaching was not only to prohibit Aaron's entry into the Tent of the Meeting while under the influence of intoxicating beverages. Hashem was telling Aaron that he would not need the fortification of a drink to enable him to represent the Jewish people in his sublime mission, at a time when his thoughts would have to be the purest.[14]

Now we go from the vote of confidence to the actual reality of the moment. A dialogue between Moses and Aaron explodes. Moses inquires why the he-goat of Rosh Ḥodesh had not been eaten as the two other he-goats had.[15] Instead it had been burnt. Aaron replies that the two other he-goats, consisting of the offering of Nahshon b. Amminadab and the offering of the nation for the dedication ceremony, were brought only at the inauguration ceremony and could be eaten despite Aaron's state of *anninut* attributable to the death of Nadab and Abihu. The he-goat of Rosh Ḥodesh, however, is an offering for the generations and therefore the law of *anninut* should apply, which prohibits him and

---

Genesis Rabbah 19:7; R. Yehudah Aryeh Leib Alter (*Sefat Emet*, Poland, 1847–1905), *Sefat Emet, Tetzavveh* (5647/March 1887).

12. Aaron elevated the earth to the heavens by performing the service in the Tabernacle of bringing offerings and lighting the Menorah. See R. Yehudah Aryeh Leib Alter, *Sefat Emet, Tetzavveh* (5647/March 1887). Aaron is thus referred to in *Kabbalah* as the "*shushvina de-matronisa*," the "escort of the Matron." *Zohar* 3:53b.
13. Leviticus 10:8–9.
14. See R. Naphtali Tzvi Yehudah Berlin, *Ha'amek Davar*, Leviticus 10:9.
15. Leviticus 10:16–18.

his sons Eleazar and Ithamar from eating the Rosh Ḥodesh offering.[16] Moses, in the turmoil, had lost his serenity and forgotten the law.[17]

What have we here? Aaron, the distraught father, is thinking in a clear and precise manner and reminding Moses, the teacher of the Torah to the people, the course of action. Here Aaron demonstrated the great potential of man as an intellectual creator, as an interpreter of the Torah, that even in a distraught condition, he could function on the highest level.

Today, we are faced with a very formidable problem, the drug culture. It is not only a force that threatens the health of our youth, but the cult of escape and euphoria as an ideal negates man's sublime role as a creator and lowers him many rungs in the order of creation. Euphoria is for the World to Come, the world of reward. In This World, we must take an active role as a creator. To accomplish that, we must live a reality, not escape it. We must be energized with the proper purity of feeling and urgency of the moment, never to be caught in lethargy or indolence.

---

16. *Rashi* to Leviticus 10:19.
17. Leviticus Rabbah 13:1.

Torah from Heaven

April 20, 1985

One of the greatest challenges that the twentieth-century Jew faces today, living in an era of scientific discovery and critical analysis, is the intensity of his belief in the divine origin of the Torah. The technique that our rabbis use to derive Halakhah, the thirteen hermeneutical rules, is a methodology quite alien to modern scientific research.[1] Indeed, our Sages often present no explanations and simply say "*halakhah le-Mosheh mi-Sinai*," "it is the law given to Moses at Sinai."[2]

1. *Baraita de-Rabbi Yishmael.*
2. See Mishnah, *Pe'ah* 2:6; Mishnah, *Ediyot* 8:7; Mishnah, *Yadayim* 4:3. The laws of ritual slaughter are considered to have been given to Moses at Sinai. *Rashi* to *Ḥullin* 27a, s.v. "*u-kera le-mai asa*." Other examples of laws specified in the Talmud that are considered to have been given to Moses at Sinai include: the eighteen defects that render an animal a *terefah* (*Ḥullin* 42a; *Rashi* ad loc., s.v. "*shemoneh esreh terefot*"); the mitzvah to walk around the Altar with willows and the feast of water drawing on Sukkot (*Sukkah* 34a); the construction of the underside and duct of the *tefillin*, the embossing of the letter *shin* on the *tefillah* worn on the head, and the requirements that the straps of the *tefillin* be black and that the *tefillin* be square (*Menaḥot* 35a); the law that the straps of the *tefillin* should have a knot (*Eruvin* 97a); the minimum

Now, if the Sages would not be reflecting *divrei Elokim ḥayyim,*[3] would they dare to transform generality and vagueness into something very precise and expose themselves to the possible ridicule of the scientific communities throughout the ages? But this is precisely what the Sages did in connection with the pure animals that we are permitted to eat. Here, in *Parashat Shemini,* the Torah speaks in general terms, telling us just the signs of *kashrut.*[4] But in *Re'eh,* the Torah tells us that there are only ten animals that we are permitted to eat.[5]

Taking up the rule that *mi'ut poret ha-katuv,* i.e., the Torah enumerates the items in the smaller group rather than enumerating the items in the larger group, the Sages understood that there are only ten animals that we may eat.[6] The general rule that is stated after the specific rule, consisting of "every animal that has a split hoof, which is separated with a split into two hooves, that brings up its cud among animals, it you may eat" (Deuteronomy 14:6), is not taken as an expansion of the ten, but rather as telling us that if a *terefah* gives birth to an animal that has the signs of a kosher animal, the offspring is kosher,[7] or if an animal that has split hooves and chews its cud draws sustenance from a *terefah,* it also does not matter because it has the signs of a kosher animal.[8]

We begin to think, what forced *derashot,* all for the purpose of pinning the Torah down to an emphatic statement that there are only

---

quantities of forbidden foods the consumption of which constitutes an offense (*Eruvin* 4a); the rules regarding interpositions between one's body and the waters of ritual immersion that invalidate the immersion (ibid.); and the law that if damage is inflicted through pebbles kicked from under an animal's feet, the owner of the animal is required to pay an amount equal to only one-half of the damage (*Bava Kamma* 3b; *Rashi* ad loc., s.v. "*be-ḥatzi nezek tzerurot*").

3. Jeremiah 23:36.
4. Lit., "the words of the living God." Leviticus 11:1–23.
5. Deuteronomy 14:4–5. The specified kosher animals are the ox, sheep, goat, hart, deer, *yaḥmor, akko, dishon, te'o,* and *zamer.*
6. *Sifrei,* Deuteronomy 100; *Ḥullin* 63b; *Rashi* to Deuteronomy 14:4–5. The Torah specifies the names of the pure animals, implying that the rest of the animals are impure. Because the Torah specifies the items in the smaller group, the listing of the names of the pure animals signifies that the number of impure animals is greater than the number of the pure animals.
7. See *Ḥullin* 69a.
8. *Sifrei,* Deuteronomy 101.

ten kosher animals. And even the difference in the *parashot* – here in *Shemini* it says "*ḥayah*"[9] and there it says "*behemah*"[10] – is ignored. But why would someone go to such trouble to expose himself in this manner, subjecting himself to possible ridicule and the challenge of the collective genius of the scientific communities of all ages?

It is only because, I submit, they were sure that it is *halakhah le-Mosheh mi-Sinai*. It reflects the word of Hashem, who created everything and knows exactly what He created.

And in connection with fish, the Torah says that two signs – fins and scales – are necessary.[11] Our Sages tell us that any fish that has scales certainly has fins.[12] So why does the Torah state that a fish must also have fins to be kosher? *Le-hagddil Torah u-le-ha'addirah*, to make the Torah's teaching great and glorious.[13] Again our Sages twist around the Torah to make a statement subject to challenge by the scientific communities throughout the ages. Again because they are not afraid that what they say expresses *divrei Elokim ḥayyim*.

Why does the Torah choose to make the point here? It is because it is precisely with respect to the dietary laws that we can easily fool ourselves and say that by keeping these, we have established our separation from the gentiles. But no, this is not profound enough. We dare not fall into a trap and imagine that this is sufficient.

When we observe the contemporary scene, what do we find? The academic will couch his theory in the language of his discipline and then make any trivia seem profound wisdom. The businessman will always attach many disclaimers to his warranties and frame them in legal jargon. Forecasters have long learned that he who lives by the crystal ball is fated to dine on crushed glass.[14] And President Truman

9. Leviticus 11:2.
10. Deuteronomy 14:4.
11. Leviticus 11:9.
12. *Ḥullin* 66b.
13. Isaiah 42:21; *Ḥullin* 66b.
14. Statement attributed to Edgar R. Fiedler (1929–2003), an American economist who served as Vice President of the Conference Board and as Assistant Secretary of the Treasury for Economic Policy (1971–1975) during the presidencies of Richard Nixon and Gerald Ford. See Edgar R. Fiedler, "The Three Rs of Economic Forecasting – Irrational,

prayed for an economist with one hand so the economist could not say "on the other hand."[15]

We must learn to express the divine nature within us by formulating all our commitments in terms that can be challenged, in precise terms. This is divine. And paradoxically, in a *dor she-kullo ḥayyav,*[16] where no one trusts anyone, the only way to advance self-interest is to formulate commitment in objective, verifiable ways. Thus, evil is the catalyst of the highest good. And this is the process of the Redemption. "I will remember My covenant with Jacob and also My covenant with Isaac, and also My covenant with Abraham will I remember, and I will remember the Land" (Leviticus 26:42). The Redemption process begins with the character trait of truth.[17]

Irrelevant and Irreverent," *Across the Board* 14 (June 1977): 62 ("He who lives by the crystal ball soon learns to eat ground glass.").

15. N. Gregory Mankiw, *Principles of Economics,* 7th ed. (Stamford, CT: Cengage Learning, 2014), 28.
16. See *Sanhedrin* 98a.
17. Jacob represents the character trait of truth. See Micah 7:20 ("Grant truth to Jacob."). See also *Midrash Shoḥer Tov,* Psalms 117.

Subversion of the Dietary Laws

April 25, 1987

For the marginal Jew, there is perhaps no area in Jewish law that is regarded as more irrelevant in the pursuit of the ethical life than the Jewish dietary laws. Indeed, our Sages regard the dietary laws as falling into the category of *ḥukkim*, statutes that cannot be explained.[1] And these laws are counted among the laws that evoke ridicule among the nations of the world.[2]

Nonetheless, our greatest Sages have found an ethical rationale for the dietary laws. One school of thought, consisting of such diverse parties as Philo and *Rabbeinu Beḥaye*, regard the dietary laws as inculcating temperance and restraint in the physical and material realm.[3]

1. *Rashi* to Leviticus 18:4, s.v. "*ve-et ḥukkkotei tishmiru.*"
2. Ibid.
3. *Rabbeinu Beḥaye al ha-Torah*, Exodus 23:19, Leviticus 11:13, 17:11; Philo (Alexandria, ca. 20 B.C.E. – ca. 50 C.E.), *The Special Laws* 4:100–118.

Untrammeled indulgence can only be harmful for our intellectual development and spiritual wellbeing.

Nahmanides sees in the dietary laws the Torah's concern that the obnoxious traits of the prohibited species should not become part of the personality of the one who ingests them. Hence the concern that the predatory nature of the prohibited fowl might become part of the nature of the one who ingests the flesh.[4] Similarly, the *Ḥinnukh* understands the prohibition of eating the blood of an animal as deriving from the concern that the ingestor should not develop animal-like characteristics.[5]

We are living a real paradox today. On the one hand, we are striving ever more towards higher standards of *kashrut*. Witness the sometimes intense rivalry among the various *kashrut* organizations. Take the one of *ḥalav Yisrael*. Many do not rely on the leniency of the ruling that government inspection of milk is sufficient to assure us that the milk of a non-kosher animal was not added.[6] But at the same time, we are witnessing a blatant violation of Halakhah's call for the one-sixth profit rate constraint in the Necessity Sector.[7] Well, the ordinance has fallen into disuse because it does not apply when the market is dominated by sellers who do not submit to Halakhah.[8] Nonetheless, it has ready application when the sellers are exclusively Jewish and cater to an Orthodox market.[9]

The Kosher Food Price Watch, an organization that monitors pricing policy in the kosher food industry, even found that as much as sixty cents per pound of poultry and ten to seventeen cents per a half-gallon

4. Nahmanides (*Ramban*, Spain, 1194–1270) to Leviticus 11:13.
5. R. Aaron b. Joseph ha-Levi (*Ra'ah*, Spain, ca. 1235–1300), *Sefer ha-Ḥinnukh*, mitzvah no. 148.
6. R. Abraham Isaiah Karelitz (*Ḥazon Ish*, Belarus and Israel, 1878–1953), *Ḥazon Ish, Yoreh De'ah* 41:4; R. Mosheh Feinstein, *Iggerot Mosheh, Yoreh De'ah* 1:47.
7. M. Y. Melamed, "Kosher Food Overpricing: The Problem, and $ome Solutions," *Kashrus Magazine*, March 1987, 20–21.
8. R. Meir b. Todros ha-Levi Abulafia (*Ramah*, Spain, ca. 1170–1244), cited in R. Jacob b. Asher (*Tur*, Spain, 1270–1343), *Tur, Ḥoshen Mishpat* 231; *Shulḥan Arukh, Ḥoshen Mishpat* 231:20; R. Jehiel Michal Epstein (Belorus, 1829–1908), *Arukh ha-Shulḥan, Ḥoshen Mishpat* 231:20.
9. See R. Aaron Levine, *Economic Morality and Jewish Law* (New York: Oxford University Press, 2012), 109–110 (proposing regulation of prices for kosher poultry and Passover products).

of *ḥalav Yisrael* milk cannot be accounted for by the cost of rabbinical certification and supervisors.[10]

The operation of the kosher food industry in the area of poultry might be serving as a stumbling block for the marginal Jew, who would otherwise see no reason not to buy kosher poultry. Also, instead of fostering temperance, restraint, and kindness in us, it is working to encourage greed and self-interest.

The best approach is to link kosher products to comparable non-kosher products and require sellers to restrict themselves to a one-sixth profit of their extra costs. The challenge that we face is to not allow the operation of the kosher food industry to subvert the humane approach or to act as a stumbling block for the marginal Jew. Would it not be soothing and reassuring that despite the absence of any government requirement, "we answer to a higher authority"[11] and exercise restraint?

10. Melamed, "Kosher Food Overpricing," 20–21.
11. This phrase is a slogan used by Hebrew National for its brand of hot dogs.

Yom Ha-Atzma'ut

April 16, 1988

As we stand on the eve of the fortieth anniversary of the celebration of the restoration of Jewish sovereignty in the Land of Israel, our inclination is to identify with another momentous event of Jewish restoration, an event that normally would have been recited as the *haftarah* of today's *parashah,* the restoration of the Ark to the City of David.[1] After being captured by the Philistines, the Ark journeyed a wandering, deflective path, entailing much anguish for the Jewish nation. When it was finally restored, we read, "David danced with all his strength before Hashem" (II Samuel 6:14).

But today, there are many a Michal lurking in the shadows, bent on depriving us of our celebration and joy upon this anniversary.[2] There are those who would characterize the policies of the Israeli government

1. II Samuel 6:1–7:17. The *haftarah* of *maḥar ḥodesh* (lit., "tomorrow is the New Moon") at I Samuel 20:18–42 was read on that Sabbath because the first day of the month of Iyyar fell out on Sunday, April 17, 1988. See *Shulḥan Arukh, Oraḥ Ḥayyim* 425:2.
2. See II Samuel 6:20.

in the liberated territories as one of repression and domination. This generates a bleak scenario. Unless Israel seizes the moral high ground and holds it by making major initiatives and concessions to Palestinian rights, the perception that Israel is a country of moral sensitivity and transcendent vision will dissipate. Emigration will accelerate. We will be giving fodder to the anti-Semites all over the world, and support for Israel in the United States will erode. Survival itself is at stake. This is the scenario of self-destruction.

But there are those who produce for us another scenario, the scenario of self-preservation. The Arab mentality understands only suppression and force. As far as the Arabs are concerned, there is no difference in their claim for Hebron and Tel Aviv. Both are the same. Any shocking of the nations in the form of ceding something to the Arabs will only whet their appetite for more. Our incorrigible enemies will soon become intoxicated with the belief that anything is feasible. Any weakness could send us down the slippery slope, even leading to, God forbid, annihilation. This is the scenario of self-preservation.

Much confusion now exists regarding our course of action. We will only compound our confusion if we do not relate to the proper model. Now, let us not repeat the mistake made in the earlier celebration of the restoration of the Ark. The people of Beit Shemesh got excited when the Ark returned. "They rejoiced to see it" (I Samuel 6:13). But it was only an idle curiosity. They quickly returned to their agenda of everyday living. The havoc that the Ark created hence moved them to say, "Who can stand before Hashem, this Holy God?" (I Samuel 6:20). The Ark was not central to their lives.

When the Ark moved from Kiriath-jearim, again a celebration was held. This time, the attention that the people lavished on the Ark was extraordinary. Even people who were not Levites participated when they should not have. A new cart was made for the Ark, when this too should not have been made.[3]

But this sets the trigger of the Uzzah syndrome. Uzzah felt that the cart was swaying, and he begins to lunge to take hold of the Ark to

---

3. II Samuel 6:3.

stabilize it, a capital offense.[4] Why? He should have referred to history. At the crossing of the Jordan, the Ark carried its bearers.[5] The bearers were carried over the water.[6] The Ark could take care of itself.

Now, in the present difficulties, many who are guided by logic and geopolitical events feel that they are at an impasse. They begin to doubt Jewish survival. But this is so wrong. The formation of the State was a miracle. And the divine gift served, as R. Joseph B. Soloveitchik put it, to redeem an orphaned mitzvah, the mitzvah of possession and settlement of the Land of Israel.[7] The gift served to suffuse the covenant of Abraham with its meaning, the identification of every Jew with every other Jew. The multitude of miracles that we have witnessed since the establishment of the Jewish State tells us clearly that the State will remain viable because Hashem does not make miracles in vain.[8]

The challenge that we have is the same as the one that David faced. He knew that the Ark would not be a unifying force, a rallying point, and a source of inspiration for all Jews until it was perceived as a blessing, not as the Philistines perceived it, as a "panic of death" (I Samuel 5:11), not as the people of Beit Shemesh perceived it, proclaiming, "Who can stand before Hashem, this Holy God?" (I Samuel 6:20), but as a blessing. And, indeed, it was not until the Ark resided in Beit Obed-edom that it was perceived as such. Obed-edom and his wife, along with their eight daughters-in-law, were blessed with the birth of six children at a time.[9]

Our challenge is to reach out to our fellow Jews and end the terrible rifts in society between the religious and the secular, between Likud and Labor. Our model is indeed the *haftarah* of *maḥar ḥodesh*.[10] When we adopt the model of David and Jonathan, rivals who had the

4. II Samuel 6:6.
5. *Sotah* 35a; *Rashi* to II Samuel 6:7.
6. *Sotah* 35a. First the Jordan River split and the Children of Israel passed through. After the waters returned to their place, the Ark carried its bearers across the water.
7. R. Joseph B. Soloveitchik (New York, 1903–1993), *Ḥamesh Derashot* (Jerusalem: Makhon Tal Orot, 1974), 88–89.
8. See *Berakhot* 58a; Nahmanides to Exodus 13:16.
9. II Samuel 6:11; *Rashi* ad loc.
10. I Samuel 20:18–42.

most noble, tender, and loving relationship, when we end the rifts in Jewish society, the State will indeed be perceived as having the dual character of the Cherubim, the character of angels of destruction[11] to our enemies, but at the same time to everyone, including our enemies, *ke-ravya*, "like a child,"[12] as the society of moral sensitivity and transcendent vision – "their face toward one another" and "with wings spread upward" (Exodus 25:20).

11. See *Rashi* to Genesis 3:24, s.v. "*et ha-keruvim.*"
12. *Sukkah* 5b; *Ḥagigah* 13b; *Rashi* to Exodus 25:18, s.v. "*keruvim.*"

The Test of the Strength of One's *Kevod ha-Torah*

April 21, 1990

The connection between this week's Torah reading and the *haftarah* is apparently to provide parallel incidents in Jewish history of two festive occasions that were marred by calamity. In today's portion, the dedication of the Tabernacle was marred by the death of Nadab and Abihu.[1] In the *haftarah,* the recovery of the Ark from the Philistines was marred by the death of Uzzah, who saw the oxen struggle and instinctively grasped the Ark to prevent it from slipping.[2] For this, he was struck down on the spot.[3]

Permit me to suggest that the connection goes beyond parallelism. Perhaps the purpose of the *haftarah* is to provide us a clue to the answer to a very disturbing question. The Torah explicitly gives us the reason

1. Leviticus 10:1–7.
2. II Samuel 6:6–7.
3. II Samuel 6:7.

for the death of Nadab and Abihu. "They brought before Hashem an alien fire that He had not commanded them" (Leviticus 10:1). So why, asks R. Yaakov Kamenetsky, do our Sages heap upon these righteous people a litany of transgressions that are not mentioned in the Torah?[4] These transgressions include that they did not consult with Moses and Aaron;[5] they did not consult with each other;[6] they did not marry;[7] they wished for the death of Moses and Aaron so they could take over their leadership;[8] and they drank wine.[9]

But the answer is that at that ecstatic moment, the moment of the dedication of the Tabernacle, when Nadab and Abihu departed from the instructions of Hashem, there was of course an element of purity and nobility, a desire to display their affection to Hashem. But at the same time, Nadab and Abihu were at center stage, and their departure was an expression of their own individualism and creativity. It was presumptuous of them to think that they could improve upon what Hashem had commanded. For these righteous men, their act evidenced a fatal flaw of character, but it was a delicate flaw, one that they were not even aware of. Our Sages in their wisdom understood that such a flaw does not develop spontaneously, but rather must be a unified character trait. So our Sages drag in all these flaws, which are a reflection of a presumptuous nature. We then reinterpret behavioral manifestations that could be understood in a different light and now understand them as manifestations of haughtiness and presumptiveness.[10]

---

4. R. Yaakov Kamenetsky (New York, 1891–1986), *Emet le-Yaakov: Sefer Iyyunim ba-Mikra al ha-Torah, Shemini*, 3rd ed. (New York, 2007), 361–362.
5. *Eruvin* 63a. R. Eliezer b. Jacob stated that the sons of Aaron died only because they gave a legal decision in the presence of their Master Moses. They interpreted the verse "the sons of Aaron the Priest shall place fire on the Altar" (Leviticus 1:7) to mean that although fire came down from heaven, it is nevertheless a religious duty to bring ordinary fire on the Altar too.
6. Leviticus Rabbah 20:8.
7. Ibid., 20:9.
8. Ibid., 20:10.
9. Ibid., 20:9.
10. R. Kamenetsky, *Emet le-Yaakov*, 362.

It is the role of the *haftarah* to provide us with a test for the authenticity and strength of our *kevod ha-Torah*. Is it self-honor or honor of the Torah? The delicate test is seen by identifying with Uzzah. David had ordered that the Ark be placed in the wagon. There was a reasoning that the rule of *ba-kasef yissa'u*, that the sons of Kohath carry the Ark on their shoulders, applied only in the presence of the Tabernacle, to give the Ark extra status.[11] But this was an egregious mistake regarding a law that even *tinnokot shel beit rabban* knew.[12] This means that if the people who were present would have asserted themselves and questioned David why he thought that the honor of the Ark should be suspended here, he surely would have relented.

Uzzah now fell into the authoritarian syndrome because David created a relaxation of the honor due the Ark. That is, David went down one step, Uzzah went down another two steps. Uzzah was not a Levite, yet he actually touched the Ark to prevent it from slipping, forgetting that the Ark carried its bearers across the Jordan.[13]

The test is that when the authoritarian figure is lenient in honoring the Torah, we should not be dragged down with him in a mindless way, but instead, at that point, we should become assertive and questioning.

And then there is the responsibility of the *Rav* to honor the Torah. David danced with complete abandon and the breakdown of social barriers.[14] In front of Hashem, all social classes become equalized. Michal, however, understood that the presence of the King enhances the ritual ceremony, not that the King honors the Torah.[15]

Preventing the Michal and Uzzah syndromes from developing in the Torah educational institutions requires a special extra effort on the

---

11. R. David Kimhi (*Radak*, Provence, ca. 1160–ca. 1235), *Radak* to II Samuel 6:6, s.v. "*ki shamtu ha-bakar*." When the Children of Israel sojourned in the Wilderness, the Tabernacle was carried in wagons but the Ark was carried on the shoulders of the Levites, in accordance with Numbers 7:9. *Radak* explains that David thought that the requirement that the Ark be carried on the shoulders of the Levites applied only when the Tabernacle was in existence to demonstrate that the Ark possessed a greater degree of holiness than the Tabernacle.
12. *Sotah* 35a; *Rashi* to II Samuel 6:3.
13. *Sotah* 35a; II Samuel 6:6; *Rashi* to II Samuel 6:7.
14. II Samuel 6:14–15.
15. See *Malbim* to II Samuel 6:15, 6:20.

part of the both the *rebbe* and the *talmid*. Any breach in the honor of the Torah must be questioned by the *talmid*. The *talmid* must not allow himself to be dragged down into a believer syndrome. The *rebbe* must also demonstrate honor of the Torah with a complete social equality with the *talmid*.

When the Michal and Uzzah syndromes are stamped out, we witness *haramat keren ha-Torah*.

Moral Vegetarianism and Halakhah

April 13, 1991

The story is told of a gentile who was advised by a Jewish friend that if he wanted to partake of a sumptuous Jewish meal, he should masquerade as a pauper and station himself in the back row of the local synagogue on the night of Passover. Surely a wealthy patron would approach him and invite him to the Seder.

Well, things went as planned, but the gentile was dismayed when he found that instead of being treated to a feast, lively dialogue amidst rapturous singing took place for a seemingly interminable time, and the only food served was a cup of wine and a measly piece of radish dipped in salt water. His impatience grew when the matzah was served, and built to an outrage when the *maror* came. That was the last straw. The gentile left in a huff and mumbled, "These Jews are nothing but vegetarians, and they have no imagination in preparing vegetarian dishes." If the gentile would have waited but a few minutes, he would have been treated to a feast.[1]

Some note that in the formative years of our nationhood, we started with matzah at the Exodus from Egypt, and then we had the manna for forty years. The manna is described as similar to coriander seed, a vegetarian food.[2] Perhaps the ideal food for us is vegetarian food.

In a provocative book, Dr. Richard Schwartz claims that flesh-centered diets assault various Jewish values and ideals.[3] He starts with the desideratum of avoiding *tza'ar ba'alei ḥayyim*, our obligation to show compassion for animals and do nothing to cause them anguish,[4] and many laws of the Torah, such as "you shall not muzzle an ox in its threshing" (Deuteronomy 25:4) and "an ox, or a sheep or a goat, you may not slaughter it and its offspring on the same day" (Leviticus 22:28).[5] Instead of focusing on the relative humaneness of *sheḥitah* compared to other methods of killing animals, why, he asks, do we not recognize that mass production of beef and fowl subjects animals to cramped living conditions, depriving them of fresh air, sunshine, exercise, and emotional fulfillment?[6]

Schwartz assumes that Torah legislation with regard to animal welfare is rooted in animal rights – there are rights that people have, and there are rights that animals have. But Nahmanides and the *Ḥinnukh* both understand the laws to be rooted in the degenerative effect that acts of cruelty have on the human agent who performs them.[7] Just as the advancement of civilization with the explosion of population requires mass production of clothing and shelter, perforce the need to

1. See R. Ephraim Oratz, *And Nothing but the Truth: Insights, Stories, and Anecdotes of Rabbi Menachem Mendel of Kotzk* (New York: Judaica Press, 1990), 79–85.
2. Exodus 16:31.
3. Richard H. Schwartz, *Judaism and Vegetarianism* (Smithtown, NY: Exposition Press, 1982).
4. See Exodus 23:5; *Bava Metzia* 32b; *Shabbat* 128b; Maimonides, *Mishneh Torah, Rotze'aḥ u-Shemirat Nefesh* 13:9; R. Joseph Caro (Safed, 1488–1575), *Kesef Mishneh* ad loc.
5. Schwartz, *Judaism and Vegetarianism*, 10–18.
6. Ibid., 17, 22–25, 73.
7. Nahmanides to Leviticus 11:13; R. Aaron b. Joseph ha-Levi, *Sefer ha-Ḥinnukh*, mitzvah no. 148.

feed multitudes of people requires that we raise animals more roughly, abuse aside. This inhumane treatment is justified in that we are putting human welfare ahead of animal welfare.

Moreover, changing one's lifestyle in such a dramatic manner by adopting a vegetarian regimen is quite an act of protest against an evil – cruelty to animals – over which we as individuals have absolutely no control. What are we doing to change those of our faults over which we do have control? If we leave gross faults unchanged and devote our attention and energy to protest evils over which we have no control, this is *yuhara* (false piety).[8]

Another point that he makes is that a flesh-centered diet violates the spirit of the *bal tash'ḥit* prohibition.[9] The production of a unit of beef or fowl uses up resources very heavily compared to the input needed to produce a unit of vegetarian food. Observe that 80% of the grain produced in the United States is devoted to feeding animals. More than half the acreage is devoted to growing grain for animals. If we would only be vegetarians, the resources required for our food needs would be so much less, and this would free acreage to grow grain to feed the lesser-developed countries (LDCs) of the world.[10]

How noble. But the economics can be put to question. The more resources that are expended to produce beef and fowl, the more people are employed. A dramatic change in lifestyle to favor vegetarians would only cause mass unemployment, which would worsen through successive rounds of income reduction and spending reduction. It could be stopped only if we were to develop new *ta'avot*. To ascribe the unequal distribution of wealth in the world to Western man's appetite for meat is absurd.

The fundamental difference in living standards among nations is a matter of resource endowment and the relationship of the size of

---

8. *Berakhot* 17b; *Pesaḥim* 55a.
9. The principle of *bal tash'ḥit* (lit., "do not destroy") is based on Deuteronomy 20:19–20, which forbids cutting down fruit trees to assist in a siege. See *Bava Kamma* 91b–92a. The prohibition extends to destroying utensils, clothing, or food. See Maimonides, *Mishneh Torah, Melakhim* 6:10; R. Aaron b. Joseph ha-Levi, *Sefer ha-Ḥinnukh,* mitzvah no. 530.
10. Schwartz, *Judaism and Vegetarianism*, 57.

the population to the supply of natural resources.[11] If the gap in living standards between the developed nations and the LDCs is too narrow, the more developed nations will have to become more generous in their willingness to share their bounty with the less fortunate. If the United States with its present GDP per capita of over $20,000[12] is willing to do only a small bit to reduce the gap, what will it be willing to do if the standard of living is drastically reduced by becoming a vegetarian economy?

While vegetarianism on health grounds, removed of all the moral trappings, is certainly not inconsistent with the spirit of the Torah, I wonder if the health objectives could not be achieved by being a vegetarian year-round except on the Sabbath and *Yom Tov* and other festive occasions such as weddings, when it is a *mitzvah min ha-muvḥar*, a "noble act," to consume meat[13] and, according to some *Rishonim*, even an absolute mitzvah.[14]

---

11. See Michael E. Porter, *Competitive Advantage of Nations* (New York: Free Press, 1990), 564.
12. See World Bank Group, World DataBank, www.data.worldbank.org/indicator (providing that the gross domestic product per capita in the United States for 1990 was $23,954.50).
13. *Ḥiddushei ha-Ran, Sukkah* 42b, s.v. "*ve-ha-simḥah*"; *Ḥiddushei ha-Ritva, Sukkah* 42b, s.v. "*hallel ve-ha-simḥah.*"
14. Maimonides, *Mishneh Torah, Yom Tov* 6:18; *Tur, Oraḥ Ḥayyim* 529.

Tazri'a

The Birth and Development of a Nation

April 12, 1986

Without question, childbearing is the most creative act known to mankind. By giving birth, a mother perpetuates the species and adds a link to the generations. We would therefore imagine that the Torah would crown the mother with a diadem of glory and admiration when she gives birth. But instead, we find that the mother plunges into a period of impurity from which she does not fully emerge in the case of a male child until the forty-first day after childbirth and, in the case of a female child, until the eighty-first day.[1]

Far from constituting a stigma, the period of impurity thrust upon the mother reflects a recognition of the tremendous force of holiness that she brought into the world. In accordance with the principle that whenever holiness manifests itself and departs, its mirror-image counterpart, *tumah*, sets in, so, too, the child that the mother carries within

1. Leviticus 12:1–5.

her represents a tremendous force of holiness. When it is released from the mother's womb, *tumah* must set in.[2]

In a similar vein, the author of *Sefer Or ha-Ḥayyim* understands the double period of impurity for a female child as stemming from the greater holiness that comes into existence with the birth of a female child. Far from being an anti-feminist notion, it testifies to the natural creativity of women to give birth to a child that itself can bear a child, involving the bringing into the world a double dosage of holiness. Hence a double period of impurity sets in.[3]

The birth and development of a nation perhaps parallels the birth and development of a human being. When our beloved State of Israel was formed in 1948, it represented a tremendous force of holiness in the lives of the Jewish people. Yet, at its inception, what was mostly visible and perceptible to the world was the mirror image – impurity – that the birth of the State represented. Not only was the surrounding Arab population bent upon annihilating the State, making it stillborn, but many Jews, even in our circle, did not perceive its potential holiness, but instead, for various reasons, distanced themselves from it.

But our beloved State has proven its mettle. It has achieved the noble goal of being *tehorah le-ba'alah* (lit., "ritually pure for her husband"). It has served as the catalyst to encourage the ingathering of the Diaspora and certainly a good measure in the direction of being qualified to eat *ma'aser sheni*.[4]

---

2. R. Menahem Mendel Morgensztern of Kotzk (*Kotzker Rebbe*, Poland, 1787–1859), *Ohel Torah: Likkutei Amarot Tehorot* (Benei Berak: Slavita, 1959), 47, *Tazri'a*.
3. R. Joseph b. Hayyim Yavetz (*He-Ḥasid Yavetz*, Spain, ca. 1438–1504), cited in R. Norman Lamm, *The Royal Reach: Discourses on the Jewish Tradition and the World Today* (New York: Feldheim, 1970), 291–294.
4. During the time of the Temple, *terumah* and *ma'aser* were required to be taken from agricultural produce to render it fit for ordinary consumption. First, *terumah* was set aside for the Priests. Next, *ma'aser rishon* (the first tithe), consisting of one-tenth of the remainder, was given to the Levites. Numbers 18:21–24. A second tithe was then given. In the first, second, fourth, and fifth years of the Sabbatical cycle, the second tithe was called "*ma'aser sheni*." Deuteronomy 14:22–26. In the third and sixth years, the second tithe was called *ma'aser ani*, which was given to the poor. Deuteronomy 14:28–29, 26:12. *Ma'aser sheni* was required to be eaten in Jerusalem. If it was too difficult to carry the produce to Jerusalem, *ma'aser sheni* could be redeemed for money,

What does *ma'aser sheni* represent? More than the sanctification of one's material possessions, more than bringing one's own foodstuff to Jerusalem, *ma'aser sheni* represents the experience of Jerusalem and Torah scholars, which are by-products of the mitzvah. So, too, the Jewish State serves as a catalyst to reawaken Jews to their roots, serving as an identification symbol. The Jewish State is one of the very few nations in the world that actively subsidizes family dependents.[5]

But as we get close to the next stage of purification, the eligibility to eat *terumah*,[6] we must have a heightened sensitivity toward the holiness of the Land. Therefore, we must enthusiastically applaud the persistence of Shas to try again to introduce their amendment to *mi yehudi*,[7] and we should feel all the vehemence against the Mormon pollution of the holiness of Jerusalem.[8]

---

consisting of the value of the produce plus one-fifth. The money would then be taken to Jerusalem where the owner would spend it on food or *shelamim* offerings. Leviticus 27:31; Deuteronomy 14:25–26; Mishnah, *Ma'aser Sheni* 1:3, 2:1; Jerusalem Talmud, *Ma'aser Sheni* 1:2, 2:1.

5. See Abraham Doron and Ralph M. Kramer, *The Welfare State in Israel: The Evolution of Social Security Policy and Practice* (Boulder, CO: Westview Press, 1991), 119–134; Gary S. Schiff, "The Politics of Fertility Policy in Israel," in Paul Ritterband, ed., *Modern Jewish Fertility* (Leiden: Brill, 1981), 268–270.
6. See *Niddah* 71b; *Rashi* ad loc., s.v. "*masnisim, u-modim she-okhelet*"; *Yevamot* 74b–75a. The woman who gives birth immerses in a *mikveh* on the seventh day after the birth of a boy and the fourteenth day after the birth of a girl. For the next thirty-three days in the case of the birth of a boy, and sixty-six days in the case of a birth of girl, the mother has the status of a "*tevulat yom arukh*" (lit., "one who immersed on an extended day"). During that time, she is eligible to eat *ma'aser sheni*. After nightfall on the thirty-third or sixty-sixth day, as applicable, if the woman is the wife of a *Kohen*, she becomes eligible to eat *terumah*, according to *Beit Hillel*. According to *Beit Shammai*, she is required to immerse again after nightfall on the thirty-third or sixty-sixth day to be eligible to eat *terumah*.
7. Lit., "who is a Jew." The proposed amendment provided that all conversions to Judaism performed outside the State of Israel would require the endorsement of a rabbinical court in Israel, and that a rabbinical court would be the sole arbiter of whether a person is considered Jewish. Asher Wallfish, "Hillel Battling Shas over New 'Who's a Jew'-Type Bill," *Jerusalem Post*, March 6, 1986, 2.
8. Brigham Young University's planned construction of a center on Mount Scopus in 1985 sparked controversy in Israel over concern that the center would be used to convert Jews. See William Clairborne, "Israeli Jews Fight New Mormon Center;

But perhaps this should extend to having a sympathy with the fanatical Kahaneism movement, with its obsession to evict the Arab population because, after all, they do not belong in *Eretz Yisrael.* No! There is an astonishing *halakhah* of "'*ki yokhal kodesh*' *perat le-mazzik*" (lit., "'one who eats the holy' excludes one who damages the holy").[9] This means that as far as Torah law is concerned, in the entire gamut of civil and tort law, no Jewish court will demand payment for the damage of the property of Hashem – *nezikin le-hedyot ve-ein nezikin le-hekdesh*[10] – whether it pertains to *ona'ah,*[11] or the obligation to pay double,[12] four-fold, or five-fold damages for stolen property.[13] This is saying that God needs no human agent to represent Him in invoking punishment of the one who causes damage.

Brigham Young Presses Construction, Denies That It Intends to Seek Converts," *Washington Post,* December 24, 1985, A10.

9. *Bava Metzia* 99b; *Yoma* 80b. The Torah states, "If a man will eat of the holy [i.e., *terumah*] inadvertently, he shall add a fifth to it and repay the holy to the Priest" (Leviticus 22:14). From the phrase "if a man will eat," the Sages understood that the obligation to pay an additional fifth applies only to one who eats the *terumah,* not to one who damages the *terumah.* The same principle is extended to one who damages *hekdesh,* i.e., items consecrated to the Temple treasury or as offerings. See *Tosafot* to *Bava Metzia* 99b, s.v. "*perat le-mazzik.*"
10. Mishnah, *Bava Kamma* 4:3; *Tosefta, Bava Kamma* 4:3; Jerusalem Talmud, *Gittin* 5:1; *Tosafot* to *Bava Kamma* 6b, s.v. "*shor re'ehu*"; *Tosafot* to *Bava Metzia* 99b, s.v. "*perat le-mazzik.*"
11. *Bava Metzia* 56b; Maimonides, *Mishneh Torah, Mekhirah* 13:8; *Shulḥan Arukh, Ḥoshen Mishpat* 227:29. The Talmud explains that the biblical prohibition against price fraud at Leviticus 25:14 refers to one who wrongs "his brother," implying that the prohibition does not apply to a transaction involving Temple property. *Bava Metzia* 56b.
12. One who steals is required to return the stolen object, or equivalent value if the object is no longer intact, and pay an additional penalty equal to its value. Exodus 22:3; *Rashi* ad loc., s.v. "*ḥayyim shenayim yeshallem.*" In connection with this law, the Torah specifies that the thief shall pay double "to his fellow." Exodus 22:8. From the words "to his fellow," the Sages derived that the obligation to pay double does not apply to theft of property consecrated to the Temple (*hekdesh*). *Bava Kamma* 62b; Maimonides, *Mishneh Torah, Geneivah* 2:1.
13. If one stole a sheep or goat and slaughtered or sold it, he must pay back four times the value of the animal. Exodus 21:37. If the thief stole an ox and slaughtered or sold it, he must pay back five times the value of the ox. Ibid. The four-fold and five-fold penalties are not applicable to theft of consecrated property. See *Bava Kamma* 76a; Maimonides, *Mishneh Torah, Geneivah* 2:1.

This is the best proof of the divine origin of the Torah. Which clerical institution would not resist the temptation to use the secular court to ensure its viability and guarantee its protection?

As far as Torah law is concerned, one who damages *terumah* is completely exempt.[14] Only according to rabbinic law is he liable for the *keren*, the "principal."[15] This tells us clearly that as far as our approach towards those who seek to harm us, we do not invoke the religious law of *ein ha-kohen yakhol limḥol*.[16] No, it is entirely a practical matter, a military consideration, weighing the consequences of action and inaction, direct or subtle, discreet action.

May we merit to clearly perceive the leap from *ma'aser sheni* to *terumah*, the realization of the difference in orientation from the self being the center to the concept of commitment associated with elevation that the *terumah* implies. We must also realize that an increase in our faith must accompany our heightened perception of the holiness of *Eretz Yisrael*.

The balanced growth of our ideal system – on the one hand, the greater sensitivity to *kedushah* and, on the other hand, the greater belief in the divine aspect of our destiny – will bring about a much better understanding between all factions. Then we move toward greeting the Messiah.

---

14. *Bava Metzia* 99b.
15. Ibid.
16. Mishnah, *Terumot* 6:1. This refers to the principle that if one inadvertently ate *terumah*, the Priest may not waive the obligation of the offender to repay the principal and one-fifth to the Priest.

He Will Know that There Is a Prophet in Israel

April 8, 1989

The quest for power, like most human traits, comes in the decadent and virtuous varieties. This stark contrast leaps in front of our eyes in today's *haftarah*. On the one hand, we encounter the mighty warrior Naaman. We are told at the outset that he was merely an instrument of Divine Providence. "Through him Hashem had granted victory to Aram" (II Kings 5:1). Fearing the veracity of the prophecy that he would be slain in the battlefield, Ahab disguises himself as a commoner.[1] But the King of Aram, also hearing of the prophecy, orders his troops to do battle only with the King of Israel, Ahab.[2] Yehoshafat, King of Judah, is mistaken to be Ahab. He is nearly killed,

1. I Kings 22:30.
2. I Kings 22:31.

but miraculously survives.[3] Naaman shoots an arrow in his innocence and it finds Ahab and kills him.[4]

Naaman is clearly only an instrument of Divine Providence, but the masses make him into a hero, and he does nothing to deflect the glory from himself. In fact, all the honor goes to his head. He becomes very haughty and is afflicted with leprosy.[5]

For the man of decadent power, getting healed from the hideous disease is all a matter of using his influence and paying the necessary price. So when word filters to him from the captive Jewish girl that he should offer supplication to the prophet of Israel – "My master's prayers should be brought before the Prophet who is in Samaria" (II Kings 5:3) – he decides that its import is merely that there is a specialist available to heal him. What is needed is merely a plan to manipulate that specialist to treat him. He goes to the King of Aram, who in turn twists the arm of the King of Israel to heal him. The prophet is only another pawn in the scenario for healing the hideous disease, nothing more.

In sharp contrast, power of the virtuous variety is displayed by Elisha. He too craves power. "Let him come to me now, and he will realize that there is a prophet in Israel" (II Kings 5:8). But Elisha summons every ounce of his resourcefulness to heal Naaman in a manner that it will be evident to all that the healing is an act of God and Elisha's role is merely that of an instrument.

Toward this end, Elisha incurs the risk of greatly antagonizing Naaman by refusing to come out personally to meet him, as would befit a dignitary of Naaman's stature. Instead, Elisha sends a messenger to pronounce the cure of bathing seven times in the waters of the Jordan.[6]

Why can Elisha not meet Naaman? Because personal contact might give the impression that Elisha's skill was in part responsible for healing Naaman. Elisha would not touch him or even speak directly to

3. I Kings 22:32–33.
4. I Kings 22:34; *Rashi* ad loc.
5. II Kings 5:1.
6. II Kings 5:10.

him, as doing so might create the impression that he had some role to play in curing Naaman.[7]

Also, of course, Elisha refuses remuneration, doing so most emphatically with an oath, so as not to commercialize the healing of Naaman, so as not to deflect the Glory of Heaven.[8]

Today's *haftarah* is the story of the triumph of "he will know that there is a prophet in Israel" over "the man was a great warrior" (II Kings 5:1). But two people made the utterances "he will know that there is a prophet in Israel." One explicitly, Elisha. But there was another, the anonymous Jewish girl from the Land of Israel. She is doubly anonymous because neither her name nor her city of origin is mentioned. She is described only as an Israelite girl, captured by Naaman in a marauding raid.[9]

I ask you: Which triumph was greater? Was it Elisha's, or was it the anonymous girl's? Elisha was a giant of the spirit. He received the command from Hashem "*lekh taher*," "go heal," and used his genius to devise an intricate plan to deal with Naaman.[10] He focused on the fact that Naaman's name begins with a *nun* and ends with a *nun*. His computer mind then told him that only three verses in the Torah begin with a *nun* and end with a *nun*.[11] This was enough to figure out the intricate plan.[12]

---

7. *Malbim* to II Kings 5:10.
8. II Kings 5:16.
9. II Kings 5:2.
10. The *gematria* of *lekh taher* (go heal) (לך טהר) is 264, the same as that of *yarden* (Jordan) (ירדן). Based on this numerical equivalence, Elisha understood that Naaman should immerse in the Jordan River. R. Moshe Weissman, *The Midrash Says: The Book of Vayikra* (Brooklyn: Benei Yaakov Publications, 1982), 129. See also R. Yaakov Gellis, ed., *Tosafot ha-Shalem: Otzar Perushei Ba'alei ha-Tosafot* (Jerusalem: Makhon Harry Fischel, 2009), Leviticus 13:9, p. 213.
11. The three verses are Leviticus 13:9 ("If a leprosy affliction will be in a person, he shall be brought to the Priest."); Numbers 32:32 ("We shall cross over, armed, before Hashem to the land of Canaan, and ours shall be the heritage of our inheritance across the Jordan."); and Deuteronomy 18:15 ("A prophet from your midst, from your brethren, like me, shall Hashem, your God, establish for you – to him you shall hearken."). Based on these verses, Elisha deduced that Naaman would be healed from his leprosy by bathing in the waters of the Jordan, at the direction of the Prophet.
12. See R. Alexander Zusha Friedman (Poland, 1897–1943), *Ma'ayanah shel Torah*, vol. 3 (Tel Aviv: Pe'er, 1956), 77–78 (citing R. Eleazar b. Judah of Worms [*Roke'aḥ*, Germany,

But Elisha never achieved complete satisfaction and total triumph. For all his meticulous attention to detail and efforts to deflect the glory of triumph away from himself and maximize the Glory of Heaven, Naaman was still not overwhelmed to the extent that he was ready to sanctify Hashem. He acknowledged Hashem and wanted to serve Him, but at the same time, not give up his position and lifestyle, begging forgiveness for not being *moser nefesh* and giving the appearance of serving idols out of fear.[13] And regretfully, the impact that he made on Naaman is further diminished by the venality of Gehazi, who falsely seeks reward in the name of Elisha, commercializing the miracle and hence deflecting glory away from Hashem.[14]

But the triumph of the anonymous girl is beyond her wildest expectations. Her aspiration is "my master's prayers should be brought before the prophet who is in Samaria" (II Kings 5:3). Naaman should supplicate and humble himself before Elisha. Only a humbling experience would heal him.[15]

But what chance was there that Naaman would ever listen to her advice, let alone get word of it? She was, after all, a real nonentity in the profoundest sense, far away from the love of parents and family, being deprived of even a rudimentary education, not important enough that she could hope for ransom. In fact, her message is distorted and is almost the cause of another open war between Aram and Israel based on the King of Israel's response. He thinks that the epistle from the King of Aram requesting that he heal Naaman is a pretext for war.[16]

But somehow, her inner yearning for "he will know that there is a prophet in Israel" is not lost or dissipated. It wends its way through

---

ca. 1176–1238]); R. Nosson Nota Shapira (Cracow, 1585–1633), *Megaleh Amukot, Va-Et'ḥanan* 215.

13. II Kings 5:17–18.

14. II Kings 5:20–24.

15. See R. Samuel b. Abraham Laniado (Aleppo, d. 1605), *Keli Yakar,* II Kings 5:20. R. Laniado notes that other symbols of humility inherent in the cure of Naaman were that the miracle was effected through water and specifically through the waters of the Jordan River. Water is symbolic of humility in that it always flows downwards (*Ta'anit* 7a), and the Hebrew word for Jordan, *Yarden,* is similar to the word "*yeridah,*" a decline in stature.

16. II Kings 5:7.

the many obstacles and hurdles, and the boundary of government. And what is the end result? Naaman does humble himself. He makes a grand acknowledgment of Hashem, greater than Jethro's,[17] and indeed humbles himself as no non-Jew had ever done before. He requests permission to remove the earth on which he stood for the purpose of building an altar, permission to remove something of absolutely no value at all.[18] What submission and awe Naaman evokes for the Prophet!

The anonymous little girl would never dare to add to her yearning of "he will know that there is a prophet in Israel" the preface "let him come to me." Of course not. Naaman would never come to her for the advice. Never. But when Naaman returned home, he did come to the maiden and what he saw in her was the image of God itself. The young girl, despite her bitterness and lugubrious plight of hopelessness, would not begrudge him a favor. The concept of the greatness of the miracle would hence become detached from the miracle of the healing itself.

Yes, the sincere yearning and noble deeds of even the most ordinary people never dissipate. Hashem will weave them into a web and a scenario of events that will culminate in the grand sanctification of Hashem's Name.

17. See Deuteronomy Rabbah 2:28.

18. II Kings 5:17.

Metzora

Death and Life Are in the Hands of the Tongue

April 7, 1984

We are all familiar with the teaching of our Sages that honoring one's parents, the performance of deeds of loving-kindness, and promoting peace are counted among the mitzvot that bring dividends for us in This World, while the main reward is stored up for us for the World to Come.[1] To this, the Mishnah adds that *talmud Torah* is equivalent to all of them.[2] Corresponding to this teaching is another teaching that the three cardinal sins of idolatry, forbidden sexual relations, and murder are punished in This World, but the main punishment is reserved for the World to Come.[3] To this is added that the sin of *lashon ha-ra* is equivalent to all

1. Mishnah, *Pe'ah* 1:1.
2. Ibid.
3. *Tosefta, Pe'ah* 1:2.

of them.[4] We have here a parallel. *Talmud Torah* is the loftiest mitzvah, while *lashon ha-ra* is the most degrading sin.

Why is *lashon ha-ra* singled out and regarded as equivalent to the three cardinal sins? Perhaps the answer lies in the fact that in the good society, transgressions always separate the sinner from the moral climate of society. Moreover, sin often elevates the moral climate of society by arousing within those who take notice a greater revulsion to sin, awakening in them a grain of decency, a greater respect for human life, and a greater commitment towards our beliefs. With the moral climate of society intact, no matter how far the individual strays, he is close to repentance.

Not so when it comes to *lashon ha-ra*. We have an instinct that telling the truth is always somehow to the benefit of society and to all concerned, at the very least in the long run. If Pachaz enters into a partnership with Chaim and finds him to be totally incompetent, it is his duty to inform someone who inquires about Chaim's business acumen to this effect. Disclosure of the truth hence is a mitzvah.[5]

Well, when it comes to a mitzvah, many think that the principle "*zerizin mak'ddimin*"[6] should be invoked. Pachaz makes a preemptory disclosure to everyone he encounters, reasoning that he is only extricating these innocent people from possible financial loss in the eventuality they would consider doing business with Chaim. Despite the fact that there is no urgency or immediacy, the disclosure is made.

Without the interdict of *lashon ha-ra*, we would think that disclosure of an evil report is a mitzvah. Without us being aware of it, *lashon ha-ra* drags down the moral climate of society. Disclosure of *lashon ha-ra* immediately contributes to creating an atmosphere of distrust. At the

---

4. *Arakhin* 15b (recording that the school of R. Yishmael taught that one who speaks slander increases his sins even to the degree of the three cardinal sins). Cf. *Midrash Shoḥer Tov*, Psalms 52:2.

5. R. Israel Meir ha-Kohen Kagan (*Ḥafetz Ḥayyim*, Radin, 1838–1933), *Sefer Ḥafetz Ḥayyim, Tziyyur* 2:1.

6. Lit., "The zealous are early to perform their religious duties." *Pesaḥim* 4a. Our Sages derive the concept that one should perform mitzvot with alacrity from Abraham, who arose early to fulfill Hashem's commandment regarding the Binding of Isaac. See Genesis 22:3 (stating that "Abraham arose early in the morning").

very moment that an individual might be delighting himself in hearing a juicy piece of *lashon ha-ra,* he is subliminally thinking that he may be the next victim of *lashon ha-ra*. When the secret part of someone's life is revealed, there is no longer an atmosphere of harmony.

In Exile, Jews are compared to the dust of the earth,[7] and the gentiles are compared to on-rushing water.[8] As the *Netziv* points out, on-rushing water will disintegrate sand.[9] Only when the particles of dust coalesce and form a stone is there security from the inundating waters. A stone is only rolled by the gushing waters but cannot be disintegrated. *Lashon ha-ra* causes the grains of sand to stand apart, preventing them from coalescing. *Lashon ha-ra* thus attacks our social fabric and we are not even aware of it.

The atonement procedure prescribed for the leper, as the *Shem mi-Shemuel* notes, based on Nahmanides, is very similar to the two he-goats of Yom Kippur.[10] The usual atonement procedure of "turn from evil and do good" (Psalms 34:15) is not followed on Yom Kippur.[11] On this holiest day of the year, we focus not only on remorse for our transgressions, but a reconceptualization of our ideals themselves. We aim for a more noble concept of good.

It is therefore not appropriate to start with a concentration on departing from evil. First we offer the *sa'ir la-Hashem* deep in the Sanctuary, in the Holy of Holies, symbolic of a deeper commitment to the ideal of good. Only then do we attend to the *sa'ir ha-mishtale'aḥ,* which represents the turning away from evil.[12]

---

7. Genesis 28:14.
8. Song of Songs 8:7 ("Many waters [of heathen tribulation] cannot extinguish the fire of this love."); *Rashi* ad loc., s.v. "*mayim rabbim.*"
9. R. Naphtali Tzvi Yehudah Berlin, *Ha'amek Davar,* Genesis 49:24, s.v. "*mi-sham ro'eh even Yisrael.*"
10. R. Shmuel Bornsztain (*Shem mi-Shemuel,* Poland, 1855–1926), *Shem mi-Shemuel: Al Seder Parshiyyot ha-Torah u-Mo'adei Kodesh,* 9th ed., vol. 3 (Jerusalem, 1992), *Metzora* (5763/April 1913), p. 241.
11. Ibid., 244–245.
12. Ibid.

Similarly, in the atonement process of the leper, the leper is bidden to take two birds.[13] Just as the two he-goats must be identical,[14] the two birds must be identical in appearance, height, and value.[15] First our attention is turned toward revitalizing our concept of good, refurbishing society's lost innocence and lower concept of good. To accomplish this, one of the birds, which are wild birds, representing man's untrammeled nature,[16] is slaughtered on top of an earthenware receptacle in *mayim ḥayyim*, the life-giving water.[17]

The ceremony that follows, according to R. Samson Raphael Hirsch, is laden with powerful symbolism. A piece of cedar wood, representative of the highest form of plant life, and the hyssop, representative of the lowest form of plant life, are joined with the wool dyed with the blood of a worm. The wool is from a mammal, the highest form of animal life, and the blood is from a worm, the lowest form of animal life. All this is combined into a single unit. This combination of elements is held separately from the wild bird, as if to say that the leper's behavior resembled the plant and animal kingdoms. Before he can re-enter human society, seven sprinklings must be performed, representing the ever-increasing energetic striving toward achieving the ideal.[18]

Only now after this rededication to the ideal of good do we commit him to depart from evil. The live bird that was dipped in the blood of the other bird and in the *mayim ḥayyim* is now sent away to an uninhabited, desolate place.[19] If the bird returns, it must be driven away again, even a hundred times.[20]

But there is still one more message for the leper before he can re-enter human society. Lest he think that his lot is now to be in a perpetual state of silence, the ceremony includes tying the rest of the

13. Leviticus 14:4.
14. Mishnah, *Yoma* 6:1; *Yoma* 62a.
15. Mishnah, *Nega'im* 14:5; Maimonides, *Mishneh Torah, Tumat Tzara'at* 11:8.
16. R. Samson Raphael Hirsch, Leviticus 14:8.
17. Leviticus 14:5.
18. R. Samson Raphael Hirsch, Leviticus 14:8.
19. Leviticus 14:7.
20. Maimonides, *Mishneh Torah, Tumat Tzara'at* 11:1; R. Aaron b. Joseph ha-Levi, *Sefer ha-Ḥinnukh*, mitzvah no. 173.

elements with a piece of cedar wood. This delivers the message that one must have arrogance and impudence when it comes to speech too, but for the right purpose. Not only death, but life too, is in the hands of the tongue. To encourage a friend, to defend him against attack, to elevate his spirit, speech is fine. There is a place for the piece of cedar wood too.

And to what extent? The Second Temple was destroyed because of *sin'at ḥinnam.*[21] R. Kook says that the Third Temple will be built only through *ahavat ḥinnam.*[22]

21. *Yoma* 9b.
22. R. Abraham Isaac Kook (Palestine, 1865–1935), *Orot ha-Kodesh*, ed. R. David Cohen (*Rav ha-Nazir*, Israel, 1887–1972), Part II, vol. 3 (Jerusalem: Aguddah le-Hotza'at Sifrei ha-Ra'iyah Kook, 1950), 324.

The Moral Climate of Society

April 27, 1985

Perhaps there is no transgression for which an individual is made to feel so acutely the measure-for-measure aspect of divine retribution than the offense of *lashon ha-ra*. One guilty of this sin is afflicted with the appearance of a white spot on his skin. This sign of impurity will carry with it a quarantine only if the color falls in the range of snow-white to egg-white,[1] and the disease will not be pronounced a *nega*, an "affliction," unless the diseased area contains either two white hairs or

1. The Torah mentions three types of spots: *se'et*, *sapaḥat*, and *baheret*. Leviticus 13:2. *Se'et* is the color of the fleece of a newborn lamb, and *baheret* is snow-white. The term *sapaḥat* denotes a derivative form of *tzara'at*. The *sapaḥat* of *se'et* is the color of the skin of an egg, and the *sapaḥat* of *baheret* is the color of the plaster of the Temple. Mishnah, *Nega'im* 1:1; Maimonides, *Mishneh Torah*, *Tumat Tzara'at* 1:2.

raw red meat.[2] It is as if we are saying that even a small misjudgment can cause the ruination or isolation of one's friend.

And if the *nega* is pronounced *tamei,* what occurs to the leper? It is nothing less than isolation and the sense of abandonment that a mourner feels. His hair must grow wild, he must cover his lips, and he may not even associate with other lepers.[3]

Now, at the purification ceremony, we give him a parting admonition regarding his sin. The Priest assembles the *erez,* a twig from the cedar tree, and the *ezov,* the hyssop grass, together representing the highest and lowest forms of plant life, and ties them with a piece of wool dyed in crimson. The wool is from the lamb and the crimson dye from the worm, representing the highest and lowest forms of animal life, to tell the leper that he forfeited living in human society on account of his transgression. The wild bird is also held in his hand, as if to say, "You have much in common with the twittering, chirping bird." All this is dipped into the earthenware vessel, which is filled with the blood of the other bird and the *mayim ḥayyim.* Seven sprinklings are necessary,[4] to indicate the seven-fold rededication to the value of the *mayim ḥayyim,* i.e., the Torah.[5]

Well, if the transgression of *lashon ha-ra* is punished with such an acute dosage of measure for measure, why do our Sages tell us that the *ketoret* and the sound of the bells of the High Priest's robe atone for the sin of *lashon ha-ra*?[6] What kind of atonement can be expected?

The answer is that if we want to purify ourselves from the sin of *lashon ha-ra,* we must focus not only on the naked sin itself, but also on the elements that foster the moral climate that encourages it. So our

2. Leviticus 13:10–11; Mishnah, *Nega'im* 3:7, 4:4; Maimonides, *Mishneh Torah, Tumat Tzara'at* 1:10, 2:1.
3. Leviticus 13:45–46.
4. Leviticus 14:7.
5. See *Keli Yakar* to Leviticus 14:6; *Moshav Zekenim al ha-Torah: Kovetz Peirushei Ba'alei ha-Tosafot* (Jerusalem: Keren Hotza'at Sifrei Rabbanei Bavel, 1982), Leviticus 14:7. According to one view, the Torah consists of seven books. *Shabbat* 116a (citing Proverbs 9:1: "With all forms of wisdom did she build her house; she carved out its seven pillars.").
6. *Zevaḥim* 88b.

focus is on the tingle of the bell of the High Priest. This imparts the message that what might encourage *lashon ha-ra* is not only what we say, but how loudly or softly we say it. How vigorously do we defend our friend? Not defending him vigorously is tantamount to allowing him to falter!

And we focus not on the phrases and words that we say, but rather on an inarticulate sound, the tingle of the bell, that is, the impression that our words leave.

Then we concentrate on an even more delicate dimension of the intangible realm, on something that affects our sensitivities, a fragrance. Our sensitivity to someone else's feelings often spells the difference between encouraging a moral climate and failing to do so.

By concentrating on these elements that are responsible for creating the moral climate, we are brought to a need to perfect ourselves in this dimension, especially as it pertains to speech about our leaders!

Mayor Koch's Dilemma

April 23, 1988

This past week, Mayor Koch was lambasted for the role that he chose to assume in the Democratic Presidential primary in New York City. The Mayor's frequent and vitriolic attacks on both the character and the positions of Jesse Jackson managed, critics claim, to polarize the city and heighten racial tensions.[1] When the results were in, more critics joined the fray. Koch's endorsed candidate was thoroughly thrashed and soon dropped out of the race.[2] The Mayor also seemed to have done some damage to his own political aspirations.[3]

Every Jew, bounded by Halakhah, can well identify with the Mayor's dilemma. The Torah prohibits us from engaging in talebearing, i.e.,

1. Joyce Purnick, "Koch and Fallout from the Primary," *New York Times*, April 21, 1988, D26.
2. Bernard Weinraub, "Gore Suspends Presidential Campaign: The Senator Says He Will Retain His Delegates," *New York Times*, April 22, 1988, A16.
3. John J. Goldman, "Could Boomerang at Reelection Time in '89; Koch Hurt by Attack on Jackson," *Los Angeles Times*, April 21, 1988, C20; Howard Kurtz, "Koch May Be a Victim of His Brickbats," *Washington Post*, April 21, 1988, A17.

from disclosing scandalous but true information regarding our fellow.[4] The prohibition may come into conflict with another dictum of the Torah, *lo sa'amod al dam re'ekha*, "do not stand idly by when the blood of your brother is being shed" (Leviticus 19:16). Our Sages interpret this dictum to extend beyond the life-threatening realm to the monetary sphere.[5] If we know that our fellow is about to enter into a partnership with *A*, or become engaged to a woman, offer a job to *A*, or seek the services of a particular professional, and we have information and a knowledge that the association would be detrimental, we cannot be silent; we must intervene and provide the timely information.

The *Ḥafetz Ḥayyim* devotes much analysis to reconcile these two conflicting obligations. He tells us that we may not set aside the prohibition against talebearing unless several very stringent conditions are met.[6]

First, there must be an immediacy. If we are convinced that *A* is either dishonest or incompetent, we cannot broadcast this to the world so the information can be drawn upon when needed. No! And even if we know that our friend is in the market for a service, a partner, or an employee, we cannot tell him our negative information about *A* unless we know that our friend is contemplating entering into an association with him.[7]

Second, we must not exaggerate. Relatedly, we cannot present what we know only second-hand as first-hand information.[8]

Third, if the penalty would be greater than the person deserves, we cannot make the disclosure.[9]

Finally, if we assess that our advice will not be taken, we cannot make the disclosure.[10] How often is the advice of an acquaintance, and certainly of a stranger, ignored and is even counter-productive with respect to a personal matter?

---

4. Leviticus 19:16.
5. Maimonides, *Sefer ha-Mitzvot, mitzvat lo sa'aseh* no. 297.
6. R. Israel Meir ha-Kohen Kagan, *Sefer Ḥafetz Ḥayyim, Hilkhot Lashon ha-Ra* 10; *Hilkhot Rekhilut* 9.
7. Ibid., *Hilkhot Lashon ha-Ra* 10:2, 10:4; *Hilkhot Rekhilut* 9:1–2.
8. Ibid., *Hilkhot Lashon ha-Ra* 10:2; *Hilkhot Rekhilut* 9:2.
9. Ibid., *Hilkhot Lashon ha-Ra* 10:2; *Hilkhot Rekhilut* 9:5–6.
10. Ibid., *Hilkhot Lashon ha-Ra* 10:4; *Hilkhot Rekhilut* 9:2.

Now, if we would put ourselves in Mayor Koch's position, I think the case against silence is overwhelming. The immediacy test was met. Koch's remarks were made only in the heat of the New York City primary itself, not before. Second, no exaggeration or misstatements were made. He only reminded people of the public record, and no more. Third, with respect to penalties, Jackson deserves nothing less than the maximizing of his political defeat. Fourth, Koch is likely to be listened to. He is the Mayor of New York City, our political leader. We look up to him.

Now, there are two forms of *lashon ha-ra*. There is the type that we are proud of, the self-righteous type, which has a *kol* and can be easily traced back to us. For this type, we need atonement, represented by the bells of the High Priest's robe.[11] He counteracts open evil by visible and open good and nobility. He is "one who loves peace and pursues peace, and loves people."[12]

But there is also another variety of *lashon ha-ra*, the devious type, when we engage in a whispering campaign. We play one person against another. The atonement for this is *davar she-be-ḥashai*, the *ketoret*.[13] The *ketoret* represents using our creativity to produce noble and beautiful combinations.

If there are two varieties of prohibited *lashon ha-ra*, then there are two varieties of the permitted kind. Koch was too crude, negative, and direct and open. He should have used more *ketoret* and less *kol*.

But there is another dimension here. Koch could have viewed himself primarily as a governmental leader with political aspirations and secondarily as a Jew. He could have made an overwhelming case for silence and taken the safe course. He could have reasoned that there is no immediacy here because Jackson will never get the nomination anyway. There is exaggeration because Jackson is contrite and has not been seen lately either embracing Arafat[14] or associating with

11. *Zevaḥim* 88b; *Arakhin* 16a.
12. Mishnah, *Avot* 1:12.
13. *Yoma* 44a; *Zevaḥim* 88b; *Arakhin* 16a. The *ketoret* is referred to as a *davar she-be-ḥashai*, lit., "something in private," because it was offered by the designated Priest in private.
14. See "Jackson in Beirut, Declares Support for Palestinian Cause," *Hartford Courant*, September 30, 1979, 11; "Jackson and Arafat Confer in Lebanon: Civil Rights Leader

Farrakhan.[15] He could have reasoned that no one would listen to him; the electorate is independent and politically sophisticated. And finally, any rhetoric might set an oppressed group, African Americans, back more than is warranted. Any issue of Israel is in the realm of national, not local, politics.

No, the Mayor felt his Jewishness so intensely that he forgot about his political life and felt first and foremost that he was a Jew. And as a Jew, he was being attacked personally by Jackson. He looked upon Jackson as a *rodef* and had no recourse but to speak up.

We are all human, and we will always err in reconciling the obligation to remain silent with the obligation to speak up. I, for one, pray that any mistake I make should be in the direction of over-defending the Jewish people, rather than in over-defending myself.

Later Suggests That He Serve as a Mediator between U.S. and P.L.O., *New York Times*, September 30, 1979, 7; *Jerusalem Post*, September 30, 1979, 1 (photograph of Jesse Jackson embracing Arafat).

15. See Bruce Buursma, "Black Muslim Leader Sharing Jackson Limelight," *Chicago Tribune*, February 26, 1984, C1.

Aḥarei Mot–Kedoshim

The Building Blocks of the Good Society

April 28, 1984

The Torah apparently fully appreciates that the emotional claim is the most taxing demand on man. Accordingly, the Torah discriminates. When it comes to our fellow Jew, the Torah demands nothing less than love, "Love your fellow as yourself" (Leviticus 19:18). When it comes to a brother, however, we do not expect love, only "You shall not hate your brother in your heart" (19:17). When it comes to the *Rav*, the Torah demands neither love nor restraint from hatred, only "*Elokim lo tikallel*," "you shall not curse God" (Exodus 22:27).[1] Finally, when it comes to the *Nasi*, the Torah does not demand love, or restraint from hatred or cursing. We ask only that we not curse the *Nasi* in a way that we would physically

1. See *Sanhedrin* 66a (explaining that the commandment "you shall not curse God" (Exodus 22:27) includes a prohibition against cursing a judge).

injure him, "*nasi be-ammekha lo sa'or,*" "you shall not curse a leader among your people" (ibid.).[2]

In all seriousness, when the Torah makes an emotional demand on the Jew in his interpersonal relations, the claim is never total and all-encompassing.[3] Yet, when it comes to *bein adam la-Makom,* the emotional claim on the Jew is total and all-encompassing. We are bidden to love Hashem and to fear Him.[4] Throughout the generations, the commentators have grappled with the question: How can we be demanded to love and fear that which we have never seen and recognized?[5] More fundamentally, how can we be commanded to love and fear? Emotions are not within our control. Actions, yes. But emotions?

Several approaches have been advanced to answer these questions.[6] We would like to suggest a somewhat novel approach. Man is created in the image of God.[7] Though all men reflect God's image, the image of God is more evident in some types of people than in others. By focusing on and imposing *halakhot* with respect to the types of people who reflect the divine image more clearly, the Torah capitalizes on the natural impulse and ensures that the impulse spreads upward to a fear and love of Hashem Himself. Recognition of the handiwork of the Creator leads to the recognition of the Creator Himself. Two categories of people who

---

2. The root word *kalal* signifies a less severe curse than the root word *arar*. *Kalal* denotes denigration whereas *arur* is a curse accompanied by physical harm. R. Baruch ha-Levi Epstein (*Torah Temimah*, Belarus, 1860–1941), *Torah Temimah*, Exodus 22:27, n. 213.
3. For example, the obligation to love one's fellow is to love him "as yourself" (Leviticus 19:18).
4. Deuteronomy 6:5 ("You shall love Hashem, your God, with all your heart, with all your soul, and with all your resources."); Deuteronomy 6:13 ("Hashem, your God, shall you fear.").
5. See, e.g., *Sifrei*, Deuteronomy 33; Maimonides, *Sefer ha-Mitzvot*, no. 3; Maimonides, *Mishneh Torah, Yesodei ha-Torah* 2:2; R. Joseph Albo (Spain, ca. 1380–1445), *Sefer ha-Ikkarim, ma'amar* 3, ch. 36.
6. One approach is that the obligation to love Hashem can be understood as commanding that the Name of Heaven become beloved through one's actions. In particular, one should read Scripture, learn Mishnah, and serve Torah scholars, and his dealings with others should be conducted in a pleasant manner. See *Yoma* 86a. According to *Sifrei*, one can achieve love of Hashem by reflecting upon the words of the Torah. *Sifrei*, Deuteronomy 33.
7. Genesis 1:26.

especially reflect the divine image because of their role are parents and the married couple.

Parents reflect the divine image on a simple level because there are three partners in the creation of man.[8] But, in addition, the commandment to honor one's parents in the Decalogue appears immediately after the commandment to keep the Sabbath.[9] Parents, by virtue of their role, are Sabbath creatures. The *Beit ha-Levi* points out that the Torah says that "by the seventh day, God completed His work that He had done" (Genesis 2:2). This proves that the Sabbath did not represent merely a cessation from work, but that the Sabbath itself was a creation.[10]

The creation on the Sabbath was the routinization of what was created on the previous six days. "Who renews in His goodness every day perpetually the work of Creation."[11] Such action is not apparent, but it is very important. It represents stability. Parents are truly the stabilizing force in their children's lives. When their children are very young, parents set routines for them. Parents are always the crisis managers in their children's lives. They therefore assume the role of a stabilizer.

There is one more aspect of the divine image in parents that is like the Sabbath. Just as on the Sabbath, we turn our creative energies away from the environment and instead direct those energies inward for the purpose of recreating ourselves, enhancing our spiritual lives, so, too, parents sacrifice their own development and turn their creative energies toward fashioning the character of their children. That sacrifice and devotion nurture the element of *hakkarat ha-tov* in children. Because parents reflect the divine image in such an exemplary manner, the Torah treats them as God-like creatures.

Kavod and *mora* characterize the filial obligation toward one's parents.[12] *Kavod* is service, and *mora* is fear and awe. *Mora* manifests itself in the form of not contradicting the words of one's father and *lo*

---

8. *Niddah* 31a.
9. Exodus 20:8–12.
10. R. Yosef Dov Soloveitchik (*Beit ha-Levi*, Belarus, 1820–1892), *Beit ha-Levi al Derush u-Milei de-Aggadata, Bereshit* (Jerusalem, 1985), 5–7.
11. Morning Prayer, Blessings of the *Shema*.
12. Exodus 20:12 ("honor your father and your mother"); Leviticus 19:3 ("every man shall revere his mother and father").

makhri'o, not tipping the scales.[13] *Rashi* understands *lo makhri'o* to mean that a child may not support an opponent of his father in a Talmudic debate.[14] But R. Meir b. Todros ha-Levi Abulafia says that not supporting his father's opponent in a Talmudic debate is part of the prohibition against contradicting a parent's words.[15] In his view, *lo makhri'o* means instead that one should not be presumptuous to chime in to the dispute by saying "I would agree with Father," for who are you to presume that your father's position is enhanced by the fact that you agree with him?[16] In short, the child must do nothing to depreciate the authoritarian image of his father.

The scope of *meḥilah* is also limited. A particular act of *kavod* may be excused,[17] but a father may not abrogate the role that the Torah assigns to him as a father.[18] Parents must define the role for the child. Parents cannot tolerate abuse or cursing by their child. Since parents reflect the divine image to such a great degree, the honor and fear of parents that the Torah demands of a child will spread to the fear of Hashem, as the Creator is always recognized by His handiwork.

But the Torah says, "Therefore a man shall leave his father and his mother and cling to his wife, and they shall become one flesh" (Genesis 2:24). This statement is understood by *Onkelos* to refer to the fact that man leaves the physical residence of his parents.[19] But *Pirkei de-Rabbi Eliezer* understands this to refer to the emotional state of love.[20] When a man marries, the love that he has for his parents is transferred to his wife, and he becomes one entity with her. What appears to be said

---

13. *Kiddushin* 31b; Maimonides, *Mishneh Torah, Mamrim* 6:3; *Shulḥan Arukh, Yoreh De'ah* 240:2.
14. *Rashi* to *Kiddushin* 31b, s.v. "*lo makhri'o.*"
15. R. Meir b. Todros ha-Levi Abulafia (*Ramah,* Spain, ca. 1170–1244), cited in *Tur, Yoreh De'ah* 240.
16. R. Abraham Danzig (Prague, 1748–1820), *Ḥayyei Adam, Kibbud Av ve-Em* 67:8.
17. *Kiddushin* 32a; Maimonides, *Mishneh Torah, Mamrim* 6:8; *Shulḥan Arukh, Yoreh De'ah* 240:19.
18. R. Ahai Gaon (Palestine, 8th cent.), *She'iltot de-Rav Aḥai Gaon, Mishpatim,* no. 60; R. Isaac b. Sheshet Perfet (*Rivash,* Spain, 1326–1408), *She'elot u-Teshuvot ha-Rivash,* no. 220.
19. *Targum Onkelos* to Genesis 2:24.
20. *Pirkei de-Rabbi Eliezer* 32.

here is that the highest level of love is achieved in the marital relationship, as in connection with no other relationship does the Torah employ the phrase "they shall become one flesh."

Now, the marital relationship, unlike the parent-child relationship, is one of equality. Oneness in the marital relationship is achieved on three reinforcing levels. First, man is not fulfilled until he marries, as our Sages comment that a man who has no wife lives without joy, without blessing, without Torah, and without peace.[21] Second, marriage is a friendship of sharing. A joy shared is intensified, and a sorrow shared is lessened. Finally, when a couple is united in their commitment to an ideal, and both partners work to achieve it, they are fused in a metaphysical, transcendent way.

Now, only when man is content with himself, fully loves himself, and recognizes his own divine image, is he capable of loving his friend. When a wife sees the divine image of selfless devotion and oneness with her in her husband, and when the husband sees the same in his wife, each has recognized the handiwork of the Master of the Universe. This selfless love is then capable of spreading to society at large and to Hashem Himself.

Parenthood, with its aura of fear and honor, and marriage, with its aura of love and oneness, are therefore the building blocks of the moral climate of society. Today we are witnessing a perversion of these two ideals. Parenthood sometimes fosters permissiveness instead of honor and fear, and marriage is sometimes not characterized as a complementary relationship, but instead as one of fear and competition. When the institutions of parenthood and marriage achieve their ideal states, however, the resulting docility and love permeate society, and the religious climate is intensified.

21. *Yevamot* 62b.

Love Your Fellow as Yourself – This Is the Entire Torah

May 9, 1987

The great Sage Hillel, as we all know, summarized to a convert the entire Torah with the succinct principle: "What is hateful to you, do not do to your neighbor. That is the whole Torah. The rest is commentary. Go and learn it."[1]

Now, if the guidepost for interpersonal behavior is for us to imagine what our reaction would be if we ourselves would be the target of our own conduct, would not many commercial transactions be defeated? How could a salesperson allow a customer to buy a product that he himself would never buy? Could a man in good conscience offer to sell a financial asset or a parcel of real estate when the offer is motivated by a firm conviction that the price will subsequently plunge?

1. *Shabbat* 31a.

Indeed, the story is told of R. Eliyahu ha-Kohen Dushnitzer (1876–1949), the *Mashgiaḥ* of the Lomza Yeshiva in Petach Tikvah, who sought to sell an orchard that he owned near Tel Aviv. On his way to inspect the property with a prospective buyer from America, R. Elya learned that the buyer was not planning to settle in Israel and would therefore not personally manage the orchard. R. Elya began discouraging him from buying the property, citing R. Yohanan's dictum, "If someone wishes to lose his money, he should hire workers and not supervise them."[2]

R. Elya went on to describe all the orchard's defects. The buyer was still interested. When they arrived at the orchard, R. Elya insisted on taking him around to point out the property's defects, invoking the dictum "hearing is not the same as seeing."[3] The buyer was still interested. But when R. Elya observed the buyer swallowing a few pills because of a heart condition, he simply refused to sell the property. Over the protests of the buyer, R. Elya gently but firmly stated that owning the orchard would entail too much aggravation for an absentee owner who was also in such delicate health.[4]

I would submit that there are two aspects of the commandment "love your fellow as yourself" (Leviticus 19:18). One aspect comes into play when we are directly asked by our fellow to advise him in a matter and tell him what we would do if confronted with the same circumstances. Another example is when we feel as parents that we should intervene in a situation and impose our values, our approach, and our feelings. Here, we must imagine ourselves in the situation of our friend.

But there are many situations when we have no right to invade someone's privacy or assume a paternalistic role. Quite the opposite, we are bound to respect our friend, to give him enough credit to respect his individuality, his maturity, and his independence. We cannot mold him in our image.

---

2. *Bava Metzia* 29b.
3. *Mekhilta, Yitro* 2.
4. R. Paysach J. Krohn, *The Maggid Speaks: Favorite Stories and Parables of Rabbi Shalom Schwadron Shlita, Maggid of Jerusalem* (New York: Mesorah, 1987), 66–71.

This occurs in the commercial setting. It is our duty to make forthright disclosure, provide our client or customer with the pertinent facts, and let him decide for himself what is in his best interests.[5] Removing ourselves from paternalism comes to an extreme in the investment area. Participation here carries with it an implied assumption that it is only contrary expectations that make the transaction possible.

When we are in doubt if we should exercise paternalism or respect our opposite number's independence, we should probably have a bias toward paternalism. But there is one circumstance when our bias should certainly be in the opposite direction, and this is where we exercise our charity obligation. When our fellow is thrust into a state of dependency, we should do nothing to rub into him his state of dependency by instructing him how he should use the aid that we give him. It is degrading to presume that the recipient does not have his priorities set straight. We should grant him the presumption that he has the maturity and the intelligence to know what to do with the money.[6]

Regrettably, the Jewish community has been recently victimized by an action taken by the Jewish Agency requiring all *yeshivot* to take a pledge of loyalty to Zionism as a condition to continue receiving financial aid from the Jewish Agency.[7] This amounts to a requirement to send their students to the army and the equivalent for girls. This is paternalism with respect to charity giving. Moreover, the principle is a blatant

5. *Ḥullin* 94a; R. Isaac b. Jacob Alfasi (*Rif*, Algeria, 1013–1103), *Rif* ad loc.; *Mishneh Torah, Mekhirah* 18:1; R. Asher b. Jehiel (*Rosh*, Germany, ca. 1250–1327), *Rosh, Ḥullin* 7:18; *Tur, Ḥoshen Mishpat* 228; *Shulḥan Arukh, Ḥoshen Mishpat* 228:6; *Arukh ha-Shulḥan, Ḥoshen Mishpat* 228:3. See generally R. Aaron Levine, *Case Studies in Jewish Business Ethics* (Hoboken, NJ: Ktav, 2000), 116–137.
6. See *Rema* to *Shulḥan Arukh, Oraḥ Ḥayyim* 694:2 (stating that a poor person is entitled to spend the money he receives as charity on Purim as he wishes); R. Moses Sofer (*Ḥatam Sofer*, Hungary, 1762–1839), *She'elot u-Teshuvot ha-Ḥatam Sofer, Yoreh De'ah* 238, s.v. "*ve-amnam be-teshuvot Rashba*"; R. Ezra Batzri, *Dinei Mamonot*, vol. 4 (Jerusalem: Haktav Institute, 1982), *sha'ar* 4, ch. 5, p. 227, ¶ 3 (stating that one who gives charity to a *gabbai* of *tzedakah* is not entitled to dictate to the *gabbai* how the money should be spent).
7. Asher Wallfish, "*Yeshivot Hesder* Head for Clash with Agency," *Jerusalem Post*, April 27, 1987, 2.

violation of Halakhah, as it denies the primacy of Torah study for the survival of Israel. We cannot stand by idly and allow the Jewish Agency to grossly pervert the commandment "love your fellow as yourself."

Plant Closings

April 30, 1988

This past week, as the trade bill waded its way through Congress and it became apparent that not enough support could be found to override the expected Presidential veto, one of its provisions emerged as a major issue in the 1988 Presidential campaign. This was the provision that called for employers to give employees sixty days' notice of plans to close plants or implement widespread layoffs. As the bill affects mostly huge corporations with billions of dollars of assets, Republicans are opposed to the proposal. They regard it as an unnecessary intrusion into the private affairs of business and detrimental to the competitiveness of U.S. business in world markets. Democrats, however, regard it as a necessary social reform, softening the impact of economic dislocation.[1]

1. Clyde H. Farnsworth, "Trade Bill Voted in Senate by 63–36 but Is Facing Veto," *New York Times*, April 28, 1988, A1. The proposal requiring advance notification of plant closings was passed by a veto-proof Democratic majority in Congress and was enacted as the Workers Adjustment and Retraining Notification Act (WARN Act) without President Reagan's signature on August 4, 1988. Pub. L. No. 100–379, 102 Stat. 890 (1988) (codified at 29 U.S.C. §§ 2101–2109 (1988)).

What perspective does Halakhah provide for this issue? We are dealing here with vehicles of enormous economic power and leverage. What therefore comes to mind is R. Yohanan's dictum that "wherever you find mention of the power of the Holy One, Blessed is He, you find His humility."[2] He demonstrates this with three different proofs. Why three? Because each adds something to the lesson of how we should emulate divine conduct in human relations.

First, we get the image of Hashem as a powerful judge, who is impervious to graft, "Who does not show favor and Who does not accept a bribe" (Deuteronomy 10:17). So we would think that some cases are too trivial or petty to warrant attention by Hashem. We are told otherwise. "He executes the judgment of the orphan and widow, and loves the proselyte to give him bread and garment" (Deuteronomy 10:18).

Then we see the image of Hashem as one occupied in exalted matters beyond human intelligence and ken, "exalted and uplifted One," but nevertheless interested "to revive the heart of the despondent."[3] We can relate to this on the level that society is obliged to show empathy towards the victims of power although the plight of the victims was not the side effect of society's actions.

Finally, we can relate to R. Yohanan on a legislative level. We get the image of Hashem as "*rokhev ba-aravot*," "riding upon the highest heavens."[4] *Aravot* is where the deeds of the most righteous are stored. And we would be tempted to think that when Hashem, in a manner of speaking, is turning His attention to the most righteous, He would have no interest in the small deeds of little people. To this we say, "Father of orphans and Defenders of widows is God in the abode of His holiness" (Psalms 68:6). Legislators who are addressing priorities will be concerned with exalted matters such as disarmament and tax reform, but not necessarily the problems of workers outside the protection of unions and the civil service.

2. *Megillah* 31a.
3. Isaiah 57:15.
4. Psalms 68:5.

You may very well think that what I have said relates only to the realm of *lifnim mi-shurat ha-din,* not to the realm of legislative mandate. And what if the firm is faltering, and the sharing of the information of the plant closing will compromise the finances of the firm? What the arguments do, I contend, is only make a case for the sharing of the costs of disclosure or the shifting of those costs after the disclosure is made, depending upon the case.

What we are dealing with is not merely labor relations, but Judaism's basic social welfare philosophy. Our society recognizes that if an individual is laid off, he is impoverished and must be given unemployment compensation. But we are bidden not only to take care of our fellow's physical needs, but to provide him with "*dei maḥsaro asher yeḥsar lo*" (lit., "sufficient for his requirement, whatever is lacking to him") (Deuteronomy 15:8). If Hillel could provide the pauper who had previously been wealthy with a horse to ride on and a servant to run before him,[5] we surely should recognize that to maintain his self-worth, man aspires for a job, the knowledge that his skill is demanded and, if his skill is no longer in demand, that we will re-train him so that he can again become valuable to society.

If we do not relate on an emotional level to this issue, it is because, I submit, our concept of justice is much too narrow. Hashem's justice, in contrast, is global and cosmic. Now, when a huge firm locates in a neighborhood, it puts into motion a whole welter of relationships. The municipality expands services and water facilities. The school plants and facilities expand to accommodate the children of the workers. The government builds roads, bridges, and trains, and an educational system to train the workers. The firm derives such enormous benefits from society. If it now abruptly relocates, it leaves everyone in the lurch. Where is the *hakkarat ha-tov* akin to *va-yiḥan et penei ha-ir* (Genesis 33:18)?[6]

5. *Sifrei,* Deuteronomy 116; *Ketubbot* 67b.

6. When Jacob arrived at the city of Shekhem from Paddan-aram, the verse states, "*va-yiḥan et penei ha-ir,*" "he encamped before the city." Connecting the word "*va-yiḥan,*" "he encamped," to "*ḥanan,*" "he conferred benefit," the Midrash explains that Jacob established bazaars and sold merchandise cheaply as a display of gratitude to the city for providing shelter and peace. From this conduct, we learn that one must be grateful to a place from where he derived benefit. Genesis Rabbah 79:6.

And finally, what about the "sweet smell of pollution"?[7] As Governor Wallace pointed out, it is sweet because it represents the smell of money.[8] The EPA sets ceilings on pollution levels, but it is up to the municipalities to confer licenses to fill their quota.[9] In the name of economic progress and jobs, huge corporations are given licenses to pollute. There is an implicit contract. We will tolerate pollution up to a point and suffer a reduction in our health standards and an increase in the mortality rate because you provide us with jobs and a decent standard of living. There is a *quid pro quo*. And now the firm ignores the implicit contract and abruptly, without notice, refuses to share vital information. It is a callous disregard of an implicit contract. And the pollution, of course, is here to stay and will continue to wreak havoc.

In the Holocaust, we saw the use by the Nazis of the inventions of modern society to minimize the cost of killing Jews. So our challenge is to sanctify the engines of economic concentration and leverage by infusing in them a soul.

---

7. The sweet smell of pollution refers to benzene, a clear colorless liquid that has a sweet odor. Benzene is used primarily as a raw material for synthesizing chemicals and for manufacturing rubbers, lubricants, dyes, detergents, drugs, and pesticides. Industrial processes are the main source of benzene in the environment. Agency for Toxic Substances and Disease Registry, *Toxicological Profile for Benzene*, U.S. Public Health Service, U.S. Department of Health and Human Services, Atlanta, GA, August 2007, 1–2.
8. Governor George Wallace is reported to have said after taking a deep breath outside a rural Alabama paper mill in the early 1960s, "Yeah, that's the smell of prosperity. Sho' does smell sweet, don't it?" David R. Goldfield, *Promised Land: The South Since 1945* (Arlington Heights, IL: Harlan Davidson, 1987), 197.
9. See Robert J. Marineau and David P. Novello, eds., *The Clean Air Act Handbook*, 2nd ed. (Chicago: American Bar Association, 2004), 13; Environmental Protection Agency, "Air Pollution and Operating Permit Program Update: Key Features and Benefits," February 1998.

The *Ḥok* Test for the Gentile Society

April 29, 1989

There is perhaps no law in the Torah that evokes a heavier image of a social barrier between us and the non-Jewish world than the prohibition of *be-ḥukkoteihem lo telekhu*, "do not follow their traditions" (Leviticus 18:3). The formulation of this prohibition advanced by the fifteenth century Italian halakhist R. Joseph Colon b. Solomon Trabotto is widely adopted today.[1] In his view, a *ḥok* should be understood in the familiar sense of a practice or custom that defies logic or reason. Adopting such a practice reflects a desire on our part to imitate the gentile. Adopting a custom, as long as it is not idolatrous, even if there is some advantage for us in the adoption, is not, however, objectionable.

On this basis, *Maharik* ruled that it was permissible for Jewish physicians to wear the special frock that gentile physicians wore at the

1. R. Joseph Colon b. Solomon Trabotto (*Maharik*, Italy, ca. 1420–1480), *She'elot u-Teshuvot ha-Maharik*, *shoresh* 88. See also *Rema* to *Yoreh De'ah* 178:1 (citing *Maharik*).

time, since the motivation was to identify oneself as a physician rather than to imitate the ways of the gentiles.[2]

After World War II, the European refugees in America asked R. Mosheh Feinstein if adopting American dress would entail any prohibition. Assuming the standards of modesty are met, R. Mosheh found no violation of "do not follow their traditions" (Leviticus 18:3). Granted that styles and fashion defy logic, it is not the *ḥok* of the gentile. Rather it is just nonsense generally of society. Fashions are made indiscriminately for all, for Jews and gentiles alike.[3]

With respect to the American custom of not covering one's head indoors, not wearing a *kippah* at work does not constitute a violation of "do not follow their traditions." When our motive is purely monetary, to land and keep a job, by not wearing a *kippah,* we are not acknowledging the gentile. We are motivated merely by monetary gain.[4]

For some, Thanksgiving is a problem. In their view, if the celebration of a few Pilgrims evolved into a national holiday, this is a *ḥok*. But for me, Thanksgiving is a happy reminder that we enjoy religious freedom in America. It is reminiscent of the call of the *rav ha-ḥovel,* "How can you sleep so soundly? Arise! Call to your God!" (Jonah 1:6). It is a call made not in a time of life-threatening crisis, but in ordinary times. It is a call to give thanksgiving for the ordinary blessings of life, blessings that we often take for granted.

Now, if research and analysis remove the *ḥok* element of a practice and legitimize it for us, then *a fortiori,* it is our obligation to put to question the presupposition of the gentile culture. It is our duty to examine the underlying logic and rationale behind the attitudes of the gentile culture. We should not mindlessly accept everything at face value and assume that since many people follow it, there simply must be a logic to it.

A case in point is the distinction between public and private ethics. The recent John Tower confirmation hearings showed that the American public freely embraces the concept of the compartmentalized

2. *She'elot u-Teshuvot ha-Maharik, shoresh* 88.
3. R. Mosheh Feinstein, *Iggerot Mosheh* (Jerusalem, 1996), *Yoreh De'ah* 4:11, ¶ 3.
4. See ibid. and *Iggerot Mosheh, Oraḥ Ḥayyim* 4:2.

personality. The issue was whether a man whose private morality is out of control should be suspect regarding the execution of his public duties. In the view of the majority of Americans, as long as discretion is exercised, we can overlook private immorality.[5]

But for us, the public servant is the first citizen of nobility. There is no such thing as the compartmentalized personality.

5. Richard Morin, "Majority in Poll Says Tower Not Disqualified by Drinking," *Washington Post,* March 1, 1989, A11.

Rights or Duties?

May 5, 1990

It has often been said that the essential difference between the American legal system and the legal system prescribed by the Torah is that in the former, everything revolves around rights – constitutional rights, legislated rights, and the assertion of rights – but in the Torah society, everything revolves around duties and responsibilities. Built on top of this system of duties is legislation that adjures us not to abuse our responsibilities and duties.

Highlighting in a very poignant way the difference between a society that bases itself on rights and one that bases itself on duties is the treatment of the borrower. Halakhah makes no bones of this. The debtor is called a servant. "A debtor is a servant to the creditor" (Proverbs 22:7). And we need not go far afield to discover why. The debtor need only think of what will happen to him if he repudiates a lawful debt that he has the ability to pay. The Jewish court will seize his assets – *mesadderin le-ba'al ḥov* – and leave him with precious little.[1] If it is a debt that he owes his spouse, the *ketubbah* will be enforced, "*Ve-ana eflah... yasikhi likhi,*" "I will work so that I can provide financial support for you," and he will be forced to take a job.

But if we move to corporate America, protected under limited liability, there is no fear of being a servant. Moreover, executives perched in high places in corporate America feel insecure if their company carries very little debt because that makes the company a likely candidate for a hostile takeover. So what do they do? They pile on debt to make any potential suitor uninterested.[2]

Another difference is that in the society based on duties, the debtor would be abusing his position if he would borrow on *bittaḥon,* without providing collateral. Why? Only in connection with the needs of the Sabbath is there is a dispensation on the basis of "*loveh alai... ve-ani pore'a,*" "borrow on My account and I will pay."[3] But in the international financial markets, we have been witnessing the spectacular phenomenon of Third World debt. Seventy percent of the debt lent by major banks is syndicated loans, which drag in the small banks.[4] But it has resulted in widespread unilateral suspension of interest and principal, in other words, in default. And why? It is the theory of the greater fool.[5]

---

1. *Bava Metzia* 113b–114a; *Tur, Ḥoshen Mishpat* 97; *Shulḥan Arukh, Ḥoshen Mishpat* 97:23; *Arukh ha-Shulḥan, Ḥoshen Mishpat* 97:26. *Mesadderin le-ba'al ḥov* refers to the process by which *beit din* inventories the assets of the debtor and allows the debtor to retain basic necessities.
2. See Milton Harris and Artur Raviv, "The Theory of Capital Structure," *Journal of Finance* 46, no. 1 (March 1991): 319–325; Richard G. Clemens, "Poison Debt: The New Takeover Defense," *Business Lawyer* 42, no. 3 (May 1987): 747–760.
3. *Beitzah* 15b.
4. See Victoria Ivashina and David Scharfstein, "Loan Syndication and Credit Cycles," *American Economic Review: Papers and Proceedings of the One Hundred Twenty Second Annual Meeting of the American Economic Association* 100, no. 2 (May 2010): 59 (illustrating through a graph the percentage of U.S. loans retained by banks each year from 1990 through 2009).
5. The theory states that any price can be justified if a buyer believes that there is another buyer, i.e., a "greater fool," who will pay an even higher price for the same item. See Burton G. Malkiel, *A Random Walk Down Wall Street: The Best Investment Advice for the New Century* (New York: W. W. Norton, 1999), 32.

The final difference between these two societies is that in Jewish law, we have the concept of "the wicked one borrows but repays not" (Psalms 37:21), which means that the debtor may not engage in reckless behavior to endanger his ability to pay back the loan. If he does, the lender can get a court order to seize collateral, a *mashkon she-lo be-sha'at halva'ah*.[6]

But in America, we have the phenomenon of the leveraged buyout, which results in the downgrading of the existing debt of the target corporation. What American society has done on the order of the spectacular is to eviscerate the servitude part of being a debtor and hence denude this role of any capability to generate *hakkarat ha-tov*. Cultivating the delicate sensitivity of *hakkarat ha-tov* is the essential ingredient in forming the moral personality.[7] Joseph overcame the wiles of Lady Potiphar only by invoking *hakkarat ha-tov* to Potiphar[8] and to Jacob.[9] Hence, he personalized the moral dilemma.

If the national setting of debtor-creditor relations does not produce *hakkarat ha-tov*, the vital sentiment is blunted even in the compelling setting of honoring one's parents. And for teachers, even their relationships lapse into *quid pro quo* encounters. Our sensitivity to *hakkarat ha-tov* is blunted.

Our Sages were well aware of the trickle-down effect when it comes to abusing the duties and responsibilities that the Torah imposes on us. When R. Shimon asked R. Yishmael why he deserved to die at the hands of the Romans, R. Yishmael explained that even trivial oppression is prohibited by the Torah, and thus R. Shimon must have been guilty of abusing his authority by making people wait a bit before adjudicating their case, causing them anguish.[10] If the great Sage abuses his authority, then it trickles down to every segment of society.

Now, think of the *kiddush ha-Shem* that could result if we would move a little bit away from *ona'at devarim*, inflicting less abuse, and take our duties and responsibilities much more to heart.

---

6. Lit., "collateral taken not at the time the loan is made." *Bava Metzia* 113a; *Mishneh Torah, Malveh ve-Loveh* 3; *Tur, Ḥoshen Mishpat* 97; *Shulḥan Arukh, Ḥoshen Mishpat* 97:6; *Arukh ha-Shulḥan, Ḥoshen Mishpat* 97:5.
7. See R. Aaron Levine, *Economic Public Policy and Jewish Law* (Hoboken, NJ: Ktav, 1993), ch. 5.
8. Genesis 39:8–9.
9. *Sotah* 36b.
10. *Mekhilta, Mishpatim* 18, s.v. "*im anneh si'anneh*."

His Mercies Are on All His Works

April 27, 1991

With the rate of unemployment in the current recession reaching almost the highest level of this decade, many pained people are demanding that business firms, especially huge corporations, demonstrate that they are not just legal personalities, but have a heart and a soul. Restraint should be shown in layoff policy. At other times, these same voices would call for the firm to sacrifice some of its profits to show restraint in pricing, abuse the environment less than the law allows, and be less brutal in labor negotiations than profit considerations dictate. All these demands fall under the rubric of social responsibility, which we would call *lifnim mi-shurat ha-din*.[1]

1. The obligation to act *lifnim mi-shurat ha-din* is derived from the verse "You shall make known to them the path in which they shall go and the deeds that they should do" (Exodus 18:20). In this passage, "deed" refers to strict law, and "that they must go" refers to *lifnim mi-shurat ha-din*. *Bava Kamma* 100a. See generally R. Aaron Levine,

Well, Milton Friedman calls this approach a dangerous one, no less than fundamentally subversive to a free society. As individuals, working on their own time and spending their own resources, people are in a free society. But as agents of an organization set up to make profits, the managers can run the business only to promote their goal. Besides, they are not expert at achieving the goals of social responsibility. If business managers would attempt to promote social goals, they would be acting like civil servants imposing taxes on their shareholders and using their concept of social justice to spend their money. In the long run, society would be much better off if all firms would pursue a policy of profit maximization and this larger base of wealth would allow people as individuals to pursue what they feel constitutes social justice.[2]

At first glance, Friedman's view finds support in Halakhah. We cannot coerce anyone to conduct himself *lifnim mi-shurat ha-din*.[3] And in the Jewish society, a coercive tax levy for charitable causes is the domain of the public sector,[4] so a business firm that adopts this goal would be usurping the function of the public sector.

Permit me to suggest that Friedman's approach assaults cherished Jewish values. The highest ideal in the Torah society is to imitate

---

Case Studies in Jewish Business Ethics (Hoboken, NJ: Ktav, 2000), 258–262; R. Aaron Levine, *Economics and Jewish Law* (Hoboken, NJ: Ktav, 1987), 26–31.

2. Milton Friedman, *Capitalism and Freedom* (Chicago: University of Chicago Press, 1962), 133–135; Milton Friedman, "The Social Responsibility of Business Is to Increase Its Profits," *New York Times Magazine*, September 13, 1970, 32–33, 122–124.
3. See R. Hananel b. Hushi'el (*Rabbeinu Ḥananel*, Kairouan, 990–1053), *Bava Metzia* 24b; *Rosh*, *Bava Metzia* 2:7; R. Yom Tov Ishbili (*Ritva*, Spain, ca. 1250–1330), *Ḥiddushei ha-Ritva*, *Bava Metzia* 24b; R. Joseph Caro, *Beit Yosef* to *Tur*, *Ḥoshen Mishpat* 12; R. Shabbetai b. Meir ha-Kohen (*Siftei Kohen* or *Shakh*, Lithuania, 1621–1662), *Siftei Kohen* to *Shulḥan Arukh*, *Ḥoshen Mishpat* 259, n. 3; *Arukh ha-Shulḥan*, *Ḥoshen Mishpat* 304:11. But cf. R. Mordecai b. Hillel (*Mordekhai*, Germany, 1240–1298), *Mordekhai*, *Bava Metzia* 2:257 (validating judicial coercion of *lifnim mi-shurat ha-din* conduct if the individual who is asked to give up his rights is wealthy); R. Joel Sirkes (*Baḥ*, Poland, 1561–1640), *Baḥ* to *Tur*, op. cit., n. 4 (validating the practice even when the individual who is asked to give up his rights is an employer seeking damages against an employee).
4. *Rema* to *Shulḥan Arukh*, *Ḥoshen Mishpat* 163:1; *Arukh ha-Shulḥan*, *Ḥoshen Mishpat* 163:1.

Hashem.[5] And we must immediately identify with R. Yohanan's statement that "wherever you find mention of the power of the Holy One, Blessed is He, you find His humility."[6] When there is an awesome power, there must be at the same time a delicate sensitivity. "For thus said the exalted and uplifted One, Who abides forever and Whose Name is holy: I abide in exaltedness and holiness, but I am with the despondent and lowly of spirit, to revive the spirit of the lowly, and to revive the heart of the despondent" (Isaiah 57:15).

The most delicate sensitivity is *hakkarat ha-tov*, and the ideal here is gratitude to Hashem.[7] *Va-yiḥan et penei ha-ir* (Genesis 33:18).[8]

What makes for the success of business? It is the legal environment of society. It is the certainty that contracts will be honored and no gross discrimination will be allowed. Those who fled persecution appreciate this very much.

Then there are the roads, bridges, and communication networks, which allow for minimizing the cost of the distribution of goods, and education, which provides training of the labor force and produces a literate population.

But it is more than *hakkarat ha-tov*. When you give a waiter or a taxicab driver a gratuity, do you regard it merely as a kindness to the one who provided the service? Surely not. It is almost an implicit contract. The practice is so prevalent as to make the expectation almost a quasi-contract. So, too, there is almost a quasi-contract between the business firm and society. Society deliberately lowers its pollution standards, sacrificing aesthetics and even health, to allow firms to increase output and employment. There is almost a *quid pro quo* here. Also, the license

5. Deuteronomy 8:6, 10:12, 11:22, 13:5, 26:17, 28:9, 30:16. R. Naphtali Tzvi Yehudah Berlin, *Emek ha-Netziv, Sifrei*, Deuteronomy 10:12, *piska* 13.

6. *Megillah* 31a.

7. See R. Bahya b. Joseph ibn Paquda (Spain, 11th cent.), *Ḥovot ha-Levavot, Sha'ar Avodat ha-Elokim*.

8. Genesis Rabbah 79:6. When Jacob arrived at the city of Shekhem from Paddan-aram, the verse states, "*va-yiḥan et penei ha-ir*," "he encamped before the city." Connecting the word "*va-yiḥan*," "he encamped," to "*ḥanan*," "he conferred benefit," the Midrash explains that Jacob established bazaars and sold merchandise cheaply as a display of gratitude to the city for providing shelter and peace. From this conduct, we learn that one must be grateful to a place from where he derived benefit.

to operate with limited liability will of course harm society, particularly creditors. But this will be tolerated because this organizational structure will maximize employment opportunities and be a vehicle to raise huge amounts of capital. So again, there is an element of *quid pro quo*.

"The son of David will come only in a generation that is either entirely righteous or entirely wicked."[9] This tells us that a generation that rejects spiritual striving and is interested only in material striving is very close to repentance because it can imitate Hashem in a way that the society of angels cannot, that is, to fulfill "His mercies are on all His works" (Psalms 145:9). The colossal engine of commercial power can find a heart of delicate sensitivity and take pity on its workers and community, and should share the burdens of the recession.

9. *Sanhedrin* 98a (statement of R. Yohanan).

Emor

Hallel on Yom Ha-Atzma'ut

May 5, 1984

Jewish history has been graced with forty-eight Prophets and seven Prophetesses.[1] These inspired men and women neither added to nor subtracted from the Torah aught. They fully appreciated the divine origin of the Torah, both the Written and Oral Law. It was perfect and self-sufficient. Indeed, it would be presumptuous of man to change the character of a single mitzvah or to add a single mitzvah to the 613 mitzvot. The ordinances enacted by the Sages, as Maimonides points out, were

1. *Megillah* 14a. *Rashi ad locum* lists forty-six of the forty-eight prophets: Abraham, Isaac, Jacob, Moses, Aaron, Joshua, Pinhas, Elkanah, Eli, Samuel, Gad, Nathan, David, Solomon, Ido, Mikhahu b. Yimlah, Obadiah, Ahijah the Shilonite, Yehu b. Hanani, Azariah b. Oded, Haziel the Levite, Eliezer b. Dodavahu, Hosea, Amos, Micah the Morashite, Amotz, Elijah, Elisha, Jonah b. Amitai, Isaiah, Joel, Nahum, Habakkuk, Zephaniah, Uriah, Jeremiah, Ezekiel, Shemayah, Barukh, Neriah, Shiryah, Mahseiyah, Haggai, Zechariah, Malakhi, and Mordecai Bilshan. According to the *Turei Even*, the additional two prophets were Eleazar b. Aaron the Priest and Elihu b. Berakhel the Buzite. R. Aryeh Leib b. Asher Gunzberg (*Sha'agat Aryeh*, Lithuania, ca. 1695–1785),

intended only to put a fence around the Torah, to preserve and guard the commandments of the Torah.[2]

Surveying the entire record of the Prophets, the Sages came up with only one piece of disturbing legislation, the reading of the Megillah. Did this not constitute an addition to the mitzvot of the Torah? To this, the Talmud answers that the Sages of the time reasoned that if our ancestors, upon experiencing the ecstasy of the Exodus, instituted song on account of a change in status from servitude to freedom, then *kal ve-ḥomer*, we should institute a commemoration in the form of a Megillah to mark our deliverance from death to life![3]

Now, on the other hand, we must exhibit the proper awe and reverence for the Torah. We must not tamper with it. But at the same time, it is the duty of the Sages of every generation to demonstrate the relevancy of the Torah to changing socio-economic and political circumstances and to show the responsiveness of the Torah to the great and momentous events of history.

But the *kal ve-ḥomer* must operate within parameters. We are told that we cannot appoint an individual to the Sanhedrin unless he can purify a *sheretz* in accordance with the Torah.[4] Now, *Tosefot* ask, "What benefit is there in worthless syllogisms?"[5] We all know that a *sheretz* is *tamei*. The answer, I believe, is that the logician who is true to Torah principles knows that despite the beauty and power of his edifice of creative genius, he must reject it as it is clearly against the Torah. Even school children know that a *sheretz* is *tamei*, not *tahor*. It is only the man who is infused with the intellectual honesty of a scientist and the reverence and awe for the divine doctrines who will check and recheck with exhaustive thoroughness and make sure that

---

Turei Even to *Megillah* 14a. The Vilna Gaon, however, states that the two additional prophets were Oded the Prophet and Hanani the Seer. R. Elijah b. Solomon Zalman (Vilna Gaon or *Gra*, Vilna, 1720–1797), *Haggahot ha-Gra* to *Megillah* 14a. The seven Prophetesses were: Sarah, Miriam, Deborah, Hannah, Abigail, Huldah, and Esther. *Megillah* 14a.

2. Maimonides, *Mishneh Torah, Mamrim* 2:9.
3. *Megillah* 14a.
4. *Sanhedrin* 17a.
5. *Tosafot* to *Sanhedrin* 17a, s.v. "*she-yode'a le-taher.*"

his logic does not violate any Torah principles, to make sure that his analysis is connected with the divine doctrine and is not separate from it.

Indeed, the *kal ve-ḥomer* mentioned earlier to establish the reading of the Megillah operated within these parameters. The Early Prophets established that for every distress from which we are saved, we say *shirah*.[6] That is, *Hallel* was established for all time. The criteria established by our Sages had only to be met.

We are standing at the threshold of a momentous event of the modern era, the thirty-sixth anniversary of the establishment of the State of Israel. Regrettably, some people in our circles regard the event as devoid of any religious significance. Some claim it is a cause for mourning, as the declaration of independence and Statehood so incited the surrounding Arabs that war against Israel intensified and many *korbanot* fell.

But to this, I would say that we cannot look upon the declaration as an isolated event in the past, but rather, we must look upon it from a historical perspective. No single event could have been more important in contributing to the long-term security of the State. If not for the protective wing of *Tzahal*, could the country have attracted the ingathering of the exiles? Without the achievement of Statehood, would secular Jews have identified with the State and immigrated there, contributing their enormous talents? Achievement of Statehood is what enabled the Jewish State to receive foreign aid and grants as a sister nation among the nations of the world.

Some circles argue that the establishment of the State should be ignored because it was established by secular Jews; if indeed it was a divinely-inspired event, it should have been undertaken by *Gedolei Torah*. To this, R. Ahron Soloveichik replies that the City of Samaria was saved by four spiritual lepers.[7]

---

6. *Pesaḥim* 117a.
7. R. Aaron Soloveitchik (Chicago, 1917–2001), "Israel's Day of Independence: Reflections in Halacha and Hashkafa," *Gesher: A Publication of Student Organization of Yeshiva Rabbi Isaac Elchanan Theological Seminary* 4, no. 1 (1966): 9–10. The story of the four lepers is recorded at II Kings 7:1–20.

Now, that is a powerful *kal ve-ḥomer* to mark the day with appreciation and thanksgiving. If *Tu be-Av* is a *yom tov* because permission was granted to bury the victims of Beitar,[8] then certainly if the remnants of the Holocaust are given a chance to return to their homeland, it is cause for celebration. We cannot say *Taḥanun* or recite *la-minatze'aḥ mizmor le-David, ya'anekha Hashem be-yom tzarah* (Psalms 20).[9] And we should mark the day with the traditional form of thanksgiving, that is, the recitation of *Hallel*.

But there are those who have another *kal ve-ḥomer*. They go back to the *Gemara* in Megillah and note that the *Gemara* asks why should we not go one step further and say *Hallel* on Purim as well. The answer is that we do not recite *Hallel* for a miracle that occurred outside the Land of Israel,[10] and we were still servants of Ahasuerus.[11]

All these answers do not apply to the establishment of the Jewish State. But are we really giving the Torah all the awe and reverence that it is due? The *Turei Even* asks: What does *Hallel* have to do with the Megillah? He suggests that the *kal ve-ḥomer* is from the Song at the Sea of Reeds to the reading of the Megillah.[12] The reasoning is that if we recited *shirah* in the form of a story at the Exodus, we should surely compose a *megillah* as a story that relates the event of Purim.

Now, if this is the *kal ve-ḥomer*, then we must note that at the Sea of Reeds, the highest level of faith was also achieved. "A slavewoman saw at the Sea what even Ezekiel b. Buzi did not see."[13] If so, we can be very thankful for the progress of the State in the form of the government of the State of Israel. The government has progressed from being merely a framework for population growth and development to a conduit for

8. *Berakhot* 48b.
9. "For the conductor, a psalm by David. May Hashem answer you on the day of distress." Psalms 20.
10. *Megillah* 14a. As long as the Children of Israel did not yet enter the Land of Israel, all lands were appropriate venues for the recitation of *Hallel*. Thus, although the miracle of the Splitting of the Sea of Reeds occurred outside the Land of Israel, the Children of Israel were permitted to recite *Hallel*. Ibid.
11. Ibid. After the Exodus from Egypt, by contrast, the Children of Israel were no longer slaves of Pharaoh.
12. R. Aryeh Leib b. Asher Gunzberg, *Turei Even* to *Megillah* 14a.
13. *Mekhilta, Be-Shallaḥ* 3; *Rashi* to Exodus 15:2, s.v. "*zeh Keli*."

enormous sums of money to develop and defend the Land. We look upon it as a vehicle for Torah observance, and then at the highest level, to be the essence of Torah itself.

To recite *shirah* before we feel the religious climate erupting is premature. It amounts to us being satisfied with mere crumbs when the State itself can progress to become a vital, active force in the scenario to produce the Messiah. Now it is "I trust in Your kindness… I will sing to Hashem, for He has dealt kindly with me" (Psalms 13:6)!

Kindness in Truth, and Truth in Kindness

May 17, 1986

Anticipation of the event of *Mattan Torah,* which capsulates for many commentaries the essence of the mitzvah of *sefirat ha-omer,* was marred, as we all know, by the occurrence of a historical tragedy for our people. According to Tradition, 24,000 disciples of R. Akiva perished during this period.[1] The Talmud contends that their death was attributable to their failure to show proper respect for one another.[2]

We do not presume to pass judgment when the Torah relates of a bygone era. "The Holy One, Blessed is He, is exacting with the righteous even to a hair's breadth."[3] Nevertheless, permit us to suggest a possible root cause of their misconduct.

---

1. *Yevamot* 62b.
2. Ibid.
3. *Yevamot* 121b.

Those who regard themselves as the authorities and the guardians of our cherished Tradition are sometimes prone to regard truth as an absolute value. In their monomaniacal pursuit of truth, they may forget such niceties as gentility and politeness. They may gloat over the defeat of their opponent, to say nothing of displaying magnanimity in victory. To prevent society from being led astray by erroneous doctrines, personal vindication must be added if necessary. What cannot be accomplished by means of scholarship can be made up in personal attacks.

But this is not the way of Torah. "Its ways are ways of pleasantness" (Proverbs 3:17). The more that scholarly debate moves away from the realm of abstraction and turns to personal attack, the less likely one side will concede, for concession is tantamount to self-repudiation. Moreover, the Torah welcomes severe challenges. This is the rationale of *kullam ḥayyav patur*,[4] because a position that is not challenged is less certain to represent fact and truth.

Finally, the great *roshei yeshivah* will always react to a comment and question of a student, which may be shallow and inane, and read all kinds of brilliance into it. The *ḥelbbenah* is blended into the spices to produce the pleasing fragrance of *ketoret*.[5] Just as there is the need to sometimes inject *ḥesed* into *emet*, there is the equal challenge of restraining oneself from injecting *emet* into *ḥesed*.

We are told, "Always should the disposition of man be pleasant with his fellow."[6] If one made a bad purchase from the marketplace, and the buyer engages in a glowing self-assessment of his purchase, how should we react? We should praise the purchase, based on the principle that the disposition of a person should always be pleasant with his fellow.[7] We can interpret the requirement to be pleasant and withhold our true feelings very narrowly. R. Samuel b. Joseph

4. If a Sanhedrin opens a capital case with a unanimous guilty verdict (*kullam ḥayyav*), the accused is exempt (*patur*) until some merit is found to acquit him. *Sanhedrin* 17a; Maimonides, *Mishneh Torah, Sanhedrin* 9:1.
5. Exodus 30:34; *Keritot* 6b.
6. *Ketubbot* 17a.
7. Ibid. (opinion of *Beit Hillel*). Talmudic decisors follow *Beit Hillel*'s view. *Tur, Even ha-Ezer* 65; *Shulḥan Arukh, Even ha-Ezer* 65:1; *Arukh ha-Shulḥan, Even ha-Ezer* 65:1.

Strashun says that the case speaks to the instance where the buyer has no idea from whom he bought the article, so a return is impossible.[8] Therefore, no benefit can proceed from telling our friend our true feelings.

So we may say that the whole interdict applies only to an acquaintance, not a friend. For a friend, *adderabba,* we must be honest and tell him our true feelings; we must adopt a paternalistic attitude towards him. But such an attitude would entirely emasculate the interdict of *ona'at devarim,* as we would always claim that we are acting in the long-term interests of our friend. The dignity of our friend is harmed when we always inject *emet* into *ḥesed.*

During the seven weeks of *sefirah,* we concentrate on the perfection of *middot.* The attribute of *gevurah,* withholding *ḥesed,* can be a glorious trait, provided that we also perceive beauty flowing from it. *Gevurah* is glorious when we perceive *ḥesed she-be-gevurah* and it is motivated by love.

And *gevurah* is glorious if we perceive *gevurah* in *gevurah,* that is, we perceive that the withholding of *ḥesed* is not motivated by hatred or a sense of superiority, but rather by an awesome feeling of fear of Heaven.

And *gevurah* is glorious if we perceive the *tiferet,* the synthesis of love and fear, in *gevurah.*

And *gevurah* is glorious if we perceive *netzaḥ* in *gevurah.* What is *netzaḥ*? It is the after-glow of fear of Hashem. Not only do we perceive the fear when we are engaging our friend, but the motive of fear in the distancing is evident if after the encounter is over, and we think about it, it still lingers.

---

8. R. Samuel b. Joseph Strashun (*Rashash,* Lithuania, 1794–1872), *Ketubbot* 17a. R. Strashun draws support for his thesis by pointing out that the Talmud refers to the bad purchase as having come not from any specific seller, but rather from the marketplace (*min ha-shuk*). The indication is that the buyer has no recollection of the identity of the seller. Because returning the item to get a refund or adjustment based on a defect or excessive price is not an option for the buyer in that case, it is permissible for the buyer's friend to lie and praise the buyer for his selection. Understanding the bad-purchase case in the same manner as R. Strashun is R. Israel Meir ha-Kohen Kagan, *Sefer Ḥafetz Ḥayyim, Hilkhot Rekhilut* 9:12, ¶ 2.

And the *gevurah* is glorious if we perceive the *hod* in it, that the motive of love is what we feel when we think about our friend after the encounter with him is over.

And *gevurah* is glorious if we perceive the *yesod* in *gevurah*, the outreaching, the bond that the individual is trying to maintain with us, not just the *tiferet* as a distant entity.

And finally, *gevurah* is glorious if we perceive the *malkhut* in the *gevurah*. We perceive that the distancing all fits into a cosmic scheme. It is all for the purpose of promoting the Kingdom of Heaven.

The National Holocaust Museum

May 13, 1989

Indicative of the Torah's demand on us to behave compassionately is the observation that the Torah's legislation in this area extends to concern for the welfare of the animal kingdom.[1] Indeed, it would be tempting to collect all the Torah's regulation of human conduct vis à vis the animal kingdom and build a theory that the Torah advocates animal rights.

This approach is, however, fraught with danger. It could lead to the assertion that eating meat is immoral, for how dare we kill an animal just to satisfy our hunger when plant life is available to us? Ancillary to this, we might subconsciously regard the standard of morality that we are subject to as no more than that of an animal. According to this theory, we, too, have urges and instincts, and we must inexorably

1. See *Bava Metzia* 32b (deriving a biblical prohibition against inflicting pain on living creatures from the commandment at Exodus 23:5 to assist in unloading burdens from animals).

submit to them; our conduct, whatever it is, must be excused. Finally, conceptualizing the Torah's legislation regarding the animal kingdom in terms of animal rights runs the risk of us becoming concerned with animal rights in a very exaggerated form. We become champions of animal rights but callous to man's inhumanity toward our fellow men.

Instead of viewing the Torah's regulation of conduct vis à vis the animal kingdom as recognizing animal rights, the approach of the *Ḥinnukh* is inviting. Actions shape character.[2] By refraining from forbidden actions and fulfilling our positive duties toward the animal kingdom, we purge our inclinations toward cruelty and cultivate a sensitivity to compassion.[3]

"You shall not muzzle an ox in its threshing" (Deuteronomy 25:4). It is a callous act to muzzle an animal while it is engaged in threshing. Depriving an animal a portion of the produce of its travail is cruel. And what are we to say of the Nazis' confiscation of the life's property of Jews in the 1930s[4] and the gall to impose a penalty in the many millions of dollars on the Jews to clean up the mess of Kristallnacht?[5]

In connection with the commandment of covering the blood of an animal, a distinction is drawn between fowl and beasts on the one hand, and domesticated animals on the other. The former require

2. R. Aaron b. Joseph ha-Levi, *Sefer ha-Ḥinnukh*, mitzvah no. 16 (prohibition against breaking a bone of the paschal offering). See also ibid., mitzvah no. 40 (prohibition against building an altar from hewn stone); mitzvah no. 99 (commandment that Priests wear the Priestly Vestments); mitzvah no. 264 (obligation for a Priest to become impure for a close relative); mitzvah no. 299 (obligation to bring a *Musaf* offering on Passover); mitzvah no. 324 (commandment to take a *lulav* on Sukkot); mitzvah no. 401 (commandment to bring two lambs as a burnt offering daily).
3. Ibid., mitzvah no. 148.
4. See generally Martin Dean, *Robbing the Jews: The Confiscation of Jewish Property in the Holocaust, 1933–1945* (Cambridge: Cambridge University Press, 2010); Richard Z. Chesnoff, *Pack of Thieves: How Hitler and Europe Plundered the Jews and Committed the Greatest Theft in History* (New York: Doubleday, 1991); Götz Aly, *Hitler's Beneficiaries: Plunder, Racial War, and the Nazi Welfare State* (New York: Metropolitan Books, 2007), ch. 7.
5. The German government imposed a fine of one billion Reichsmark, the equivalent of approximately $400 million, on the German Jewish community. See Dean, *Robbing the Jews*, 113–114.

covering of the blood, but not the latter.[6] R. Abraham Isaac Kook explains that with respect to foul and beasts, which are not domesticated, we gave them nothing. We should therefore feel some guilt when we kill them to satisfy our hunger and should cover up the evidence of the slaughter. But with respect to domesticated animals, we at least give them something, so the guilt is not warranted.[7]

If we should feel some guilt when we slaughter foul and beasts, what is to be said of the negligent slaughter of noncombatants in military operations in a world war? And what is to be said of the Nazi murderers who targeted the Jewish population when engaged in war with the Allies, even doing so when the war was being lost?

And the crescendo – "an ox, or a sheep or goat, you may not slaughter it and its offspring on the same day" (Leviticus 22:28). It is cruel because it might lead to the slaughter of the offspring in the presence of the mother.[8] And it also in a microcosmic way smacks of genocide, destroying two generations in one day. What is to be said therefore of the Nazi murderer who, as an ordinary matter, killed whole families and designed genocide against our people?

The challenge to civilization is not only to legislate what is right and what is wrong, but also to create an environment in which man purges his cruel instincts and cultivates a sensitivity to compassion. Toward that end, a great milestone took place at the National Rotunda at the ninth annual celebration of Holocaust Remembrance Day. Construction will finally begin of the National Holocaust Museum. After nine years of planning, the $100 million project will finally begin.[9]

It was very moving for me to read the story of the architect. He visited Auschwitz and walked near the crematoria. His foot kicked up dirt and, to his amazement, a fragment of human bones was exposed. He said that he never felt so Jewish in his whole life. It was as if it were

6. Leviticus 17:13.
7. R. Abraham Isaac Kook, *Ma'amarei ha-Re'iyah: Kovetz Ma'amarim me-et ha-Rav Avraham Yitzḥak ha-Kohen Kook* I (Jerusalem: Keren Goldah Katz, 1988), 26–27.
8. R. Aaron b. Joseph ha-Levi, *Sefer ha-Ḥinnukh*, mitzvah no. 294.
9. Robert S. Greenberger, "$100 Million Memorial to the Living … and the Dead," *Jewish Herald*, May 5, 1989, 4–5, 18.

an omen that even after forty-four years, the earth refused to cover up the crimes of the Nazis.[10]

Nine years of infighting between the pragmatists and the dreamers have passed. Time has its way of blunting our sensitivities and enabling us to forget the pain and anguish of previous generations. Nefarious revisionists are teaching the new generation that the Holocaust is a fraud, a figment of our imagination, a hoax.[11]

The rise of the museum is a lethal blow to these revisionists and will arouse the conscience of the world. The museum will feature video cassettes bearing the testimony of survivors, witnesses, and liberators. It will also exhibit the artifacts of the era, such as the railroad cars that transported Jews to the concentration camps and the gas chambers.[12]

Some say that there were other victims of Hitler's madness. There were Polish intellectuals, other Slavic people, Gypsies, and political dissidents.[13] Their memory should also be preserved. But where is perspective and proportionality? If the Torah's legislation vis à vis the animal kingdom is supposed to summon up in us a revulsion toward actions that the Torah brands as cruelty, then the Holocaust represents for us a blending of a whole panorama of horrors, all mixed together in a harrowing brew. How dare we compare the other victims to the Jewish trauma?

The problem was solved in the Museum. The story of the Holocaust will be told in stages. From 1933 to 1938, the stories of Jewish victims and gentile victims will be told together. But from 1938 onward, the Holocaust will be presented as a uniquely Jewish trauma.

Perhaps the greatest potential of the museum is in the area of technology. The Germans marshalled technology to efficiently torture and decimate a people. In Treblinka, 150 Germans managed to kill

10. Ibid., 18.
11. See Deborah E. Lipstadt, *Denying the Holocaust: The Growing Assault on Truth and Memory* (New York: Free Press, 1993); Kenneth S. Stern, *Holocaust Denial* (New York: American Jewish Committee, 1993).
12. Greenberger, "$100 Million Memorial," 18.
13. Ibid., 5.

900,000 people in eighteen months.[14] Now technology will be used to arouse in man a sensitivity to compassion and a remembrance of the suffering of the past. And the catalogue of the Holocaust archives will allow scholars worldwide to gather this information and the story of the Holocaust well into the future to be able to teach with ever-increasing scholarship, lucidity, and attention to detail, all for the purpose of Never Again, Never Again.

---

14. Ibid., 18.

Be-Har

The Double Standard of Morality

May 12, 1984

A double standard of morality is always a source of disturbance for us. How can a prescribed mode of conduct be regarded as meritorious when directed toward a Jew but as reprehensible when directed toward a non-Jew? Yet, the Torah apparently prescribes a double standard. With respect to lost property, when it comes to a Jew, it is a positive duty to restore the property.[1] When, however, the property belongs to a non-Jew, a Jew may generally not return the property unless keeping the property would result in a *ḥillul ha-Shem*.[2] Concerning one who returns lost property, the Torah states "*le-ma'an sefot ha-ravah et ha-tzeme'ah*" (lit., "adding the drunk with the thirsty") (Deuteronomy 29:18).[3] Hashem will add on a punishment for him for

1. Deuteronomy 22:1–3.
2. *Bava Kamma* 113b; *Shulḥan Arukh, Ḥoshen Mishpat* 266:1.
3. *Sanhedrin* 76b.

sins committed until now unintentionally, as he causes that Hashem should combine them with intentional sins.[4]

With respect to *ribbit*, charging interest to a Jew is most reprehensible; one who does so is considered a denier of the Exodus from Egypt.[5] But Maimonides says that it is a mitzvah to charge *ribbit* to a gentile – *la-nakhri sashikh* (Deuteronomy 23:21).[6] Finally, the *Tur* tells us that *ona'at mamom* is not operative with respect to a gentile.[7]

Maimonides' categorization of friendships helps us see the difference.[8] There is a utilitarian relationship, entered into for mutual benefit. Then there is the relationship of confidants. But the highest form of friendship is when two people are committed to common goals and ideals. The ideal relationship with the gentile is the utilitarian one. The Torah is indeed concerned that our relationship with the gentile should not become intimate. "The Sages decreed a prohibition on their bread and their oil on account of their wine, and on their wine on account of their daughters."[9] Also, we are not a proselytizing people, and it is forbidden to teach Torah to a gentile.[10]

It follows naturally that it should be a mitzvah to lend them money on interest. The Talmud says that *gemilut ḥasadim* is greater than *tzedakah*.[11] This is utterly not understandable. If we are concerned

4. *Rashi* to Deuteronomy 29:18, s.v. "*le'ma'an sefot ha-ravah.*"
5. *Torat Kohanim, Behar, parashah* 5; Maimonides, *Malveh ve-Loveh* 4:7; *Tur, Yoreh De'ah* 160; *Shulḥan Arukh, Yoreh De'ah* 160:2; R. Abraham Danzig, *Ḥokhmat Adam* 130:4.
6. Maimonides, *Sefer ha-Mitzvot, mitzvat aseh* no. 198; *Mishneh Torah, Malveh ve-Loveh* 5:1. Cf. *Bava Metzia* 70b. The Talmud *ad locum* explains that the word "*sashikh*" means to cause someone to take interest, i.e., to pay interest, rather than to charge interest. Maimonides, however, based on *Sifrei* to Deuteronomy 23:20, understands "*sashikh*" to mean to charge interest.
7. *Tur, Ḥoshen Mishpat* 227.
8. Maimonides, *Perush ha-Mishnayot, Avot* 1:6, s.v. "*u-keneh lekha ḥaver.*"
9. *Shabbat* 17b.
10. *Ḥagigah* 13a.
11. *Sukkah* 49b. Our Sages taught that *gemilut ḥasadim* is superior to charity in three respects. First, charity can be done only with one's money, but *gemilut ḥasadim* can be done with one's person and one's money. Second, charity can be given only to the poor, but *gemilut ḥasadim* can be performed for both the rich and the poor. Lastly, charity can be given only to the living whereas *gemilut ḥasadim* can be done for both the living and the deceased by attending to their funeral and burial. Ibid.

about the dignity of the poor, then an anonymous gift of $1,000 should be greater than a loan of $1,000. The answer must be that the following circumstances are referred to: A poor man (*P*) approaches a fellow Jew (*R*) and asks him for assistance. *R* responds by taking out $100 and giving it to *P*. *P* says that he does not want charity and argues that if *R* is willing to give him a gift of $100, he should be willing to lend him $1,000 for a year and *R*'s opportunity cost for allowing him the use of the capital is only $100.

R is nonplused by the argument. He only planned to give *P* $100, and now he is risking his capital. To accede to *P*'s request, *R* is showing a very intimate regard for him, trusting him that he will return the money and at the same time trusting in the Al-Mighty that he will not lose for performing a mitzvah.[12]

The Torah does not want this initiation of intimacy and trust with respect to a gentile.[13] Therefore, the Torah prescribes interest for a loan to the gentile. But this is not a discriminatory relationship, as we have no objection, according to our law, for the gentile to charge us interest.[14]

Now, the Jew is conferred the 613 mitzvot. This is a heavy claim on his time and energy. It must have the effect for the ideal Jew of blunting his materialistic drive. A similar spiritual claim is not made on the gentile. His material desire is therefore typically much greater. Returning to the gentile a lost item enhances the gentile's material possessions and causes him to covet other people's property with a greater intensity. "One who has one hundred coins wants two hundred."[15] For the Jew, returning lost property is an act of kindness. But restoring it for the gentile generates societal harm.[16]

---

12. *Keli Yakar* to Leviticus 25:36; Nahmanides to Deuteronomy 23:20–21.
13. See R. Aaron b. Joseph ha-Levi, *Sefer ha-Ḥinnukh*, mitzvah no. 545.
14. *Tosafot*, *Bava Metzia* 70b; Maimonides, *Mishneh Torah*, *Malveh ve-Loveh* 5:2; R. Hayyim Joseph David Azulai, *Birkei Yosef* to *Shulḥan Arukh*, *Yoreh De'ah* 159:1; R. Abraham Danzig, *Ḥokhmat Adam* 130:6; R. Ezra Batzri, *Dinei Mamonot*, 2nd ed., vol. 1 (Jerusalem: Machon ha-Ketav, 1990), 170.
15. Ecclesiastes Rabbah 1:34.
16. See Maimonides, *Mishneh Torah*, *Avedah* 11:3.

Finally, *ona'ah* is a claim based on opportunity cost.[17] The aggrieved party claims in essence that had he known of the competitive norm, he would have modified the transaction or voided it. The claim is based on imperfect knowledge. With the spiritual claim on the gentile limited, more precise knowledge of the marketplace is expected of him.

Now, all the discussion is theoretical because our Sages have introduced the concept of *eivah* (lit., "animosity").[18] We may do nothing to antagonize or incite the wrath of the gentile, or do something to tarnish our reputation. A new variable enters the discussion. Will our action cause a *ḥillul ha-Shem*? This is prohibited. On this account, we may profane the Sabbath to save a gentile.[19] The element of *eivah* is especially intensified in our modern era of mass transportation and communication.

If in practice, our relations with the gentile are very much the same as with a Jew, is there any real difference? Yes. When our obligation is all for the sake of not antagonizing someone, then our mind begins to think along lines of subterfuge and deviousness. We begin to concentrate on appearances rather than substance.

One of the biggest tragedies in America today is the problem of intermarriage. What this segment of our brethren has done is to drastically invert the prescribed relationship. For the gentile, there is a craving to be accepted and a resort to ingratiating conduct to accomplish this. For the Jew, is there a mysterious need to define ourselves to the world as universal people? The Exodus is associated with freedom from tyranny and nothing more. We should be proud of our singularity and emphasize our universality within the framework of singularity.

Let us remember that Benjamin was the only biblical personality who achieved the title "*yedid Hashem,*" "friend of Hashem."[20] He demonstrated extraordinary character *bein adam le-ḥavero,* recognizing the

---

17. See R. Aaron Levine, "*Onaa* and the Operation of the Modern Marketplace," *Jewish Law Annual* 14 (2003): 225–258.
18. In the view of R. Moses Sofer, if a prohibition is rabbinical rather than biblical, one is permitted to violate the prohibition to prevent the generation of *eivah* against Jews. See *She'elot u-Teshuvot ha-Ḥatam Sofer, Yoreh De'ah,* no. 131.
19. R. Mosheh Feinstein, *Iggerot Mosheh, Oraḥ Ḥayyim* 4:79.
20. Deuteronomy 33:12.

proper selection and role of friends, the relationship of *yedid le-de'agah* the "empathetic friend," and the *yedid le-de'ah*, the "friend with a common, noble ideal."[21] The great sentimentalist who named his ten children after the character traits of his lost brother Joseph,[22] and the man who never bowed down to Esau,[23] was the one who merited that the Temple should be built in his portion.[24] May this be our portion too.

21. See Maimonides, *Perush ha-Mishnayot, Avot* 1:6, s.v. "*u-keneh lekha ḥaver*"; Abraham R. Besdin, *Man of Faith in the Modern World: Reflections of the Rav; Volume Two* (Hoboken, NJ: Ktav, 1989), 63–64.
22. Genesis Rabbah 94:8. The names that Benjamin relayed to Joseph were: (1) *Bela*, signifying that Joseph had been swallowed (*nivla*) by strangers; (2) *Bekher*, because Joseph was the first-born (*bekhor*) of their mother Rachel; (3) *Ashbel*, because Joseph was taken captive (*nishbah*); (4) *Gera*, because Joseph lives in a strange land (*she-gar be-eretz aḥeret*); (5) *Naaman*, connoting that Joseph's deeds were beautiful and pleasant (*ne'imim*); (6) *Eḥi*, because Joseph was Benjamin's brother from the same mother and father (*aḥi vaddai*); (7) *Rosh*, because Joseph was Benjamin's leader (*rosh*) and was also destined to be the leader of the other brothers; (8) *Muppim*, because Joseph was physically and spiritually beautiful (*yafeh me'od*); (9) *Ḥuppim*, because Joseph and Benjamin were not at each other's wedding (*ḥuppah*); and (10) *Ard*, signifying that Joseph's face was like a rose (*vered*) and that Jacob had proclaimed in grief over Joseph, "I will descend (*ered*) to the grave mourning for my son" (Genesis 37:35).
23. *Targum Sheni* to *Megillat Esther*, 3:3. Benjamin was not yet born when the other sons of Jacob bowed to Esau. See Genesis 33:6–7.
24. *Yoma* 12a.

The Relevance of *Shemittah* Today

May 24, 1986

The institution of *Shemittah,* which is described in today's *parashah,* is struggling to survive. Since the 1880s, many religious farmers in the Land of Israel have relied on the rabbinical dispensation, validated by the Chief Rabbinate of Israel since its inception, of selling their land to Arabs and leasing it back to avoid observance of the laws of *Shemittah.*[1]

1. Before the *Shemittah* of 1889, R. Isaac Elhanan Spektor (Kovno, 1817–1896) issued a statement allowing the sale of land to non-Jews for two years. R. Ephraim Shimoff, *Rabbi Isaac Elchanan Spektor: Life and Letters* (Jerusalem: Sura Institute for Research, New York: Yeshiva University Press, 1959), 134–135. R. Israel Joshua Trunk of Kutno (*Yeshuot Malko,* Poland, 1820–1893), R. Samuel Mohilewer (Russia, 1824–1898), and R. Samuel Zanvil Klepfish (Warsaw, 1820–1902) ruled similarly. The approach is known as "*hetter mekhirah*" (permission to make a sale). *Hetter mekhirah* was opposed by the Ashkenazi community of Jerusalem and its rabbis, R. Moses Joshua Judah Leib Diskin (*Maharil Diskin,* Russia and Jerusalem, 1817–1898) and R. Samuel Salant (Jerusalem, 1816–1909).

Yes, there are many religious farmers in the Land of Israel today who do not rely on this dispensation, but advances in agricultural technology in the form of hydroponic beds to produce fresh vegetables and double deep planting,[2] in addition to fundraising efforts to subsidize those who observe *Shemittah*,[3] have taken much of the anguish out of the biblical question "What will we eat in the seventh year?" (Leviticus 25:20).

If the institution of *Shemittah* is becoming moribund, we may also ask, is it not a redundant institution? The selfsame lesson that *Shemittah* imparts, that God is the Owner of the Land, is imparted by the Sabbath. We desist from the thirty-nine *melakhot*, which represent the totality of human creativity, and by doing so, we humbly testify that Hashem is the Creator and the source of all our creativity.[4] What does *Shemittah* add to that lesson? Why is it necessary to confer the character of the Sabbath on the entire seventh year and absorb the Sabbath lesson on such a grand scale?

Before the *Shemittah* of 1910, R. Abraham Isaac Kook, then Chief Rabbi of Jaffa, permitted the sale of land to non-Jews, but R. Jacob David Willowski (*Ridvaz*, Russia and Israel, 1845–1913) opposed it. R. Kook, *Shabbat ha-Aretz: Hilkhot Shevi'it* (Jerusalem: Mossad HaRav Kook, 1993), 115, and *Mishpat Kohen* (Jerusalem: Mossad HaRav Kook, 1993), 119–166; R. Willowski, *Beit Ridvaz* on R. Israel Shklov (d. 1839), *Pe'at ha-Shulḥan, Hakdamah*. During subsequent *Shemittah* years, the Chief Rabbinate continued to abide by the rabbinic rulings allowing the sale of land to non-Jews, although opposition remained. Most prominent among the opponents has been R. Abraham Isaiah Karelitz.

For a discussion of the historical development of *hetter mekhirah*, see R. Yehiel Michel Tykocinski (Israel, 1872–1955), *Sefer ha-Shemittah*, pt. 2 (Jerusalem: Mossad HaRav Kook, 2006); R. Shlomo Yosef Zevin (Israel, 1888–1978), *Le-Or ha-Halakhah: Ba'ayot u-Veirurim* (Jerusalem: Mossad HaRav Kook, 1946), 89–90; R. Dovid Marchant, *Gateway to Shemittah: A Comprehensive and Practical Guide to the Halachos of Shemittah*, rev. 3rd ed. (Jerusalem: Feldheim, 2014), 320–338.

2. See Walter Frankl, "Sabbatical Year for the Soil," Gardener's Corner, *Jerusalem Post*, June 18, 1979, 7 (reporting use of hydroponics in Ein Gedi, Kibbutz Hafetz Hayim, and Eilat).
3. An international fundraising effort is undertaken by *Keren ha-Shevi'it*, the financial arm of Israel's National Center for *Shemittah*-Observing Farmers. The organization was founded in 1979 by R. Binyamin Mendelsohn, Rav of Komemiyut. Yaakov Chaim Dinkel, *The Story of Shemittah* (Jerusalem, 2006), 181.
4. See R. Moses Isserles (*Rema*, Poland, 1525 or 1530–1572), *Torat ha-Olah*, *ḥelek* 1, ch. 5.

Rather than being moribund or redundant, *Shemittah* carries a powerful message for contemporary man. We tend to take our economic environment as a given. If we would act ethically and virtuously within this framework, most people would regard us as virtuous. The Sabbath tells us to recognize Hashem and act morally as much as we can as individuals. But *Shemittah* tells the Jew to develop a social conscience and look at the economic environment, to take a hard look at the mechanisms and institutions that create wealth for us, and to suffuse them with a divine spark. Things are indeed beyond our control as individuals, but we can change our environment as a collective.

First, *Shemittah* addresses itself to institutions of private property. The produce of *Shemittah* is available to all on an equal basis, to the rich and poor alike, not just the poor, as is the case with *lekket, shikheḥah,* and *pe'ah*.[5] And there is the custom of dismantling fences, the leveling of society,[6] to say nothing of the release of debts.[7] Instead of private property, we have economic chaos.

If we do not repudiate the institution of private property today because we do not practice *Shemittah,* we must nevertheless take a long-term look at the direction in which the institution is going and not regard it as an absolute good, or take any of its failures in stride. Is private ownership of property an absolute good? Regarding it as such may make us believe that we can use it in any way we desire, regardless of its effect on society. Do we regard our use of an automobile as a *mazzik*? Of course not, even though the exhaust fumes generate harm to society and threaten our health. Why? Because the use of a car does not pose any threat unless everyone uses their cars at the same time in stop-and-go traffic. And what about industrial noise and pollution from airports? The Jew must have a social conscience. He must extrapolate the trend before the effects of the trend become intolerable.

Shemittah deals with technology. The produce of the Sabbatical year may be harvested, but man must purposely deny himself his

---

5. Deuteronomy 25:6.
6. *Mekhilta, Mishpatim* 31, s.v. "*ve-ha-shevi'it tishmetennah be-avodatah*"; Maimonides, *Mishneh Torah, Shemittah ve-Yovel* 4:24.
7. Deuteronomy 15:2.

technological achievement. The fig may not be harvested with a fig knife, only with an ordinary knife. Grapes cannot be pressed in a wine press, but rather only in a kneading trough.[8]

Now, if we do not practice *Shevi'it* and therefore do not purposely blunt our technology, we nevertheless must have a social conscience and suffuse technology with a divine spark. Technology will cause the displacement of many workers who worked a lifetime to develop skills. Masses of people then find their jobs rendered meaningless, and people are unhappy.

Shemittah deals with commercial institutions. "The Sabbath produce of the land shall be yours to eat, for you, your slave, and your maidservant, and for your laborer and your resident who dwell with you" (Leviticus 25:6). Money earned selling produce of the Sabbatical year must be used only to buy foodstuff.[9] Commerce has now developed to such a sophisticated level. We no longer produce for the local market. It is for the regional, national, and international markets. The unit of business today is the corporation. But there is widespread ownership of the corporation, so ownership does not control management. Today, a little company can swallow up a big one by issuing junk bonds. Do the managers run the corporation in the interests of the shareholders or maybe only respond to threats of takeovers?

We may not be faced with the supreme test of faith today of "What will we eat in the seventh year?" but we are faced with the challenge of instilling a humaneness and a divine spark in the institutions and mechanisms that are the vehicles for creating wealth for us. And this could be the meaning of "the land shall observe a Sabbath rest for Hashem" (Leviticus 25:2), to sanctify Hashem in all our secular institutions.

---

8. *Torat Kohanim, Behar,* ch. 1, ¶ 3; Mishnah, *Shevi'it* 8:6; Nahmanides to Leviticus 25:5.
9. Mishnah, *Shevi'it* 7:1; Maimonides, *Mishneh Torah, Shemittah ve-Yovel* 6:1.

Be-Ḥukkotai

The Value of Human Life

May 19, 1984

The quality of life, we read today, may vacillate, *Raḥmana le-tzelan*, between the horrors of deprivation, with the accompanying feelings of abandonment, helplessness, and disillusionment described in the Reproof, and the coveted crescendo of blessing, consisting of perfect serenity amidst overflowing prosperity, robust health, and peace. While the quality of life may vary, the value of human life in Jewish law never changes. Human life has an inestimable value, an infinite value. All the prohibitions of the Torah are suspended to preserve human life, except for the prohibitions of idolatry, murder, and forbidden relations.[1] Even for the purpose of restoring temporary life, we are bidden to profane the Sabbath.[2]

Yet, when an obligation is viewed as abstract and hypothetical, it fails to impart the feeling of the sanctity, preciousness, and dignity of life. Indeed, we are told that if two people find themselves in a desert

1. *Sanhedrin* 74a; Maimonides, *Mishneh Torah, Yesodei ha-Torah* 5:2; *Tur, Yoreh De'ah* 157; *Shulḥan Arukh, Yoreh De'ah* 157:1.
2. *Yoma* 85a.

and only one has a canteen of water, ben Petura says that the one with the water should share it and not witness the death of his friend.[3] But R. Akiva says that "*ve-ḥei aḥikha immakh*," "your brother shall live with you" (Leviticus 25:36), implies that *ḥayyekha kod'mim*, "your life takes precedence."[4] The Halakhah is according to R. Akiva.[5]

If we would contemplate the underlying basis of the dispute, we might conclude that preservation of another man's life is never quite operational. This follows from the explanation of the dispute offered by the *Netziv*. Ben Petura opines that one must place himself in a *safek sakkanah*, "possibility of danger," to rescue someone else from a *vaddai sakkanah*, a "danger that is certain." If *A* denies *B* the water, *B* will surely perish. *B*'s condition is a mortal danger. If *A* shares the water, he will put himself in danger, but he may be rescued and survive. Ben Petura is of the opinion that *A* must share the water with *B*, as it is his obligation to put himself in a *safek sakkanah* to avert *B*'s *vaddai sakkanah*.[6]

R. Akiva disagrees. Now, if the obligation to save a human life is suspended for even a *safek sakkanah*, a lot is left to subjectivity and the obligation appears considerably attenuated.

Another interpretation is that ben Petura holds that it is permissible for one to wrest away something from a friend in order to save his own life, provided that he will make compensation.[7] The Halakhah therefore makes *A*'s property right inoperative and *A* has no more right in the water than *B*. Both must share it for this reason.[8]

R. Akiva, however, holds that while normally it is permissible for one to save himself with another's property, this does not apply when the property of the friend has infinite value.[9] Since the flask of water

3. *Bava Metzia* 62a.
4. Ibid.
5. Ibid.
6. R. Naphtali Tzvi Yehudah Berlin, *Ha'amek She'elah* on R. Ahai Gaon (Palestine, 8th cent.), *She'iltot de-Rav Aḥai Gaon, Re'eh*, no. 147.
7. See *Tosafot* to *Bava Kamma* 60b, s.v. "*mahu le-hatzil atzmo*"; *Rosh, Bava Kamma* 6:12; *Tur, Ḥoshen Mishpat* 359, 380; *Shulḥan Arukh, Ḥoshen Mishpat* 359:4, 380:3.
8. Ben Petura as understood by R. Hayyim Ozer Grodzinski (Lithuania, 1863–1940), *Aḥiezer, Yoreh De'ah* 16.
9. See R. Abraham Isaiah Karelitz, *Ḥazon Ish, Yoreh De'ah* 69:2.

will preserve life, it has infinite value. *B* therefore will never be able to pay it back.

If we interpret R. Akiva in this manner, we are left with the thought that in a life-and-death situation, not only does our own life take precedence over our friend's life, but we also enjoy an absolute right to use property that is necessary to preserve our own life. What seems to emerge is a feeling that selfishness is the prevailing norm under conditions of dire emergency.

Given this impression, the individual's obligation to preserve human life will never, in our view, be elevated to a consciousness of the sanctity of human life unless society creates the proper environment. Take the principle of the case of one flask of water and translate it into societal ethics. We have the following result: If we should not enter into a *safek sakkanah* to extricate someone from a *vaddai sakkanah*, the implication for society is that we should never negotiate an exchange of prisoners with terrorists. Even though our brothers are in mortal danger, releasing prisoners puts society at large in a *safek sakkanah*. The long-run effect is to generate a powerful feeling regarding the value of human life. Those who would hold human life in contempt will never gain through their actions. The second explanation we offered regarding the dispute leads to the societal law that even when man is at war, non-combatants have rights. There is a certain degree of sanctity even under the most drastic situations of war. Witness the Geneva Convention.

Society can do more on a compulsory basis. It can make people feel the sanctity of human life by forcing people to contribute to security measures until it is felt in a powerful way. The members of a city can force even the majority to defer to the minority to establish security measures.[10] Society could also provide the proper deterrent for criminals.

In the Mishnah in *Makkot*, all agree that deterrents are desirable, but R. Akiva holds that extra legal procedures are sufficient, while R. Shimon b. Gamliel holds that only the legal process itself of executing criminals can serve as a deterrent.[11]

10. Mishnah, *Bava Batra* 1:5; *Bava Batra* 7b.

11. Mishnah, *Makkot* 1:10; *Makkot* 7a. R. Tarfon and R. Akiva said that if they had been members of the Sanhedrin when the Sanhedrin still performed executions, no person

The structure of the Decalogue was two columns. There is a correspondence between the first and the sixth commandments.[12] In order to arouse a sense of Godliness in a people, it is necessary to first arouse a deep respect for human life.[13]

would have ever been executed. *Tosafot* understand this statement to mean that R. Tarfon and R. Akiva would have questioned the witnesses so relentlessly that the witnesses would have eventually contradicted themselves, rendering their testimony invalid. *Tosafot* to *Makkot* 7a, s.v. "*dilma bi-mekom sayyif nekev.*"

12. *Mekhilta, Yitro* 8.

13. The First Commandment is "I am Hashem, your God, Who has taken you out of the land of Egypt, from the house of slavery." Exodus 20:2. The Sixth Commandment is "You shall not kill." Exodus 20:13.

Numbers

Be-Midbar

Retirement in Jewish Law

May 26, 1984

We are living in a society that has displayed an increasing veneration for its senior citizens. Consider the Age Discrimination in Employment Act as amended in 1978.[1] The amendment provides that an employer may not force his employee to retire before the age of seventy.[2] As another example, an attempt by the Reagan Administration to reduce Social Security benefits had to be abandoned in the face of overwhelming opposition.[3] Finally,

1. The Age Discrimination in Employment Act of 1967 (ADEA) prohibits employers of twenty or more individuals from discriminating against employees or prospective employees on account of age. 29 U.S.C. § 621–634. The 1978 amendment to the ADEA increased the maximum age of individuals protected by the Act from sixty-five to seventy. Discrimination in Employment Act Amendments of 1978, Pub. L. No. 95–256, §3(a), 92 Stat. 189 (1978). A further amendment generally removed the age limitation of seventy. Age Discrimination in Employment Act of 1986, Pub. L. No. 99–592, § 2, 100 Stat. 3342 (1986).
2. Pub. L. No. 95–256, 92 Stat. 189 (1978) (codified at 29 U.S.C. § 631(a) (1982)).
3. Helen Dewar, "Senate Unanimously Rebuffs President on Social Security," *Washington Post*, May 21, 1981, A1; Barry Sussman, "By 3 to 2, Americans Disapprove of Reagan

witness the bid for reelection of an incumbent President at the age of seventy-three.[4]

Given the Torah's well-known veneration for the aged, we experience apparent disquietude when we read that the Torah proclaims with regard to the Levites, "From fifty years of age, he shall withdraw from the legion of work and no longer work" (Numbers 8:25). Why does the Torah call for compulsory retirement at the age of fifty for the Levites?

A little closer examination of the issue of retirement of the Levites reveals, however, a rather strong linkage between the right of continuation of service and productivity, with age being mostly an irrelevant factor. Take the position of *Rashi* in this matter. In his view, the disqualification of age applies only to *avodat massa ba-kasef*, the work of carrying on the shoulders, but not to singing, guarding the gates, or loading wagons.[5] With regard to those other functions, there was indeed quite a brutal link between the right to occupy the service and performance. The *Rosh Av* would assign those functions, and a supervisor of the singers would decide who should be in his twelve-man choir.[6] For those chosen as the guardians of the gates, a surprise inspection was made.[7] Those found slothing were beaten over the head and their clothes were burned.[8] What emerges is a picture of a rather strong link between productivity and the right to occupy a position.

Plan for Social Security," *Washington Post*, May 16, 1981, A8.

4. "Reagan Proclaims He's in Good Shape: He Declares His Age or Health Will Not Become an Issue," *New York Times*, March 31, 1984, 1.28.
5. R. Solomon b. Isaac (*Rashi*, France, 1040–1105), *Rashi* to Numbers 8:25.
6. See *Arakhin* 13b; Maimonides (*Rambam*, Egypt, 1135–1204), *Mishneh Torah, Kelei ha-Mikdash* 3:3, 3:9.
7. Mishnah, *Middot* 1:2. The Priests stood guard at three places in the Temple: the Chamber of Abtinas; the Flash Chamber (*Beit ha-Nitzotz*); and the Fire Chamber (*Beit ha-Moked*). The Levites stood guard at twenty-one places in the Temple: five at the five gates of the Temple Mount, four at its four corners on the inside, five at the five gates of the Courtyard, four at its four corners on the outside, one at the Offering Chamber (*Lishkat ha-Korban*), one at the Chamber of the Veil (*Lishkat ha-Parokhet*), and one behind the Place of the Mercy Seat (*Beit ha-Parokhet*). Mishnah, *Middot* 1:1.
8. Mishnah, *Middot* 1:2.

The disqualification of age with regard to the work of carrying on the shoulders, in our view, can be explained by the connection that the *Ḥinnukh* makes with respect to why interference with someone else's work incurs the death penalty. The *Ḥinnukh* explains that in any team effort, there is always a tendency to shift the burden to someone else. This endangers performance of the work. If a Levite could rely on someone to step in and help him, he might sloth on the job. To reduce this loss in productivity, the Torah prohibits assistance.[9]

Now, the same principle may be operative with regard to the disqualification based on age. Since productivity with regard to physical labor naturally declines at age fifty,[10] the Torah was fearful that allowing the Levites to continue after that age might result in the older worker shifting the burden to his co-workers. Why should all share in the glory associated with the work, yet contribute unequally to the necessary physical exertion?

Maimonides follows *Rashi*'s approach and goes one step further. In Maimonides' view, the disqualification of age for *massa be-kasef* applied only when the Tabernacle was transported in the Wilderness from place to place. The age disqualification did not apply in Shiloh or *Beit Olamim*, the permanent Temple.[11] We can only surmise why. Perhaps the reason is that until the tranquility and inheritance of the Land were reached, the harried conditions under which the Children of Israel lived resulted in physical debilitation at the age of fifty. In the Wilderness, the Children of Israel had to be prepared to march with no prior notice; at the sound of the trumpets, they were to prepare to march.[12] Now, in the first year in the Wilderness alone, they traveled to fourteen different stations, and

---

9. R. Aaron b. Joseph ha-Levi (*Ra'ah*, Spain, ca. 1235–1300), *Sefer ha-Ḥinnukh*, eds. R. Yitzhak Yeshayah Weiss, R. David Zicherman, and R. Yitzhak Weinstein (Jerusalem: Makhon Yerushalayim, 1992), mitzvah no. 393. The Torah prohibits the Priests from performing the work of the Levites and the Levites from performing the work of the Priests. The prohibition is based on the verse "every man to his work and his burden" (Numbers 4:19).
10. See *Rashi* to Numbers 4:3.
11. *Mishneh Torah, Kelei ha-Mikdash* 3:8.
12. Numbers 10:2, 10:5. The signal for traveling of the camps was a *tekiah, teruah, tekiah,* i.e., a long blast followed by short blasts, followed by a long blast. *Rashi* to Numbers 10:5.

in the last year, to eight.[13] That meant an unsettled state. When we at last come to Shiloh, although not permanent, it is already called *menuḥah*, "tranquility,"[14] because once we have realized our aspiration as a people to achieve conquest of our Promised Land, some quieting of the spirit already occurs, some of the restlessness already gives way.

Nahmanides takes the extreme opposite view of Maimonides. According to Nahmanides, retirement is forced on all Levites in the time of the Tabernacle at age fifty, and with regard to physical labor, the prescribed retirement age of fifty remained in Shiloh and *Beit Olamim*. Now, Nahmanides explains his position somewhat. Since the Levites were assigned tasks according to families, the family of Kohath was assigned the most important task of carrying the Ark. With the retirement age for the work of carrying necessary, it was absolutely essential to impose the age limit for the singers of Kohath, and by extension, to the families of Gershom and Merari for all their work as well.[15]

As it seems to us, Nahmanides is saying that we are concerned that we will not be able to attract Levites from the family of Kohath for the most important work of carrying if we are not meticulous in avoiding creating a disincentive to do this type of work. This will surely happen if we allow the singers to continue working beyond fifty but force those engaged in carrying to retire at age fifty. To avoid creating dissension among the entire Levite families, a uniform retirement act must be instituted.

This institution has much relevance for contemporary society. If workers are employed performing more or less homogeneous work, we must have a uniform retirement age for all, so as not to cause dissension.

All *sidrot* end on an optimistic note.[16] Our *sidrah* appears to be an exception.[17] The last verse forewarns the Levites not to be impetuous,

13. *Rashi* to Numbers 33:1.
14. *Rashi* to Deuteronomy 12:9; *Megillah* 10a; *Zevaḥim* 119a.
15. Nahmanides (*Ramban*, Spain, 1194–1270) to Numbers 8:25.
16. See Jerusalem Talmud, *Megillah* 3:8; Maimonides, *Mishneh Torah, Tefillah* 13:5; *Rema* to *Shulḥan Arukh, Oraḥ Ḥayyim* 138.
17. According to one view, the last twenty verses of *Parashat Be-Midbar* (Numbers 4:1–20) were originally included in the succeeding *parashah, Naso,* but were subsequently appended to *Parashat Be-Midbar* to shorten *Parashat Naso,* which is the

that is, not to be summoned to their task before the holy vessels are entirely covered. If they avoid this, they will escape death. "But they shall not come and look as the holy is inserted, lest they die" (Numbers 4:20).

When we read the next-to-last verse in conjunction with the last verse, the last verse turns out to be a beautiful blessing. "Every man to his work and his burden" (Numbers 4:19). If everyone will carry the banner and man his station, bearing the burden of commercial responsibility, he will enjoy the blessing of never having to witness the swallowing up of the holiness, that is, the demise of Judaism as we know it today.

---

longest *parashah* of the Torah. If those twenty verses had remained in *Parashat Naso, Parashat Be-Midbar* would have ended with the verse "Moses gave the money of the redemptions to Aaron and his sons according to the word of Hashem, as Hashem had commanded Moses" (Numbers 3:51). R. Mordecai Judah Leib Zaks (Jerusalem, d. 1963), cited in R. Aharon Yaakov Greenberg, *Iturei Torah*: *Likkut, Nisaḥ u-Biur*, vol. 5 (Tel Aviv: Yavneh, 1971), p. 29.

Achieving Optimality in the Service of the Levites

June 7, 1986

If we were asked to summarize in a single phrase the Torah's approach to everything in life, we would instinctively respond, "Its ways are ways of pleasantness" (Proverbs 3:17). It is therefore with some disquietude that in today's portion, where we are introduced to the function of the Levites, we are told that mandatory retirement at age fifty is prescribed for them.[1] Shouldn't the decision to retire be voluntary? As long as the Levite can perform his duties, he should not be made to retire.

Far from being an instance of age discrimination, mandatory retirement at the age of fifty constitutes another demonstration of "its ways are ways of pleasantness."

Rashi's view on the matter is very telling. The Levites' functions were manifold. They did guard duty at the gates, loaded wagons with the appurtenances of the Tabernacle, and carried the Ark. It was in

1. Numbers 4:3, 4:23, 4:30.

connection with only the last service, called *avodat ha-kasef*, that retirement at the age of fifty was prescribed.[2]

We need not venture far to find the reason for this. R. Eleazar b. Pedat (d. 279) tells us in *Be-Midbar Rabbah* that the service of *avodat ha-kasef* was fraught with danger.[3] If the family of Kohath, which was the only family assigned to this task, did not display the proper reverence and awe for the Ark, the Ark would strike them down. Many shied away from this service in favor of the other services. It was therefore necessary to assign certain Levites to the *avodat ha-kasef*. The early retirement age can therefore be looked upon as a concession for those who undertook the dangerous work.

We should note, however, the view of R. Samuel b. Nahman that in spite of the grave danger, Levites from the family of Kohath were eager to do the *avodat ha-kasef*, and the reason for the assignment was that other services were neglected.[4] Following this line, the early retirement requirement for *avodat ha-kasef* can be regarded as another means that the Torah uses to prevent the setting in of pride and vanity. Just as the *halakhah* of "they shall not come and look as the holy is inserted, lest they die" (Numbers 4:20) is intended to impress upon the Levites that they are subordinate, they cannot directly gaze upon the appurtenances in their pristine state, so, too, we must deflate the self-image of the Levites who engage in *avodat ha-kasef* and force them to retire at age fifty.

Nahmanides, however, posits that the disqualification of age fifty applies to the work of singing as well. Singing is a function of the Levites. What is left for them to do at fifty is only the subsidiary functions of guarding the gates and loading the appurtenances. Nahmanides explains his view. To be counted for the work of singing, the Levite would have to be qualified for all the services of the Levites. So the Levites from the family of Kohath who are disqualified from performing *avodat ha-kasef* at age fifty cannot perform the work of singing as well. Since the Levites

2. *Rashi* to Numbers 8:25.
3. Numbers Rabbah 5:1 (statement of R. Eleazar b. Pedat in the name of R. Yose b. Zimra).
4. Numbers Rabbah, loc. cit.

from the family of Kohath are disqualified from being singers at age fifty, it would be unseemly to allow the other two families, Gershom and Merari, to do the work of singing beyond age fifty, so everyone became disqualified to do the work of singing at fifty.[5]

Nahmanides apparently understands that the disqualification of age at fifty is rooted in some form of danger that the optimal level of fear of Heaven could not be produced if the Levites would continue to work beyond age fifty.

What Nahmanides says is astonishing! Everything revolves around the relatively few Levites who were concerned with *avodat ha-kasef*. If optimality with regard to the Levite service requires disinflation of self-worth, we must do the same to everyone in society. Society, in other words, is required to pay a price to achieve optimality with respect to the most holy work of the Levites.

The price goes beyond this. We are told that the Levites began their training at age twenty-five and began performing their service at age thirty.[6] But what did they need five years of training for? I would submit that it was also to produce in them the optimal blend of "the lofty praises of God are in their throats, and a double-edged sword is in their hands" (Psalms 149:6). Those who were retired at age fifty were by no means out of this – "A fifty-year old can offer counsel" (*Avot* 5:21). According to R. Obadiah b. Abraham of Bertinoro, this statement refers to the Levites.[7]

The story is told of person lost in the forest who meets an elderly man. The lost person's joy quickly evaporates when the man tells him that he has no idea how to get out of the forest. But then the elderly man adds,

---

5. Nahmanides to Numbers 8:25.
6. Numbers 8:24 ("From twenty-five years of age and up, he shall join the legion in the service of the Tent of Meeting); Numbers 4:3 (recording that Hashem instructed Moses and Aaron to count the sons of Kohath "from thirty years of age and up, until fifty years of age, everyone who comes to the legion to perform work in the Tent of Meeting); *Rashi* to Numbers 8:24, s.v. "*mi-ben ḥamesh ve-esrim*" (explaining that the Levites studied the laws of the Temple service for five years and began service at age thirty).
7. R. Obadiah b. Abraham of Bertinoro (*Bartenura*, Italy, ca. 1450–1515), *Bartenura* to Mishnah, *Avot* 5:21, s.v. "*ben ḥamishim la-etzah*."

"At least I know where *not* to go."[8] So, too, the Levites over fifty can serve as role models par excellence and can make a major contribution too.

What a powerful message for contemporary society. There is no shortage today of zealotry, but it is often simply the product of spontaneous circumstances rather than an expression of considered thought or the instinct of a long training period designed to cultivate the appropriate response that should inspire rather than antagonize.

Today's *sidrah* seems to end on a bad note: "But they shall not come and look as the holy is inserted, lest they die" (Numbers 4:20). What a way to end the *sidrah*! But if we connect this verse to the last phrase of the previous verse, "every man to his work and his burden" (Numbers 4:19), the last verse becomes a blessing. If each person regards his role with great reverence and awe, and does not look upon his role as a burden, then we will merit the blessing that we will never have to witness the swallowing up of what is holy and precious to the Jewish people.

---

8. R. Paysach J. Krohn, *The Maggid Speaks: Favorite Stories and Parables of Rabbi Shalom Schwadron Shlita, Maggid of Jerusalem* (New York: Mesorah, 1987), 215.

The Two Desert Trips

May 30, 1987

Part of the mystique of the Torah is that Jews of extreme persuasions are readied to accept the Torah by means of the same process, the taking of a journey in the desert.

The committed Jew who regards himself as an elitist prepares for *Mattan Torah* by relating to our Sages' statement that one's studies will be retained by him only if he allows himself to be treated as a wilderness on which everybody treads.[1] What does this mean on a practical level? It means first of all humility.[2] Just as the desert is desolate, devoid of any economic value whatsoever, so, too, he regards his own opinions and values as bereft of any importance. Second, just as the desert is devoid of any cultivation, so, too, the elitist denies himself all the pleasures and

1. See *Eruvin* 54a. The Talmud derives this principle from the biblical verse "*u-mi-midbar Mattanah*" (lit., "from the wilderness to Mattanah") (Numbers 21:18). The word *mattanah* can be understood as a "gift," signifying that the Torah will be given to the humble person as a gift and he will retain his learning. *Tosafot* ad loc., s.v. "*mi-midbar Mattanah.*"
2. R. Hayyim b. Moses ibn Attar (*Or ha-Ḥayyim*, Morocco, 1696–1743), *Or ha-Ḥayyim* to Numbers 21:17, s.v. "*ve-omru mi-midbar Mattanah.*"

allurements of this life, denying himself what is natural to man. Third, he feels the responsibility to plant something in the desert. He is driven by the need for self-improvement.

Astonishingly, three other Jews who are very far removed from the wilderness concept are prepared for the acceptance of the Torah in the same manner. These are the three siblings, Yizrael, Lo Ruhamah, and Lo Ammi.[3] Now they are brought into the fold. "I make her like a wilderness" (Hosea 2:5). They are convinced that they are governed by a special Divine Providence. How? When we reach verse eleven, we are overwhelmed by a feeling that Hosea is talking to us today as he says, "Therefore I will return and take My grain in its time and My wine in its season, and I will remove My wool and My linen [that I gave her] to cover her nakedness" (Hosea 2:11).

We are demonstrated this dramatically. The corn is denied us when we most feel entitled to it. We are productive members of society, contributing to its social welfare and higher standard of living. But this is denied to us, just wrested away from us, and we have the clothes stripped off our backs. We are subject to the worst humiliation and dehumanization. But this does not help.

We are led to another wilderness that is tender and soothing. "I will speak to her heart" (Hosea 2:16). Again we are made to feel that we are governed by Divine Providence. It is the mere survival of the Jewish people amidst the hostile forces surrounding us that is the miracle. It is the gift of *Eretz Yisrael* that should convince every Jew that he is special and occupies center stage.

We are passed through the wilderness of persecution, but are the Jewish people not terribly split into two separate wildernesses, the wilderness of the elitist and the wilderness of Yizrael, Lo Ruhamah, and Lo Ammi?

The elitist who feels humility only when he relates to God but not to man is not really humble. The humble man regards himself as finding something redeeming in every Jew. The pious man who denies himself material striving and subjects himself to only a spiritual world, who denies himself man's natural inclination, is aware of the special Divine

3. Hosea 1:1–8.

Providence. "The Torah was given only to those who ate the manna."[4] Understanding this Divine Providence on a personal level must be transcended to seeing the divine hand in the thrust of history. And finally, if the elitist sees only himself and a desolate wilderness, and finds a need only for self-improvement rather than planting Godly spirit in others, he also is missing something of the wilderness experience.

So, too, if the secular Jew sees in the State of Israel only Jewish identity rather than a catalyst to leap into the wilderness of the elitist to at least touch base with him, then we are operating as a people in two separate wildernesses.

We as a people strive for the new betrothal with Hashem, which speaks to the merger of the two wildernesses. "I will betroth you to Me forever; and I will betroth you to Me with righteousness, with justice, with kindness, and with mercy; and I will betroth you to Me with fidelity, and you will know Hashem" (Hosea 2:21–22).

---

4. *Mekhilta, Be-Shallaḥ* 2.

The Hypothetical Acceptance of the Torah

May 21, 1988

As we stand at the threshold of *Mattan Torah,* we all know that we must make an enormous leap. We must relate to a majestic event far removed from our mundane existence. We must relate to the moment when we pronounced in unison "we will do and we will obey" (Exodus 24:7), when we accepted upon ourselves lofty ideals and awesome responsibility with unparalleled enthusiasm.

If we find it very difficult to relate to the actual event of *Mattan Torah,* perhaps we can more easily relate to a hypothetical *Mattan Torah.* Our Sages tell us that if the Torah were not given through Moses, it would have been given through Ezra.[1] Now, what is the difference between the actual giving of the Torah through Moses and the hypothetical giving of the Torah through Ezra? Moses brought the Torah down from heaven to earth, but Ezra elevated earth toward heaven!

---

1. *Sanhedrin* 21b.

The essence of Ezra was his ten ordinances.[2] He addressed himself to the ordinary, common man, and his goal was to tear him away from his set patterns and entrenched way of thinking.

Most basically, what is precious in our heritage cannot be taken for granted. Everything precious in our Tradition must be given its due respect! Torah can be studied only in a state of ritual purity. The Sabbath, too, must be given its due. Laundry must be done on Thursday so that the entire eve of the Sabbath can be devoted to preparations for the Sabbath.

Then we direct ourselves to the dregs of society. Ezra introduced the reading of the Torah during the Sabbath afternoon prayer. He wants to tear man away from drunkards, who might sit around in the afternoon after prayer, the Sabbath meal, and the Sabbath naps. So Ezra says, "You must return to the synagogue in the afternoon."

Then he establishes that when a woman decides to bake challah, she should get up earlier and bake it early in the morning, so that the poor would not be lacking. Tear yourselves from your sleep so that you will fulfill *gemilut ḥasadim.*

Then we address ourselves to the man who has a *seder* in learning and ask him to expand that a little. Ezra, accordingly, expanded the institution of the reading of the Torah on Monday and Thursday beyond what Moses had prescribed. Originally, it was ordained that one man should read three verses or that three men should together read three verses, corresponding to the Priests, the Levites, and the Israelites. Then Ezra came and ordained that three men should be called up to read, and that ten verses should be read, corresponding to ten *batlanim,* to impress upon the people that the *tzibbur* can be run only when there are people dedicated to the *tzibbur.*[3]

Ezra acknowledged that to bring the common man close to Torah, something must be done to improve the quality of life of the common man. Hence, he made ordinances for peddlers.[4]

2. *Bava Kamma* 82a.
3. Ibid. The term "*batlanim*" refers to the ten men released from all obligations and thus having leisure to attend to public duties and to form the necessary quorum for synagogue services. *Megillah* 5a; *Rashi* ad loc., s.v. "*Gemara, asarah batlanim.*"
4. *Bava Kamma* 82a. Ezra instituted that peddlers of perfumes should be allowed to sell their wares in the towns to enable the women to adorn themselves for their husbands.

One of the favorite stories of the *Ḥafetz Ḥayyim* concerned a pitiful old woman who barely eked out a living from a bagel stand. One day, a group of miscreant boys schemed to rob her of all her bagels. The plan called for one of the boys to suddenly appear and topple the bagel stand. As soon as this would be accomplished and the bagels would be seen scattering in all directions, the other boys would appear and grab a bagel. Now, the plan was executed and bagels began to disperse in every direction. The poor woman was in a state of panic. It so happened that an old man was nearby. He empathized with the plight of the widow, but he called out to her, "Why don't you grab a bagel too?"[5]

The evil tempter has done quite a job of toppling our bagel stand. Everyone is grabbing bagels, but why don't we grab some too? We must tear ourselves away from our routines, from our entrenched way of looking at things, and make a step toward the spiritual – more Torah, more *gemilut ḥasadim,* and more *avodah.* The acceptance of the Torah begins with "Ezra ascended from Babylonia" (Ezra 7:6) and ends with "Moses ascended to God" (Exodus 19:3).

---

5. Cf. R. Israel Meir ha-Kohen Kagan (*Ḥafetz Ḥayyim,* Radin, 1838–1933), *Sefer Shemirat ha-Lashon,* Introduction; R. Mosheh Meir Yashar, *He-Ḥafetz Ḥayyim be-Netivot ha-Tefillah* (Jerusalem: Makhon Hatam Sofer, 1974), 29; David Zaretsky, *Mishlei he-Ḥafetz Ḥayyim,* 2nd ed. (Tel Aviv: Abraham Ziyoni, 1958), 21; R. J. Simcha Cohen, *How Does Jewish Law Work? Volume 2: A Rabbi Analyzes 119 More Contemporary Halachic Questions* (Northvale, NJ: Jason Aronson, 2000), 291.

Naso

From the Strong Came Forth Sweetness

June 2, 1984

Paradoxically, both the warrior and the peacemaker must make use of the same tactics to be successful. Suggestive of this is the identical phraseology that the Torah employs in describing the vestment of the High Priest and the most famous warrior, Samson. The hem of the robe of the High Priest is described as adorned with a repeating pattern of a *pa'amon zahav ve-rimmon,* "a gold bell and a pomegranate" (Exodus 28:34), and of Samson it is said, "*va-taḥel ru'ah Hashem le-pha'amo,*" "the spirit of Hashem began to resound in him" (Judges 13:25).

Now, for the peacemaker to be successful, he must possess two opposite types of characteristics. On the one hand, he must be resourceful, creative, and nimble-minded, even deceitful, to bring the parties together. He must play both sides of a conflict, giving the impression that he sympathizes with each position. On the other hand, and most importantly, he must remain in the background. Should the peacemaker seek prominence or publicity, he runs the risk of having all his inconsistencies exposed. Too much publicity may reflect the glory of reconciliation on him instead of on the parties involved. This may antagonize the parties and may make things worse than before. The gift of diplomacy is important, but silence and self-abnegation are even more important if the fruits of diplomacy are to be enduring. Symbolic of this is that each gold bell was surrounded by a pomegranate, as if to say "*millah be-sela mashtuka be-trein*," "words are worth one coin but silence is worth two."[1]

Now, these same twin traits must characterize the man of awesome strength if his strength is to achieve a higher purpose. Samson was invested with a holy role, the role of defender of the Jewish people. As a constant reminder of the purpose of his divine gift, he was made a *nazir* from the time that he was in his mother's womb. He was prohibited from drinking wine, so that nothing would interfere with his judgment. He was also prohibited from cutting his hair. Letting his hair grow, as Abrabanel points out, was a sign of mourning.[2] The affliction of his brethren was to remain constantly in the fore of his consciousness.

Now, Samson was a very crafty and creative man. He devises a plan to use his strength so that it will minimize the chance that the Philistines will retaliate against Jewish settlements. This he accomplishes by looking for a pretext to make his heroics appear as a personal vendetta. He wants to be regarded by the Philistines as a terrible disappointment to his family, as an outcast among the legitimate authorities, even as a madman. Toward this end, he secretly converts a Timnite woman and requests his father to arrange the marriage.[3] Samson's parents are distraught, saying, "Can't you find a nice Jewish girl to marry? Must you go to the Philistines?"[4] His parents did not know that all this was divinely inspired, for Samson sought a pretext.[5]

Samson knew that no experience in his life was merely a coincidence. He remembered that on the road toward Timnah, he had ripped

---

1. *Megillah* 18a.
2. R. Isaac b. Judah Abrabanel (Portugal, 1437–1508), Judges 13:5.
3. Judges 14:2; R. Jehiel Hillel b. David Altschuler (Galicia, 18th cent.), *Metzudat David* ad loc.
4. See Judges 14:3.
5. Judges 14:4.

a lion to pieces.[6] Now he discovers that a swarm of bees was attracted to the innards of the lion.[7] This inspired in Samson a riddle. From the eater comes food, i.e., the bees produce honey, and from the strong comes forth sweetness, i.e., honey is found in the lion.[8]

The riddle is proposed to the wedding guests, along with a wager. When they fail to come up with the solution, they decide to extract it from Samson's wife. Samson knew that the solution to the riddle would be impossible unless his wife had betrayed him. He now seeks revenge, having the pretext to do so.[9]

Samson probably selected this woman for a wife knowing well that she would be easily intimidated and, in a pinch, be disloyal to him. Samson even gives himself a touch of the madman, further isolating himself, but generating an even larger probability that his brethren would not suffer any retaliation. He visits his estranged wife and seeks reconciliation. Instead, he finds that his father-in-law has given her to a Philistine. Samson is enraged and goes on another rampage. When the Philistines inquire what is happening, they hear that Samson is causing havoc because of the betrayal by his wife and father-in-law. This leads the Philistines to take his side. They burn the woman and the father-in-law at the stake. Instead of being pleased, the Philistines took his side.[10]

Samson says that because you took my side, I will take vengeance only one more time.[11] Are these not the words of a madman? But there is a method to his madness. The legitimate authorities view him as an outcast. The Philistines encounter the men of Judah and request that they bring Samson to them. The men of Judah regard Samson as a *rodef*.[12] This is Samson's self-image and he does not turn himself over to them until they swear that they will only bind him, but not kill him.[13]

---

6. Judges 14:6.
7. Judges 14:9.
8. Judges 14:14.
9. Judges 14:12–20.
10. Judges 15:1–6.
11. Judges 15:7.
12. R. Meir Loeb b. Jehiel Michel Weisser (*Malbim*, Poland, Romania, and Russia, 1809–1879), *Malbim* to Judges 15:11.
13. Judges 15:12–13.

Samson is nimble-minded in choosing his heroic act, but always remains in the background.

The great warrior has his flaw. He occasionally lapses into moments of infatuation with his own power, but this is not irreversible. The tragic downfall, however, comes when the shock of alienation from his brethren and intimacy with the Philistine woman are no longer a charade. When he chooses to divulge the secret of his heart to Delilah – "He told her all that was in his heart" (Judges 16:17) – it is his downfall. The intimacy with the enemy is his downfall. The actual cutting of his hair is only the finale of the unraveling of the charade.

We are living in a society in which some are confusing recklessness with courage. They are people of violence and provocation, whose actions endanger the entire Jewish nation. They speak as if they have the courage to do what others should do and therefore should be lauded. Well, the opposite is true. They forget that Samson accomplished more in his death than in his lifetime. In his death, he caused the pillars to fall on himself and the Philistines, shattering their false belief that the idols were responsible for his capture and for the ending of the life of the despoiler.[14] This produced the solution to the riddle: Only when strength produces sweetness, i.e., *emunah,* is it worth anything.

---

14. See Judges 16:23.

The Limits of the Instrument of Truth: Polygraphs

May 28, 1988

This past week, conferees in the House and Senate unanimously passed a bill that bans the use of a polygraph, or lie detector, for most employers, both as a screening device for job applicants, an as a random device to discipline or dismiss employees.[1]

Halakhah, I submit, would applaud this development. Continuation of this practice amounts to a statement that one is guilty until proven innocent. We know that the principle of *ḥezkat kashrut*, the presumption of "innocent until proven guilty," should be the societal

1. The Conference Committee reported the Polygraph Act on May 26, 1988. H.R. Rep. No. 100–659 (1988) (Conf. Rep.), *reprinted in* 1988 U.S.C.C.A.N. 749. President Reagan signed the Employee Polygraph Protection Act of 1988 into law on June 27, 1988. Pub. L. No. 100–347, 102 Stat. 646 (1988) (codified at 29 U.S.C. §§ 2001–2009 (1988)).

norm.[2] The latter principle is, of course, a cornerstone of the American legal system as well.[3]

More basically, employers regard the polygraph as an instrument for discovering the truth. But the polygraph measures stress, no more. Stress can occur for no reason other than that someone is being subjected to a test that may result in him being denied a job or dismissed from his current employment. The inaccuracy rate is anywhere from 10%, which is what the polygraph industry concedes, and the 40% figure that critics of the industry mention.[4] What this means is that anyone tested is subject to an unwarranted bias. This can only increase the level of bitterness, dissension, and distress in society.

In our Tradition, the principle that stands at the very foundation of society is "its ways are ways of pleasantness" (Proverbs 3:17). The Torah goes to extraordinary lengths to remove an aura of distrust and suspicion. Hashem says, "Let My name be erased in the solution of the bitter waters of the *sotah* all for the purpose of restoring domestic harmony."[5] And Hashem instructs the Priests to bless the Children of Israel instead of bestowing His blessing Himself.[6] Why? Because of the principle of *tenu oz le-Elokim*, "acknowledge invincible strength to God" (Psalms 68:35). Hashem sets up a model where the Priests express pristine sentiments of love and wellbeing for the Jewish people, and Hashem

2. Maimonides, *Mishneh Torah, Kiddush ha-Ḥodesh* 2:2.
3. Coffin v. United States, 156 U.S. 432, 453 (1895) ("The principle that there is a presumption of innocence in favor of the accused is the undoubted law, axiomatic and elementary, and its enforcement lies at the foundation of the administration of our criminal law.").
4. See United States v. Piccinonna, 885 F.2d 1529 (11th Cir. 1989), n. 12 (noting that polygraph examiners cite accuracy rates between 92% and 100% while others suggest the accuracy rate is in the range of 63% to 72%); Douglas Carroll, "How Accurate Is Polygraph Lie Detection?," in Anthony Gale, ed., *The Polygraph Test: Lies, Truth and Science*, (London: SAGE Publications, 1988), 21–28 (reporting 8.7% to 33.3% false positives in laboratory studies, and 37% to 55% false positives in field studies). See generally Kenneth S. Broun, ed., *McCormick on Evidence*, 7th ed. (Eagan, MN: Thomson-Reuters, 2013), § 206, 1199–1202.
5. Leviticus Rabbah 9:9. See also *Shabbat* 116a; *Sukkah* 53b; *Ḥullin* 141a.
6. Numbers 6:23.

says that if you do your part, I will shower upon the Jewish people an abundance of love and blessing.[7]

Some claim that although the polygraph has no place in screening job applicants, it should be used as a tool for truth-finding in criminal investigations.[8] But this is contrary to Jewish law. Our rule is *ein adam mesim atzmo rasha*, "a person does not incriminate himself."[9] The use of the polygraph amounts to forced self-incrimination. And why not accept confessions elicited through a polygraph test? Maimonides explains that we do not accept confessions lest the confession be for a crime not committed; perhaps the confessor is just one of those bitter souls with a suicidal tendency.[10]

R. Lamm posits that Maimonides anticipated psychoanalysts by many centuries, acknowledging the "Death Wish" described by Freud.[11] This is the destructive instinct that one turns on himself. Now, it can assume a weakened, modified form, as a need to engage in self-humiliation or self-mutilation.

Maimonides, as R. Lamm points out, can be understood even more simply as saying that man could harbor exaggerated guilt. He might feel guilty about the commission of a related crime, a small infraction, or even criminal intent alone.[12] Ironically, in the Halakhic society, people with religious sensitivities may feel profound guilt about criminal intent or small infractions that they place under the rubric of major offenses – "One ladle of gold, its weight ten shekel, filled with incense" (Numbers 7:20).[13]

---

7. See R. Jacob Moses ha-Kohen Lessin (Lithuania and New York, 1889–1975), *Ha-Ma'or she-ba-Torah: Siḥot, Be'urim ve-Iyyunim be-Divrei Ḥazal ha-Nog'im le-Inyanei Da'at Torah, ve-Derekh Eretz*, vol. 3 (Jerusalem: Hathiya, 1962), *Sotah* 38a, p. 439.
8. See Donald H. J. Hermann III, "Privacy, the Prospective Employee, and Employment Testing: The Need to Restrict Polygraph and Personality Testing," *Washington Law Review* 47, no. 1 (1971): 79–81.
9. *Sanhedrin* 9b; Maimonides, *Mishneh Torah, Edut* 12:2; R. Joseph Caro (Safed, 1488–1575), *Shulḥan Arukh, Ḥoshen Mishpat* 34:25.
10. Maimonides, *Mishneh Torah, Sanhedrin* 18:6.
11. R. Norman Lamm, *Faith and Doubt: Studies in Traditional Jewish Thought* (New York: Ktav, 1971), 277–278.
12. Ibid., 281.
13. See *Ḥagigah* 23b. This verse is cited by R. Hanin as a proof text for the rule in the Mishnah, *Ḥagigah* 3:2, that a vessel consolidates all its contents with regard to *kodesh*

We are reminded of R. Yohanan. He abolished the institution of *sotah* in the time of the Second Temple.[14] In the *sotah* ordeal, the Torah goes out on a limb and unhesitantly pronounces that if the woman is guilty of adultery, she will experience a horrendous death.[15] Now, because of technicalities in the law, this may not happen. The husband may have not been faithful[16] or the woman may have a merit that postpones punishment.[17] But the cynics of the generation would say, "Oh! We know the accused. She is a person of base morals. She is guilty. Why do the waters not work?" A *ḥillul ha-Shem* would proceed, so R. Yohanan abolished the procedure. [18]

We have a *kal ve-ḥomer*. If R. Yohanan abolished a divinely mandated procedure, which is designed as a means of searching out the truth, because of what the cynics of the time might say, then surely we should not adopt a tool that is designed to find out the truth if it will have untoward consequences for the innocent.

---

but not with regard to *terumah*. Thus, if a ritually impure person touches one of the contents of a vessel, all the contents become impure for purposes of *kodashim*, but not for *terumah*. The apparently superfluous word "one" (*aḥat*) in the phrase "one ladle" (*kaf aḥat*) is interpreted to signify that all the granules of incense in the ladle are considered one entity with regard to ritual purity. R. Hananel b. Hushi'el (*Rabbeinu Ḥananel*, Kairouan, 990–1053), *Ḥagigah* 23b.

14. Mishnah, *Sotah* 9:9.
15. Numbers 5:21–22.
16. *Sotah* 28a; Maimonides, *Mishneh Torah, Sotah* 3:17.
17. *Sotah* 20b–21a; Maimonides, *Mishneh Torah, Sotah* 3:20.
18. See Maimonides, *Mishneh Torah, Sotah* 3:18.

Prohibition of Profiting from Crime

May 29, 1993

Recently, it was disclosed that President Clinton has narrowed his choice for filling the vacancy in the Supreme Court to two federal judges, Judge Newman and Judge Breyer, both of whom are Jewish.[1] When someone's candidacy advances from the level of honorable mention to the short list, two things are certain: one, the candidate's record and credentials will be scrutinized by the media; and two, the weekly portion will have something to say regarding the suitability of the candidate.

In 1977, New York State adopted the so-called "Son of Sam Law," which restricted the profits a criminal could make by talking about his crime on radio or television, or in a movie.[2] In 1990, the Second Circuit

1. Stephen Labaton, "2 New England Appellate Judges Are Finalists for High Court," *New York Times*, May 27, 1993, A1.
2. 1977 N.Y. Laws 823 (codified at N.Y. Exec. Law § 632–a(1) (McKinney 1982)). In the summer of 1977, New York was terrorized by a serial killer, David Berkowitz, popularly

upheld the law, but Judge Newman, a member of the panel, dissented.[3] He felt that the law, though well-meaning, was unconstitutional. In 1991, the Supreme Court reversed the Second Circuit, agreeing with Judge Newman.[4]

From the standpoint of Halakhah, I think there should be no doubt that restricting a criminal's commercial advantage from his crime would be roundly applauded. The relevant principle is *she-lo yehei ḥote niskhar*.[5] It is unseemly for the offender to gain from his offense. Moreover, even if it is quite clear in both content and motivation that the criminal is expressing penance and remorse for his crime in his confessions and revelations, and his commercial advantage is only incidental, the profit is unethical.

The *parashah* of *gozel ve-nishba* sheds light on this.[6] We are told that if one steals and swears falsely that he did not steal, and wants to make amends, he must compensate the victim by repaying the principal and an additional fifth as well as bringing a guilt offering.[7] But what comes first? It is compensating the victim.[8] If the violator wants to bring the offering before attending to the victim, it is nothing less than *zevaḥ resha'im to'evah*, "the offering of a wicked person is an abomination" (Proverbs 21:27).[9] And Maimonides teaches us that perjury makes

known as the "Son of Sam." To prevent Berkowitz from profiting from his notoriety while his victims and their families remained uncompensated, the New York State Legislature enacted the Son of Sam law. The law required that the profits derived by a criminal from the exploitation of his or her crime be deposited in an escrow account maintained by the New York State Crime Victims Board. The funds would then be used in satisfaction of civil judgments subsequently obtained by the victims of the exploited crimes. Simon & Schuster asserted that the statute imposed a direct restriction on speech in violation of the First Amendment.

3. Simon & Schuster, Inc. v. Fischetti, 916 F.2d 777 (2d Cir. 1990).
4. Simon & Schuster v. Members of the New York State Crime Victims Bd., 502 U.S. 105 (1991).
5. Mishnah, *Ḥallah* 2:7; Mishnah, *Shevi'it* 9:9; *Yevamot* 92b; *Ketubbot* 39b; *Sotah* 15a; *Gittin* 55b; *Bava Kamma* 38a, 38b–29a; *Avodah Zarah* 2b; *Menaḥot* 6a; *Niddah* 4b.
6. *Gozel ve-nishba* refers to one who stole an object or money worth at least a *perutah*, and swore falsely that he did not steal it. See *Bava Metzia* 55a.
7. Leviticus 5:21–26; Numbers 5:5–10.
8. *Bava Kamma* 110a, 111a.
9. See *Zevaḥim* 7b.

the victim despair and therefore "he shall follow him even to Media,"[10] the thief must pursue the owner to repay him even if the owner is in a distant land.[11]

In a similar vein, the *Ḥiddushei ha-Rim* asks why the act of confession is highlighted here in the laws of *gozel ve-nishba* when confession is an aspect of atonement for all sins. The answer is that the basis for confession is theft. Hashem gave us the gift of life and possessions and we misappropriate them.[12]

Now, I ask you: If Hashem gave the criminal commercial advantage for his crime, would it not be a gross misappropriation for him to keep the profits and not turn them over to the victim of his nefarious act?

Moreover, even an arrangement with the victim to share the profits with him should be declared null and void because, beyond the interests of the victim, society has an interest here as well. As R. Samson Raphael Hirsch points out in the complementary *parashah* in *Va-Yikra*, if one lies to his fellow regarding a pledge, a loan, or a robbery, the dishonesty in human affairs is also the commission of a "treachery against Hashem" (Leviticus 5:21).[13]

Examination of the laws of *gozel ve-nishba* reveals a hodgepodge of other issues. Why? Because if we focus only on the injury to the victim, we are prone to slide down a slippery slope. The first stumbling block is that we naturally direct our mischief toward a powerless victim, the convert, one who has no relatives to defend him. If he dies, we might think that he is considered *hefker* and no amends are necessary. No. We are told that the payment of the principal and one-fifth goes to the Priests and we still must bring the guilt offering.[14]

---

10. Mishnah, *Bava Kamma* 9:5.
11. Maimonides, *Mishneh Torah, Gezelah ve-Avedah* 7:9.
12. R. Yitzhak Meir Alter (*Ḥiddushei ha-Rim*, Poland, 1799–1866), *Ḥiddushei ha-Rim al ha-Torah, Mo'adim ve-Likkutim, Aseret Yimei Teshuvah* (Jerusalem: Mossad ha-Rim Levine, 1992), 256. See also R. Yehudah Aryeh Leib Alter (*Sefat Emet*, Poland, 1847–1905), *Sefat Emet, Naso* (5631/June 1871) (recording the statement of his grandfather, the *Ḥiddushei-ha-Rim*).
13. R. Samson Raphael Hirsch (Germany, 1808–1888), Leviticus 5:21.
14. Numbers 5:8.

The next slip is that we rationalize that what belongs to the Priest, the *bikkurim,* can be substituted with its monetary equivalence. Haven't you seen the dollar bill hanging in every store from the first sale? The first fruits man wants to reserve for himself. And this is the rationale for the Priest taking the *bikkurim* from the hand of the person who brings it,[15] because *shelo hu notel,* the Priest is taking what belongs to him.[16]

When the announcement of the Supreme Court nominees was made, I am sure that many of us felt ethnic pride. But for those of us who would like to see Jewish values permeate American society, the most important thing is not to get a Jew on the Supreme Court. No. Better a gentile Justice who thinks like a Jew than a Jewish Justice who thinks like a gentile.

15. In connection with the *bikkurim* offering, the Torah states, "the Priest shall take the basket from your hand" (Deuteronomy 26:4).
16. R. Jacob b. Solomon ibn Habib (Spain, ca. 1445–1515), *Ein Yaakov,* Mishnah, *Bikkurim* 3:2; R. Hayyim Palaggi (Smyrna, 1788–1869), *Ammudei Ḥayyim, Gemilut Ḥasadim* ¶ 9.

Fulfilling a Fantasy

June 2, 2001

Conventional wisdom has it that our religion is incompatible with democracy. A basic tenet of democracy is that institutions should be free and open, with leadership decided on the basis of merit. In our religion, the two most prominent positions of leadership are the High Priest and the King. Both have hereditary requirements. The High Priest must be a descendant of Aaron,[1] and the King must be a descendant of David.[2]

Perhaps the conflict is not as serious as it appears. In the thinking of the *Meshekh Ḥokhmah*, the *parashah* of *nazir* speaks to the person who would like to feel what it is like to be a High Priest.[3] The *Meshekh Ḥokhmah* explains that Hashem says, "*Nazir* is open to everyone, man,

1. Leviticus 6:15.
2. See Genesis 49:10; *Rashi* ad loc.; II Samuel 7:16; I Chronicles 28:5; Maimonides, *Mishneh Torah, Melakhim* 1:7.
3. R. Meir Simhah ha-Kohen of Dvinsk (*Or Same'aḥ* or *Meshekh Ḥokhmah*, Latvia, 1843–1926), *Meshekh Ḥokhmah* to Numbers 6:8.

woman, and *mufla samukh la-ish*."[4] Hashem speaks to these people and says, "Because you sincerely abstain from drinking wine and cutting your hair, I will give you the third law, the prohibition against *tumat met*, and you will have the sanctity of a High Priest. I charge you with the warning, the same way I charge the High Priest, 'He shall not come near any dead person; he shall not contaminate himself to his father or his mother'" (Leviticus 21:11). And the title of "the crown of God is upon his head" and the designation that "all the days of his abstinence, he is holy to Hashem" apply to the *nazir*.[5]

Permit me to take this one step further. There is a mysterious law that when the High Priest dies, the manslayer goes free.[6] What is the connection between the High Priest and the manslayer? The High Priest has failed in his mission of being an *ohev shalom ve-rodef shalom*, "one who loves and pursues peace."[7] Accountability is a feature of democracy, and if we demand awesome responsibility of the High Priest, we prevent the tragedy of the death of three hundred High Priests during the period of the Second Temple.[8] So, too, the sense of awesome responsibility is given to the *nazir*. If a person should die near him "*be-pesa pis'om*," "with quick suddenness," even accidentally, and contaminate his Nazirite head, "he shall shave his head on the day he becomes purified; on the seventh

4. Lit., "an informed minor who is on the verge of adulthood." See *Nazir* 29b, 62a. In general, a boy under the age of thirteen and a girl under the age of twelve are not considered adults in Jewish law. The Talmud explains, however, that in the year preceding adulthood, a minor's vows, including the vow to become a Nazir, are upheld if upon examination, the minor is found to understand the nature of vows.
5. Numbers 6:7–8.
6. Numbers 35:25.
7. According to our Sages, the High Priest should have prayed to avert the sorrows of the generation. *Makkot* 11a; *Rashi* to Numbers 35:25, s.v. "*ad mot Kohen Gadol*"; R. Ephraim Solomon b. Aaron of Luntshits (*Keli Yakar*, Łęczyca, 1550–1619), *Keli Yakar* to Numbers 35:25.
8. *Yoma* 9a. The Second Temple stood for 420 years, during which time more than three hundred High Priests served. After deducting the forty years that Simeon the Righteous served, the eighty years that Johanan the High Priest served, the ten years that Ishmael b. Pavi served, or according to another opinion, the eleven years that R. Eleazar b. Harsom served, less than three hundred years remain. This calculation indicates that the remaining High Priests did not complete their year in office. Ibid.

day shall he shave it" (Numbers 6:9).[9] He could have been very circumspect, but on the last day of his *nezirut*, he became defiled accidentally. Nonetheless, "the first days shall fall aside," and he must bring a guilt offering.[10] This is the only case where one who committed a sin *be-ones* (accidentally) is required to bring a guilt offering.[11] The *nazir* is made to feel an awesome sense of responsibility.

There is a famous story in the Talmud of the gentile who passes by a *beit midrash* and hears the Scribe pronounce "these are the vestments that they shall make" (Exodus 28:4), referring to the Priestly vestments. The gentile proclaims, "This is for me!" After his request to become a convert was rejected by Shammai, he approached Hillel. Hillel explained that only a descendant of Aaron may wear the Priestly vestments. Even King David was not permitted to wear the Priestly vestments. "An alien who approaches it shall die" (Numbers 1:51).[12]

But why did Hillel not tell him to become a *nazir* and that way, he would be able to feel what it is like to be a High Priest? The answer is that the gentile was not interested in experiencing the awesome responsibility of being a High Priest. He just wanted to experience the honor of being a High Priest. But we know that "if one runs after honor, honor flees from him."[13]

There is no mechanism that makes us feel the ecstasy that the High Priest felt when he received honor and adulation. Why? Because the ideal High Priest is consumed and preoccupied with his awesome responsibilities and therefore feels no elation or egoism when honor is bestowed upon him. Instead, he is impervious to honor.

We pray every day for the restoration of Royalty.[14] But until then, the Royalty resides in the people and in the elected officials. Now Ariel Sharon, because of his military background, evokes the image of Samson.

---

9. See *Rashi* to Numbers 6:9. See also *Keritot* 9a.
10. Numbers 6:12.
11. *Tosefta, Keritot* 1:5.
12. *Shabbat* 31a.
13. See *Eruvin* 13b.
14. *Shemoneh Esrei* Prayer ("May you establish the throne of David speedily within it [i.e., Jerusalem].").

The long hair of the *nazir* signifies mourning,[15] and abstention from wine means that we do not want his judgment to be impaired. "The spirit of Hashem began to resound in him" (Judges 13:25).

The fantasy of the *nazir* is not deficient. It is complete because honor is not felt by the High Priest and therefore every Jew can have the fantasy of being a King and a High Priest. "All Jews are sons of kings,"[16] because the essence of high office is responsibility. And this is the essence of every Jew, as Judah said, "I will personally guarantee him; of my own hand you can demand him" (Genesis 43:9).

15. R. Isaac b. Judah Abrabanel, Judges 13:5.
16. Mishnah, *Shabbat* 14:4.

Be-Ha'aalot'kha

Why Should We Be Diminished?

June 9, 1984

Any request for special treatment offends our sense of fairness. Yet this is exactly what we encounter in today's reading. Our ancestors found themselves in the second year of their wanderings in the Wilderness. The Al-Mighty suddenly commanded them to offer the *korban pesaḥ*. A group of people, who had been defiled through contact with a human corpse and anticipated that they would not be able to offer the *korban pesaḥ*, importuned, "*Lamah niggara*?" (lit., "Why should we be diminished?") (Numbers 9:7). Why should we be held back and not permitted to sacrifice in the proper time?

Now, did these people not know the clear-cut rule, promulgated at Sinai, that only if the majority of the congregation is impure, the obligation to bring the *korban pesaḥ* overrides the state of impurity? If only an individual is impure, however, he may not participate.[1]

1. *Pesaḥim* 79a; Maimonides, *Mishneh Torah, Korban Pesaḥ* 7:1.

Notwithstanding that knowledge, the impure bolted ahead to the top of the judicial hierarchy and requested that an exception be made for them. Moses does not find their request the least bit unreasonable. He says, "Stand by and I will hear what Hashem will command you" (Numbers 9:8). The *Shem mi-Shemuel* suggests that if a request for an exception was made, it must have been that the group thought that their importance was equivalent to the majority of the congregation and equivalent in stature to the case when the majority of the congregation is in a state of impurity.[2]

Who were these people who thought they were so important? One view is that they were the people who carried the remains of Joseph.[3] Joseph acknowledged his land and therefore merited to be buried in the Land of the Israel,[4] and the entire community was required to bring his remains up from Egypt.[5] Joseph found himself in the worst straits in Egypt. Then, when finally a glimmer of hope appeared that he could be united with his family through the good offices of the butler, Joseph exclaims, "For indeed I was kidnapped from the land of the Hebrews" (Genesis 40:15). Now, discretion would certainly have demanded silence and concealment of his Jewish identity, for it was an abomination for the Egyptians to eat with the Jews.[6] This was a true test of Jewish pride, whether in a moment of hope, the essence of his personality and aspirations would emerge.

Indeed, the Jewish community never forms spontaneously but requires the special traits of people of creativity, leadership, and exemplary warmth. Someone possessed of Jewish pride in its highest form is one who is fit to form the Jewish community. Such a man is certainly equivalent to the majority of the community.

Another opinion has it that the impure were Mishael and Elizaphan,[7] "*dod Aharon,*" i.e., sons of Aaron's uncle Uzziel, who carried

2. R. Shmuel Bornsztain (*Shem mi-Shemuel,* Poland, 1855–1926), *Shem mi-Shemuel: Al Seder Parshiyyot ha-Torah u-Mo'adei Kodesh,* 9th ed., vol. 4 (Jerusalem, 1992), *Be-Ha'alot'kha* (5676/June 1916), p. 194.
3. *Sukkah* 25a (opinion of R. Yose ha-Gelili); *Sifrei,* Numbers 68.
4. Deuteronomy Rabbah 2:8.
5. R. Bornsztain, *Shem mi-Shemuel, Be-Ha'alot'kha,* loc. cit.
6. Genesis 43:32.
7. *Sukkah* 25b (opinion of R. Akiva); *Sifrei,* Numbers 68.

the bodies of Nadab and Abihu out of the Sanctuary.[8] These people were able to shake the Jewish people out of being transfixed and immobilized by the tragedy of Nadab and Abihu.[9] It took people who were *dod Aharon*, that is, akin to the character of Aaron, people of a special gentleness, warmth, and sensitivity to someone else's suffering, to carry one's brothers to allow us to move forward. It is such people who are also equivalent to the majority of the community.

Now, one final view is that the people who were impure had been occupied with simple *met mitzvah*.[10] It takes the person who has a profound appreciation of human life to feel that man has a higher purpose and be motivated to form the Jewish community.

8. Leviticus 10:4.
9. Mishael and Elizaphan carried Nadab and Abihu out of the Sanctuary after they died. Leviticus 10:5.
10. *Sukkah* 25b (opinion of R. Isaac); *Sifrei*, Numbers 68.

The Ideal Community of Public Servants

June 13, 1987

As the first round of the Iran-Contra hearings drew to a close this past week, the American public came to the shocking realization that the cherished checks and balances of the Constitution for democracy had failed miserably. A group of zealous subordinates of the President literally set up an off-the-books government, consisting of an elaborate network of operatives and bank accounts stretching from Switzerland to Panama and Liberia. This network acted as a private intelligence organization conducting diplomacy and foreign policy in the name of the federal government.[1]

If Maimonides were asked why the system failed, I think he would say that it was because the relationship between the President and his subordinates displayed nothing more than the lowest level of friendship

1. See generally Theodore Draper, *A Very Thin Line: The Iran-Contra Affairs* (New York: Hill & Wang, 1991); Report of the Congressional Committees Investigating the Iran-Contra Affair, H.R. Rep. No. 100–433 (1987).

in the three categories of friendship that Maimonides identifies.[2] It was simply a *yedidut le-to'elet*, a friendship based on mutual self-interest. The President regarded his subordinates as skillful technicians to implement his policies and even his ideologies. And the subordinates looked upon their position as an opportunity to exercise power.

To the extent that the subordinates do not connect the President to the network, he will have achieved the second level of friendship, that of *yedid le-bittaḥon*, the confidant, the friend with whom he has no fear that he will be thought of anything less if he reveals his secrets and inner thoughts, with whom there is no chance of betrayal. We cannot say the same for the subordinates. They have been cut off and left to twist in the wind.

What constitutes the ideal community of public servants? It is when all are intensely committed to an ideal that supersedes personal loyalty. This can be seen in the relationship of the Levites to the Priests. The Levites were already subordinate – "They shall be joined to you and shall minister to you" (Numbers 18:2).[3] And to ensure that they would be competent, it was necessary, as *Ḥizkuni* points out, that the Levites should be completely supported by the Children of Israel so that they could devote their time exclusively towards perfection of their art, so that "there should not be a plague among the Children of Israel" (Numbers 8:19).[4]

But it was also necessary to make a special installation for them, to charge them with their high purpose and mission. We did not rely on the Priests to charge them. We charged the Levites in a separate and unique ceremony.[5] As R. Samson Raphael Hirsch notes, in the ceremony, it was not only pointed out to them their life's mission through the offerings – the *par*, the servant of Hashem; the *olah*, spiritual striving; and the *ḥattat*, mastering the height that they achieved – but they were also required to shave their entire bodies to impress upon them the need to rid themselves of isolating selfishness.[6]

2. Maimonides, *Perush ha-Mishnayot*, *Avot* 1:6, s.v. "*u-keneh lekha ḥaver*."
3. See *Midrash ha-Gadol*, Numbers 18:2; *Rashi* to *Tamid* 26b, s.v. "*ha ma ani mekayyem*."
4. R. Hezekiah b. Manoah (*Ḥizkuni*, France, 13th cent.), *Ḥizkuni* to Numbers 8:18.
5. See Numbers 8:5–22.
6. R. Samson Raphael Hirsch, Numbers 8:7–8.

But there are checks and balances. The Priests viewed the Levites as subordinates, so there was *tenufah* (lit., "waving"). Aaron physically lifted up each and every one of the Levites, all 22,000 of them.[7] As the *Ḥida* says, this was *kinyan hagbahah* but *lifnei Hashem,* "before God" (Numbers 8:10).[8] At the same time, so that they should not forget that they represent the Jewish people, the Children of Israel leaned their hands upon the Levites.[9] When people are mutually committed to an ideal, the ideal gains luster and brilliance. But when someone is not faithful to the ideal, the personal relationship means nothing, the natural affection means nothing. "The one who said of his father and mother, 'I have not favored him,' his brothers he did not give recognition and his children he did not know, for they have observed Your word, and Your covenant they preserved" (Deuteronomy 33:9).

The proof that the system works is that we have the juxtaposition of *Pesaḥ Sheni.* A group of people who had been defiled through contact with a human corpse and anticipated that they would not be able to offer the *korban pesaḥ* importuned, "*Lamah niggara*?" (lit., "Why should we be diminished?") (Numbers 9:7). Why should we be held back and not be permitted to sacrifice in the proper time? It is a *hora'at sha'ah* because the mitzvah of *Pesaḥ Sheni* is clearly connected to entering the Land of Israel.[10]

Now, the *she'elah* was on the very boundary of Halakhah. The people who posed the question were ritually impure on the eve of Passover, but would become pure the next day, on Passover itself, as the last of their seven days of ritual impurity fell on the eve of Passover.[11] With a question in the twilight zone of legality, the discretionary license could

---

7. Numbers 8:21; Numbers 3:39.
8. R. Hayyim Joseph David Azulai (*Ḥida,* Jerusalem, 1724–1806), *Ḥomat Anakh, Be-Ha'alot'kha,* ¶ 3. *Kinyan hagbahah* is the acquisition of legal rights to movable property that is effected through lifting the property. See *Shulḥan Arukh, Ḥoshen Mishpat* 198.
9. Numbers 8:10.
10. Exodus 12:25, 13:5; *Tosafot* to *Kiddushin* 37b, s.v. "*ho'il ve-ne'emra bi'ah*"; Nahmanides to Numbers 9:1.
11. *Sifrei,* Numbers 68. One who comes in contact with a corpse becomes ritually impure for seven days and requires sprinkling with purification water on the third and seventh day. Numbers 19:11–12.

have run amok. But it did not. Quite to the contrary, the *she'elah* travels up the entire hierarchy of the judicial system. Each person displays his unblemished loyalty to the Torah, and honestly admits that he does not know the answer. Moses himself says, "Stand by and I will hear what Hashem will command you" (Numbers 9:8).

May this be our refrain, "Stand by and let us hear what Hashem will command us."

Humility

June 24, 1989

The personality of Moses presents a paradox. He is described as "exceedingly humble, more than any person on the face of the earth" (Numbers 12:3). But when the Korach resurrection broke out, the rebels cried out to Moses and Aaron, "Why do you exalt yourselves over the congregation of Hashem?" (Numbers 16:3).

Moreover, how is it possible that Moses was unaware that he was a very special person? Did he not orchestrate the Ten Plagues? Did he not lead us out of Egypt and guide us in the Wilderness for forty years? Did he not ascend to the heaven to receive the Torah? Was his level of prophecy not unsurpassed?[1]

Perhaps the answer lies in the proposition that *anavah* is not self-denial with respect to one's potential and achievements. Quite to the

1. See Numbers 12:8. Unlike the other prophets, Moses received his prophecy with perfect clarity, as an "*aspaklaria ha-me'irah*" (illuminating vision). See *Rashi* to Numbers 12:6, s.v. "*Hashem ba-mar'ah elav esvadda*"; *Rashi* to Numbers 12:8, s.v. "*u-mar'eh ve-lo be-ḥidot*"; Leviticus Rabbah 1:14.

contrary, the *anav*, more so than others, is acutely aware of his divine endowment, and achievement is the fuel to drive himself to a higher level of achievement, lest he misuse his gifts and disappoint God and man. The *anav* is driven by a sense of mission and responsibility, but he is unpretentious, never putting in any claim for honor or recognition. The *anav* proves himself by the test of jealousy.

The two related episodes that immediately precede the Torah's statement that Moses was exceedingly modest are there to prove to us that he was an *anav*. It shows us how Moses dealt with jealousy. When Moses was instructed to gather seventy elders, he immediately knew the potential for the generation of jealousy. "What should I do to prevent jealousy among the Tribes? If I select six elders from ten Tribes and five from two Tribes, there will be jealousy." So he devised a scheme of lotteries, consisting of seventy-two pieces, seventy marked *zaken* (elder) and two blank.[2] This way, there could be no complaints. Moses was well aware of the human foible of jealousy.

Now, what happens next? Only tens out of thousands are invited to draw lotteries. Eldad and Medad are so humble that they feel they are not worthy, so they do not come.[3] But suddenly, Eldad and Medad begin to prophesize. What do they say? It is a test of jealousy par excellence. One opinion has it that they began to prophesize regarding the Quail, an event about which Moses had already prophesized.[4] They then became competitors. How does Moses react to a competing prophet who has visions about the same event that he spoke of?

Another opinion is that they prophesized regarding the final chapter of Jewish destiny, the War of Gog and Magog.[5] This places the horizon of Eldad and Medad on an even more important level than that of Moses, who did not relate the End of Days.

---

2. *Rashi* to Numbers 11:26, s.v. "*ve-hemmah ba-ketuvim*"; *Sifrei*, Numbers 95; *Sanhedrin* 17a.
3. *Rashi* to Numbers 11:26, s.v. "*va-yisha'aru shenei anashim*"; *Sifrei*, Numbers 95; *Sanhedrin* 17a.
4. *Sanhedrin* 17a (opinion of Abba Hanin).
5. *Sanhedrin* 17a (opinion of R. Nahman).

And finally, the jealousy of Moses was tested because they prophesized that Moses would die and Joshua would lead the people into the Land of Israel.[6]

What does Moses' alter ego, Joshua, say? "My lord, Moses, *kela'em* [i.e., silence, destroy, or imprison them]."[7] They are false prophets. They should prophesize only in the *Ohel Mo'ed,* not outside the camp.[8]

The jealous man would have readily agreed with this assessment that they are false prophets. But Moses is a true *anav*. He looks beyond superficialities and gives Eldad and Medad the benefit of the doubt. He sees in them nobility and goodness of the highest order and proclaims, "Would that the entire people of Hashem could be prophets" (Numbers 11:29).

But the test of jealousy moves to a higher plane. Moses had prophesized, "Not for one day shall you eat, nor two days, nor five days, nor ten days, nor twenty days" (Numbers 11:19). When the Quail came, the Children of Israel, as R. Samson Raphael Hirsch points out, acted as if there were no tomorrow.[9] They voraciously went after the Quail in the morning and the afternoon. This seems to cast doubt on what Moses said. Will Moses' jealousy now be aroused?

And then, as the *Ketav Sofer* points out, the way to test the authenticity of an *anav* is to accuse him of being arrogant.[10] If his modesty is only a masquerade, designed to get recognition, then at that point, the cover will explode. But if the person is a real *anav,* he will remain an *anav* even under those trying conditions. Moses is accused of arrogance by Aaron and Miriam. They say, "We, too, communicated with Hashem, yet we do not separate from our spouses."[11] Hashem Himself

6. *Rashi* to Numbers 11:28; *Sanhedrin* 17a (opinion of R. Shimon).
7. Numbers 11:28; *Rashi* ad loc. According to one interpretation, the root word is כלה, to obliterate, and according to the other interpretation, the root word is כלא, to imprison.
8. Nahmanides to Numbers 11:28.
9. R. Samson Raphael Hirsch, Numbers 11:32.
10. R. Abraham Samuel Benjamin Sofer (*Ketav Sofer,* Germany, 1815–1871), *Ketav Sofer,* Numbers 12:3.
11. Numbers 12:2; *Rashi* ad loc.; *Sifrei,* Numbers 100; *Midrash Tanḥuma, Tzav* 13.

must take up the honor of Moses because he is silent when he hears this and does not react.[12]

The *anav* manifests himself not so much with self-effacement but with a willingness to place a fellow on a pedestal when he recognizes nobility and grandeur in him. And even when goodness and nobility of his fellow are not definite, the *anav* gives the person the benefit of the doubt and heaps recognition on him.

In our society, we face a clear-cut danger that humility is all too often equated with self-denigration. But self-denigration is prohibited. Just as it is prohibited to relate *lashon ha-ra* about a fellow, it is prohibited to relate *lashon ha-ra* about ourselves.[13]

A more subtle challenge is when we deny our essential goodness because we fear that virtue is anti-social. This is akin to one who hangs *tekhelet* on his *tzitzit* and claims that it is indigo.[14] Most challenging of all is self-denigrating humor. One will say, but after all, we all know that it is just in jest and therefore it is not *lashon ha-ra*. But all too often,

12. Numbers 12:6–8.

13. R. Joseph Hayyim b. Elijah al-Hakam (*Ben Ish Ḥai*, Baghdad, 1833 or 1835–1909), *Torah le-Shemah*, no. 409; R. Mosheh Meir Yashar, *He-Ḥafetz Ḥayyim: Ḥayyav u-Po'alo*, vol. 3 (Tel Aviv: Netzah, 1961), 1075–1076; R. Hershel Schachter, *Nefesh ha-Rav* (Brooklyn, NY: Flatbush Beth Hamedrosh, 1994), 150. Cf. R. Israel Meir ha-Kohen Kagan (*Ḥafetz Ḥayyim*, Radin, 1838–1933), *She'elot u-Teshuvot le-Ḥafetz Ḥayyim, siman* 24.

A story is told of the *Ḥafetz Ḥayyim* in support of the proposition that one may not speak *lashon ha-ra* about oneself. The *Ḥafetz Ḥayyim* encountered a traveler who said that he was going to visit the great *tzaddik*, the *Ḥafetz Ḥayyim*. In his modesty, the *Ḥafetz Ḥayyim* told the traveler that the *Ḥafetz Ḥayyim* is just an ordinary Jew. Unaware that he was speaking to the *Ḥafetz Ḥayyim*, the traveler then berated the *Ḥafetz Ḥayyim* for denying the *Ḥafetz Ḥayyim*'s stature as a great *tzaddik*. Subsequently, the traveler learned the identity of the person whom he had berated and begged the *Ḥafetz Ḥayyim*'s forgiveness. The *Ḥafetz Ḥayyim* calmed the man's nerves, insisting that there was no need to ask for his forgiveness. "Moreover," added the *Ḥafetz Ḥayyim*, "on account of you, I merited to learn that it is prohibited to speak *lashon ha-ra* about oneself."

14. See *Bava Metzia* 61b. *Tzizit* threads are required to be dyed with *tekhelet*. Numbers 15:38. *Tekhelet* was derived from a sea creature, the *ḥilazon*, which appears on land only once in seventy years. *Menaḥot* 44a. Consequently, *tekhelet* was expensive. The Talmud cautions that if one dyes *tzitzit* threads with an imitation dye derived from the indigo plant and claims that the dye is *tekhelet*, Hashem will exact punishment from him. *Bava Metzia* 61b.

self-denigration is funny only because of the ring of truth in it. And still more dangerous is comedy relating to the idiosyncrasies and even warts of the Jewish people. Satire may cross the line into self-hatred.

We must remember that Moses was self-effacing when it came to himself. The Torah records that Hashem revealed Himself to Moses with the word "*va-Yikra*" (ויקרא), with a small *aleph* (א). The small *aleph* indicates that Moses did not want to record that Hashem called him into the Tabernacle to communicate with him, unlike the non-Jewish prophets, for whom the term *va-yakar* (ויקר) is used, indicating that Hashem called to them in an incidental manner. Moses requested that the *aleph* be omitted, but Hashem instructed Moses to make the *aleph* small.[15] But when Moses spoke to the Jewish people, saying, "*Ashrekha* (אשריך) *Yisrael*," "Fortunate are you, O Israel! Who is like you! A people delivered by Hashem" (Deuteronomy 33:29), "*ashrekha*" was written with a larger *aleph*.[16]

---

15. Jacob b. Asher (*Tur*, Spain, 1270–1343), *Ba'al ha-Turim* to Leviticus 1:1.
16. R. Jedidah Solomon Raphael b. Abraham Norzi (*Minḥat Shai*, Mantua, ca. 1560–1626), *Minḥat Shai* to Deuteronomy 33:29; R. Nosson Nota Shapira (Cracow, 1585–1633), *Megaleh Amukot* 91; R. Reuben Hoeshke b. Hoeshke Katz (Prague, d. 1673), *Yalkut Re'uveni, Va-Et'ḥanan*.

Shelaḥ Lekha

A Land That Devours Its Inhabitants[1]

June 16, 1984

An observed phenomenon, as we know, may evoke diametrically opposite responses or reactions. Hence, when the scouts returned from their spying mission, they all reported that they observed one funeral procession after another. Yet, they differed as to what this signified. For ten people, this meant that the climate of the land of Canaan was poisoned and the land was not habitable. But for Joshua and Caleb, it meant that they were the beneficiaries of a special Divine Providence, that the inhabitants of Canaan were made to be preoccupied with their dead and the Spies therefore went unnoticed.[2]

The disparity is, of course, no surprise. Perception is not reality but rather reflects the perspective and bias of the observer. All were righteous people at the time that they were sent. The difference, though, was

1. Numbers 13:32.
2. *Rashi* to Numbers 13:32, s.v. "*okhelet yoshveha*"; *Midrash Tanḥuma, Shelaḥ Lekha* 7.

that all but Joshua and Caleb came with the perspective of individuals. Joshua and Caleb came with the perspective of the entire Jewish nation.

Everyone wanted the Torah society of the Wilderness to continue and flourish in the Land of Israel. The Spies, however, were overcome with great fear that a Torah society in the Land of Israel was very unlikely to emerge. In the Wilderness, material needs claimed precious little of their time. Everything was provided to them with minimal effort, the manna, the Well of Miriam, the Clouds of Glory. There was a link between good behavior and reward, and between bad behavior and punishment.[3] Man had nothing to do but occupy himself in the study of Torah and spiritual growth. The Spies were overcome with fear that this would change in the Land of Israel. With the end of the supernatural existence, man would be preoccupied with material pursuits. When would he study Torah?

Moreover, the link between good conduct and reward, and between bad conduct and punishment, would no longer be obvious. The Land of Israel would not tolerate the iniquity of an entire people and would expel them only if they failed as a collective unit.[4] But this punishment would not be inflicted on an individual basis.

To demonstrate the fear of the Spies in a most spectacular manner, eight of them carried mature grapes, one carried a pomegranate, and one held a fig.[5] What message did they want to impart here? The eight who carried the grapes showed that for most people, preoccupation with materialism to achieve monstrous fortunes would be the rule of the day. Only a select few would hold the fig, the symbol of complacency, as the Prophet Micah stated, "They will sit, each man under his vine and under his fig tree" (Micah 4:4). And only a select few would preoccupy themselves with the commandments, symbolized by the pomegranate.[6]

---

3. For example, the manna took on different forms depending on the spiritual stature of the people. The righteous found the manna in the form of bread; those of average spiritual stature were required to bake it; and the wicked were required to grind the manna and then bake it to render it edible. R. Samuel Eliezer b. Judah ha-Levi Edels (*Maharsha*, Poland, 1555–1631), *Ḥiddushei Aggadot*, *Yoma* 75a, s.v. "*beinonim*."
4. Leviticus 18:25; *Keli Yakar* to Deuteronomy 29:21.
5. *Sotah* 34a; *Rashi* to Numbers 13:23, s.v. "*va-yissa'uhu va-mot bi-shenayim*."
6. See *Berakhot* 57a; *Eruvin* 19a. A Jew is compared to a pomegranate in that just as a pomegranate is full of seeds, a Jew is full of mitzvot.

Now, in a society of inequality of wealth, what would become of the unity and solidarity of our people? Each person would strike out in a different direction and the unfortunates of society would be abandoned abruptly. The outlook was very pessimistic from the vantage point of those people.

But Joshua and Caleb were visionaries. They came from the perspective of the entire nation. Joshua was the lad who "would not depart from within the Tent" (Exodus 33:11). He was the personification of Torah itself, completely lost in his own abstract world. He believed fully in the promise of the Torah and found the new materialism and environment of inequality to be a great challenge for the Torah to demonstrate its divine origin by penetrating every aspect of society, even the murkiest spots. What an opportunity! All the secular institutions of society could be infused with *kedushah*. The Jew could influence the direction of technology and social change. Even the political institutions could be penetrated and infused with Torah.

Caleb experienced his sense of commitment through a strong sense of family. He was not afraid to go to the Cave of Makhpelah in Hebron.[7] The sense of family is indeed enhanced within the framework of a society of inequality.

Paradoxically, the society of inequality offers much greater opportunity for giving than the egalitarian society of the Wilderness. Since the link between reward and punishment is at best tenuous in the Land of Israel, when giving is achieved, it produces that much more solidarity, unity, and closeness.

What could be given to a demoralized people to lift their spirits? The mitzvah of *ḥallah* and *nesakhim*.[8] As R. Shlomo Yosef Zevin puts it, *nesakhim* go down to the very core of the earth[9] and *ḥallah* goes up,

---

7. *Sotah* 34b; *Rashi* to Numbers 13:22, s.v. "*va-yavo ad Ḥevron.*"
8. *Nesakhim* are libations of wine that typically accompanied burnt offerings and peace offerings. The amount of the libation was one-fourth of a *hin* for a lamb, one-third of a *hin* for a ram, and one-half of a *hin* for a bull. Numbers 15:1–10.
9. See *Sukkah* 49a. Beneath the Altar were pits into which the wine flowed after the libation. The Talmud notes that the cavity of the pits descended into the abyss.

"*tarimu*."[10] The *korban* of Hashem can penetrate the depths of society to the murkiest areas and places of great squalor and elevate man's materialism as well.[11]

But let us remember that the conflict of views between the insular approach and the espousal of entry of the Torah into new frontiers is something that we have in our present generation as well. The penetration into new frontiers is always fraught with the gravest danger when it is attempted by an individual. But when it is undertaken by the entire Jewish community, it will surely succeed.

10. Numbers 15:19 ("It shall be that when you will eat of the bread of the Land, you shall set aside (*tarimu*) a portion for Hashem."). The mitzvah of *terumat ḥallah* requires the owner of bread-dough to give a portion of the dough to a Priest. In current times, the common practice is to burn the portion that would have been given to the Priest. See generally Maimonides, *Mishneh Torah, Bikkurim* 5; *Shulḥan Arukh, Yoreh De'ah* 322. R. Zevin interprets the word "*tarimu*" as signifying a lifting up of the bread, from the root *rom* (ר-ו-מ), to lift up. R. Shlomo Yosef Zevin (Israel, 1888-1978), *La-Torah ve-la-Mo'adim, Shelaḥ* 3 (Jerusalem, 2002), 249–250.

11. R. Shlomo Yosef Zevin, *La-Torah ve-la-Mo'adim*, loc. cit.

The Hysterical Personality

June 20, 1987

We all understand that hysteria and terror may not only distort an individual's judgment, but could lead him to irrational acts as well. Transgressions committed within this mental state should surely evoke our sympathy and compassion. It is therefore a matter of mystery that the evil report of the Spies brought on such calamity to the Jewish people. The entire generation of the Wilderness was not to enter the Promised Land. Verily, the Spies drew unwarranted conclusions from the observed facts, as for example, when they concluded that "it is a land that devours its inhabitants" (Numbers 13:32). But there is no gainsaying that they did see giants and monstrous-sized fruits.[1]

---

1. Numbers 13:22, 13:33; *Sotah* 34a. The Spies chose to bring back a cluster of grapes that was so large that eight of the Spies were needed to carry it. A ninth Spy carried a pomegranate, and a tenth Spy carried a fig. Joshua and Caleb did not bring back any fruits because they knew that the Spies would use the fruits to denigrate the Land of Israel. *Sotah* 34a.

If the evil report brought calamity upon the Jewish nation, then the mental state of the Spies that engendered the evil report was inexcusable. If only the Spies had come with the attitude of Caleb and Pinhas, the attitude of *ḥofrim*, "explorers," instead of *meraglim*, "spies," not just to gather information regarding the physical terrain and the measurements of the people, but to ascertain their mental attitude as well, they would have found out that the inhabitants of Canaan were literally terrified in anticipation of the coming of the Children of Israel. Why? Because thirty-nine years later, when Caleb and Pinhas toured the Land, Rahav told them that the inhabitants were in a state of dread over the Children of Israel, "because we have heard how Hashem dried up the waters of the Sea of Reeds for you when you left Egypt" (Joshua 2:10). Now, if this was the case thirty-nine years later, when the passage of time did not blunt the luster of the event, then certainly this would have been the case in close proximity to the event. And if there is any doubt, we say every day, "All the inhabitants of Canaan dissolved" (Exodus 15:15).[2]

So things were quite in reverse. The Canaanites were in terror of us. The Spies' state of mind was therefore inexcusable.

And why did the Splitting of the Sea of Reeds have such a pivotal effect on the mentality of the Canaanites? It is because it was a miracle for the sake of a miracle. It was not necessary for the survival of the Jewish people. So, too, we must have the *ḥofrim* attitude rather than the *meraglim* attitude toward the establishment of Jewish sovereignty after two thousand years. It was not necessary for Jewish survival. "Hashem will scatter you among all the peoples, from the end of the earth to the end of the earth" (Deuteronomy 28:64). The depths of the Reproof, the dispersion and scattering of the Jewish people, itself guarantees our survival. The establishment of the Jewish State is a divine gift.

Each generation has its challenges. Sometimes it is the challenge of conquest, whether we will adopt the attitude of a *ḥofer* or that of a *meragel*. But right now, it is with respect to the pursuit of peace. The *ḥofer* attitude realizes that negotiation can sell out the country, and therefore we can never lower our guard or be guilty of a mental lapse.

---

2. Morning Prayer, *Pesukei de-Zimrah, Az Yashir.*

This is seen in the negotiation of Caleb and Pinhas. At first, they agree to the oath that Rahav imposes on them that they should spare her and her family.[3] But then they retreat. They say that the oath was imposed under duress. But certainly she deserves to be rewarded. They shrewdly negotiate with her that they will save only the family members who are in her house at the time of the invasion, and only if they do not find the sign of the crimson cord affixed to any other house.[4] If they would not have been alert and thought to stipulate that, the entire mission of conquest of the Land of Israel would have been impossible, as every Canaanite would have claimed to be a relative of Rahav and therefore entitled to immunity.

Let us not tie ourselves up in a crimson cord!

3. Joshua 2:14; R. David Kimhi (*Radak*, Provence, ca. 1160–ca. 1235), *Radak* to Joshua 2:17.
4. Joshua 2:17–20; *Malbim* ad loc.

The Devastation of an Evil Report

June 12, 2004

One of the most troubling theological problems in the entire Torah is the severity of the punishment that Hashem meted out for the Sin of the Spies. "They brought forth an evil report on the Land" (Numbers 13:32). Consider that the Sin of the Golden Calf was a cardinal sin of idolatry, a *yehareg ve-al ya'avor*,[1] but its punishment was confined to the sinners, and the nation remained intact.[2] But for the Sin of the Spies, the punishment was for the entire nation from the age of twenty to the age of sixty to be wiped out over a forty-year period.[3] Why the horrific penalty?

1. Idolatry is one of the three cardinal sins for which one generally must allow himself to be killed (*yehareg*) rather than transgress the sin (*ve-lo ya'avor*). See *Sanhedrin* 74a; Maimonides, *Mishneh Torah, Yesodei ha-Torah* 5:2; *Tur, Yoreh De'ah* 157; *Shulḥan Arukh, Yoreh De'ah* 157:1.
2. Exodus 32:28.
3. Numbers 14:29; *Bava Batra* 121b.

Permit me to suggest an approach. I base it on the *Meshekh Ḥokhmah*.[4] The *Meshekh Ḥokhmah* points out that there was a fundamental difference between the Sin of the Golden Calf and the Sin of the Spies. The Sin of the Golden Calf was an intellectual error and a miscalculation. The Children of Israel thought that having an intermediary to God was acceptable. "Make for us a god that will go before us" (Exodus 32:1). And they made a mistake regarding Moses. "The people saw that Moses had delayed in descending the mountain" (ibid.).

If the error is intellectual, there is every hope that the consequences of the sin will not get out of hand. There is every hope that the damage will be limited. The people have not abandoned the attribute of truth, and therefore Moses can invoke *rav ḥesed ve-emet*, "great kindness and truth" (Exodus 34:6).[5] And that is the way it was when Moses returned. The reversal process began, the sinners were punished, and normalcy eventually resumed.

Not so with the Sin of the Spies. The sin here was a flaw in character. We were lacking in *hakkarat ha-tov*. Hashem promised five expressions of Redemption. Four promises were fulfilled in spectacular form, with the Ten Plagues, the Splitting of the Sea of Reeds, and *Mattan Torah*. So if we really appreciated all that, we should certainly have believed that Hashem would fulfill the fifth promise as well.

The sin of the Spies' evil report is rooted in a deficiency in *hakkarat ha-tov*. If we would have had the profound gratitude that we should have had, and applied truth to gratitude, we would have believed in the fifth promise. It was a deficiency in our attribute of truth. In praying on behalf of the people after the Sin of the Spies, Moses could not invoke truth. It is just *rav ḥesed*, but not *emet*.[6]

When the root evil is a character flaw, there is the danger that evil consequences will run amok, getting totally out of control. Just look at the sequence. It starts with an evil report and then spreads, displaying a

4. See *Meshekh Ḥokhmah* to Numbers 14:18, s.v. "*ve-rav ḥesed*."
5. Moses invoked the divine attribute of truth in his prayer on behalf of the Jewish people after the Sin of the Golden Calf by requesting that Hashem remember the oath that He had made to the Patriarchs that He would give their children the Land of Israel as a heritage forever. See Exodus 32:13; *Meshekh Ḥokhmah* to Numbers 14:18.
6. Numbers 14:18.

defeatist attitude. The defeatism moves to a wider audience, to the entire nation, including the women. "The entire assembly raised up and issued its voice" (Numbers 14:1). But it gets worse. "They said to one another, 'Let us appoint a leader and return to Egypt!'" (Numbers 14:4). And then the most frightening thing of all: When Joshua and Caleb attempted to speak to the Jewish people, "the entire assembly said to pelt them with stones" (Numbers 14:10). Hashem intervenes at that point, freezing the moment. "The Glory of Hashem appeared in the Tent of Meeting to all the Children of Israel" (Numbers 14:10).

It is frightening. If not for this intervention, just think what would have been. The mob would have killed Joshua and Caleb. Who knows what they would have done to Moses and Aaron. And "they said to one another, 'Let us appoint a leader and return to Egypt!'" (Numbers 14:4). This is self-destruction of everything, of the Exodus from Egypt, the Ten Plagues, the Splitting of the Sea of Reeds, and *Mattan Torah*. Could there be a greater tragedy?

The rule is that Hashem never interferes with free will. Witness "Reuben heard and he saved him from their hand" (Genesis 37:21). As the *Or ha-Ḥayyim* explains, Reuben saved Joseph from those who had free will to kill him, because it is possible for a person to kill another human being even if the victim does not deserve to die.[7]

And there is one final word here. Look at the difference between Hur, who was killed by the mob during the Sin of the Golden Calf,[8] and Joshua and Caleb, who were saved by Hashem from being killed after the Sin of the Spies. When fighting against an evil report, Hashem protects the person with a special blessing and majesty.

Let it be our lot to say only *lashon tov* and have no part of *lashon ha-ra*. "Death and life are in the hands of the tongue" (Proverbs 18:21). Indeed, the life and death of an entire nation or community are in the hands of the tongue.

7. *Or ha-Ḥayyim* to Genesis 37:21.
8. Leviticus Rabbah 10:3.

Koraḥ

The Sons of Korach Did Not Die

June 23, 1984

It is rare in the annals of history that a father's sin condemns him to a horrendous death yet his sons achieve immortality of sorts. This is what we find in relation to Korach and his sons. For Korach's part in the rebellion, a new death was created; the earth swallowed him up.[1] Were it not for the prayer of Hannah, Korach would have suffered eternal damnation.[2] Yet, Korach's sons, co-conspirators, recanted at the critical moment of truth and achieved immortality of sorts.[3] They became profound students of the ethics of controversy, its genesis, its remediation, and its constructive role in society.

How did they achieve immortality? They became among the select few who were authors of the Book of Psalms, and authors of not

1. Numbers 16:32.
2. Genesis Rabbah 98:2
3. *Rashi* to Numbers 26:11; *Megillah* 14a; *Sanhedrin* 110a.

some esoteric or obscure passages, but of passages recited as part of our daily rituals and in special and exalted moments of our lives.[4]

Strife, it is said, came into being on the second day of creation, when the upper waters were separated from the lower waters.[5] For this day, the sons of Korach composed a hymn, *shir mizmor le-venei Koraḥ*, Psalm 48.[6]

Now, if we look into this psalm, is there any mention of strife? No. Instead, we find the psalm relates to the Glory of God, as reflected through the beauty and power of the Land of Israel. We read such mellifluous phrases as "fairest of sights, joy of all the earth, Mount Zion, by the northern side of the great king's city" (Psalms 48:3). The Land of Israel is indestructible. "With an east wind You smashed the ships of Tarshish" (Psalms 48:8). The sons of Korach are trying to tell us how to cultivate and nurture an accommodating personality, minimizing the occurrence of strife in our lives.

How do we make our contentious nature dissipate? It is by focusing on something sublime, something of indescribable beauty, which is in the common possession of the entire Jewish nation. By focusing on the sublime, the mundane recedes into inconsequence and many of the petty causes of strife dissipate entirely. By focusing on a unifying force of stupendous beauty and power, divisiveness dissipates.

But surely there are issues that we want to take a stand on, issues that we are convinced constitute a dispute for the sake of Heaven. And a dispute for the sake of Heaven is exactly what contributes to the viability of our people. When truth is challenged and emerges unscathed, it is a truth that generates a deeper belief.

What test is there to examine our motives, to determine whether we are striving for the sake of Heaven? For this, the sons of Korach composed a hymn to be said in the house of mourning, "For the conductor,

4. *Bava Batra* 14b–15a; *Rashi* to Psalms 1:1. The Talmud *ad locum* records that King David composed the Book of Psalms in collaboration with ten elders: Adam, Malki Tzedek, Abraham, Moses, Heiman, Yedusun, Assaf, and the three sons of Korach. Psalms 42–49, 84, 85, 87, and 88 are ascribed to the sons of Korach.
5. Genesis Rabbah 4:6.
6. *Rosh ha-Shanah* 31a. See also R. Zadok ha-Kohen Rabinowitz (Lublin, 1823–1900), *Resisei Lailah* 48:3.

by the sons of Korach, a psalm" (Psalms 49:1). The psalm asks the age-old question, "Why should I be fearful in days of evil?" (Psalms 49:6). What is the source of man's feeling of self-doubt and insecurity in this world?

Now, the answer to the question, as far as the mourner is concerned, is quite simple. He has just experienced the death of a loved one. A piece of himself has died. He feels lost, demoralized, and insecure. But it is precisely at a time when the answer for the security of the mourner is crystal clear that we pose this question to humanity in general. The message here is that superficial answers will not do. We must probe beneath the surface. Instead of focusing on events in proximity, we must look at the underlying causes of the events.

Students of history may evaluate the downfall of Korach, their father, in a very simplistic way and say that he was power-hungry; he had an obsession to be recognized. But what was the underlying cause of the rebellion? The answer is the same as the answer to the question "Why should I be fearful in days of evil?" It is "the injunctions that I trod upon will surround me" (Psalms 49:6). The sins I tread under my feet. Divine Providence always works measure for measure. It is the excessive self-reliance and lack of loyalty to mitzvot, selective performance of mitzvot based on the pure logic of the mitzvot. This mentality is punished measure for measure and is inflicted with insecurity and self-doubt. This intimates that Korach's application of logic to the mitzvot by his queries of whether a *tallit* that is made entirely of *tekhelet* is still required to have a string of *tekhelet* attached to it, and whether a house that is full of holy books is still required to have a *mezuzah*, was the fundamental character flaw of Korach that led eventually to his lust for power, which was a demonstration of self-reliance.[7]

What if we pass the test? We examine our attitude towards the mitzvot and we are sure that we are not selective in the performance of mitzvot. We therefore cannot regard our restless drive to challenge an established belief or our championing of a cause to be other than for the sake of Heaven. For this, the sons of Korach authored Psalm 47, the psalm that is sung before the blowing of the

7. *Midrash ha-Gadol, Be-Midbar* 16:1; *Rashi* to Numbers 16:1, s.v. "*ve-Datan va-Aviram*."

shofar. Here, we find ourselves in an exalted moment in the Jewish calendar. We are ready to coronate Hashem, the King. At this moment, we read, "All you nations, join hands; sound the *shofar* to God with a cry of joy" (Psalms 47:2). The nations should rejoice in defeat. There is glory in defeat. Furthermore, they should rejoice that "He shall lead nations under us and regimes beneath our feet" (Psalms 47:4). They should rejoice that the Jewish people have complete control over them. Why? By admitting that their ideologies are false and misguided, and acknowledging the superiority of Torah values, the nations will be instrumental in bringing the Divine Glory into this world. They recognize the source of their spiritual elevation, the impact of the influence of the Jews, just as Korach should have realized, as the Kotzker Rebbe said, that it was only because Aaron was standing in the Holy of Holies that Korach was able to achieve his spiritual level of *al ha-dukhan*.[8] He should have realized how he fit into the scheme of things.

One final point that the sons of Korach provided us with is that, no matter what, true Torah values will ultimately triumph. Could there be a more glaring demonstration that Korach was false than the miracle that even his name in a document was erased[9] and that even needles that he lent to someone fell into the abyss?[10] Why was the test of the Staves also necessary?[11] The answer must be that this was to show that when Torah-true values are attacked, the Torah will not only survive unscathed, but will emerge with enhanced beauty and power, and with us having a deeper appreciation of its values.

8. R. Menahem Mendel Morgensztern of Kotzk (*Kotzker Rebbe*, Poland, 1787–1859), *Ohel Torah* (Benei Berak: Slavita, 1959), *Shelaḥ*, p. 58. The expression "*al ha-dukhan*" (lit., "on the platform") refers to the platform on which the Priests stood in the Temple when they administered the priestly blessing. According to one opinion, they stood on the steps of the Sanctuary, facing the people in the Temple Courtyard. See Mishnah, *Tamid* 7:2; Maimonides, *Mishneh Torah, Nesi'at Kappayyim* 14:14. According to another opinion, they stood on a platform built especially for that purpose. *Middot* 2:6.
9. Jerusalem Talmud, *Sanhedrin* 10:1.
10. Ibid.; Numbers Rabbah 18:13.
11. Numbers 17:16–24.

And this is perhaps what the sons of Korach intimate in the phrase "God has ascended with the blast" (Psalms 47:6). This means that Godliness will always ultimately emerge from factionalism, contention, and strife.

May it be our lot to sanctify the name of Heaven with the promotion of unity and not strife.

Peace for the Sake of Heaven

June 22, 1985

Our Sages regard Korach as the prototype of someone who engaged in a dispute *not* for the sake of Heaven.[1] We arrive at this conclusion not only as an article of faith, that is, on the basis of our belief that the horrendous punishment meted out to Korach was well-deserved, but also on the basis of the blatant inconsistency of his positions.

If you are a popularist and are antagonistic to a hereditary privileged class, you do not believe in leaders at all. "Why do you exalt yourselves over the congregation of Hashem?" (Numbers 16:3). Then how can you ally yourself with the sons of Reuben, who want to establish themselves as a privileged class on the basis of their

1. Mishnah, *Avot* 5:17.

being Jacob's first-born son? If you profess to be a believer by saying "the entire assembly – all of them – are holy" (ibid.) because we all heard at Mount Sinai the first two Commandments from Hashem,[2] how do you ally yourself with Dathan and Abiram, who were self-admitted scorners, proclaiming with such gall that Moses brought the Children of Israel out of "a land that flows with milk and honey," referring to Egypt?[3] How dare you openly contradict the words of the *Ribbono shel Olam* Himself, Whom all heard characterize Egypt as a "house of slaves"?[4]

And there is another indication that Korach was not sincere. That is his refusal to engage in dialogue with Moses, just as his cohorts Dathan and Abiram said, "We shall not go up!" (Numbers 16:12).

According to Tradition, the episode of Korach occurred just after the tragic incident of the Spies.[5] It is only in this context of national despair that we can understand why the naked self-interest of Korach and his band was not self-evident to all the people, how a band so small could impact such a multitude.

But an astonishing question presents itself. How much convincing did the people need to see the falseness of Korach's position? Was it not enough that a new death was created, that a fire descended from above to consume the 250 people, and that a plague broke out, all Heavenly omens that Korach was false?[6] So why the need for the test of the Staves?

If Hashem said that with the test of the Staves "I shall cause to subside from upon Me the complaints of the Children of Israel" (Numbers 17:20), perhaps this is to tell us that our ultimate goal is not to decisively crush the enemies of the Torah. No! What we want is nothing less than that those who harbor false beliefs should see the light and join our ranks with happiness and harmony. This is symbolized

2. See *Rashi* to Numbers 16:3, s.v. "*kullam kedoshim.*"
3. Numbers 16:13.
4. Exodus 20:2.
5. *Rashi* to Numbers 16:4. Cf. *Rashi* to Deuteronomy 1:1, s.v. "*bein Paran*" and "*va-Ḥatzerot*"; R. Elijah Mizrahi (*Re'em*, Constantinople, ca. 1450–1526), *Sefer ha-Mizraḥi*, Numbers 13:2.
6. Numbers 16:30–35; Numbers 17:11–12.

by the Staff of Aaron that blossomed and bore fruit. The Staff of Aaron had been the symbol of retribution par excellence in Egypt – "The staff of Aaron swallowed their staves" (Exodus 7:12). With the miracle, it did not thicken one iota, symbolic of the total defeat of the enemies of the Jewish nation.[7]

But here we find the staff placed in the middle.[8] It does not swallow up the others.[9] Quite to the contrary, it is the first to produce *shekedim* (almonds), then blossoms before leaves, symbolic of the attribute of *shekidah* (diligence), so as to say that the Tribe of Aaron would carry out its functions with great efficiency and alacrity, and would be a blessing for the entire Jewish people.[10] It blossoms fruit, and the other trees follow.

Today, we are undoubtedly living in the era of disputes for the sake of Heaven. People are sincere and present their positions with sincerity. But there is a lack of dialogue and a desire to join hands in harmony. Each Jew is a *rimmon* (pomegranate), which means that he is a spiritual *pardes*.[11] So we must understand every Jew on four different levels: the level of *peshat*, to listen carefully to what he says; *remez*, to understand what he may not have articulated well; *derash*,

7. Exodus Rabbah 9:7; *Midrash ha-Gadol*, Exodus 7:12.
8. Numbers 17:21; *Rashi* ad loc.
9. The *Ba'al ha-Turim* and the *Maharam me-Rotenburg* state that according to the Midrash, the Staff of Aaron swallowed the staves of the Princes as it had swallowed the staves of Pharaoh's magicians. *Ba'al ha-Turim* to Exodus 7:12; R. Meir b. Barukh of Rothenburg (*Maharam me-Rotenburg*, Germany, ca. 1215–1293), *Ta'amei Masoret ha-Mikra*, Exodus 7:12, reprinted in *Teshuvot, Pesakim u-Minhagim*, ed. Isaac Z. Kahana, vol. 1 (Jerusalem: Mossad HaRav Kook, 1957), *Va-Era*, 14–15. Commentators have not been able to locate this *midrash*. See *Torat Ḥayyim: Ḥamishah Ḥumshei Torah*, ed. R. Mordecai Leib Katzenellenbogen (Jerusalem: Mossad HaRav Kook, 1993), Exodus 7:12, n. 3; R. Yaakov Koppel Reinitz, *Shoham Yakar* to *Perush Ba'al ha-Turim al ha-Torah* (Jerusalem: Feldheim, 1996), Exodus 7:12, n. 21.
10. *Keli Yakar* to Numbers 17:23.
11. *Berakhot* 57a; *Eruvin* 19a. Expounding on Song of Songs 4:3, the Talmud states that even the unworthiest Jew is full of good deeds as a pomegranate is full of seeds.

to place what he said in a larger context; and *sod,* to discern his secret aspirations.[12] We must move from the era of dispute for the sake of Heaven to the era of peace for the sake of Heaven.

12. *Peshat* is the literal interpretation of a verse, *remez* (lit., "hint") is a veiled reference, such as *gematria*; *derash* is homiletical interpretation; and *sod* (lit., "secret") is a mystical interpretation. The use of the word "*pardes*" as an acronym for *peshat, remez, derash,* and *sod* dates to the late thirteenth century. See Albert van der Heide, "PARDES: Methodological Reflections on the Theory of the Four Senses," *Journal of Jewish Studies* 34 (1983): 147–159. See also *Oxford Dictionary of the Jewish Religion,* ed. Adele Berlin, 2nd ed. (New York: Oxford University Press, 2011), 552, s.v. "Pardes." For examples of references to the acronym *pardes,* see R. Hayyim Vital (Safed, 1542–1620), *Sha'ar Ru'aḥ ha-Kodesh, hakdamah* 3; R. Abraham Samuel Benjamin Sofer (*Ketav Sofer,* Germany, 1815–1871), *Ketav Sofer, Kedoshim*; R. Joseph Hayyim b. Elijah al-Hakam, *Rav Pe'alim, ḥelek* 1, *Sod Yesharim, siman* 5.

Merciful in Judgment

June 23, 1990

Moses' conduct in his confrontation with Korach presents a paradox in understanding his character. In the aftermath of national failure in the form of the Sin of the Golden Calf and the Sin of the Spies, Moses assumes the role of intercessor. He summons every means of resourcefulness to find extenuation and even petitions Hashem for leniency and mercy. Yet, he reacts with uncharacteristic vehemence and ferocity toward Korach and his assembly. Nowhere else in Scripture is Moses' emotional state described as "this distressed Moses greatly" (Numbers 16:15). The dispute seems to take on a personal tone – "I have not taken even a single donkey of theirs" (ibid.). I never took advantage of my position.

Permit me to suggest that the underlying issue of the conflict was far more important than what meets the eye. On the surface, Korach's rebellion concerns the demands of malcontents, those who were miffed and jealous because they were passed over for the appointment of positions of eminence.[1]

1. Numbers 16:3; *Rashi* to Numbers 16:1, s.v "*ve-Datam va-Aviram.*"

But if the entire dispute amounted to only this, Korach really had a good case that he was discriminated against. He should have been appointed the Prince of the Tribe of Levi.[2]

Moses' whole point was that the selection of the leaders was not his own doing, but rather instructed by Hashem.[3] If one thought that Moses made appointments on his own, he could also imagine that Moses invented some mitzvot or some interpretations. Such thinking is absolutely threatening to the future of the Jewish people.

Moses was compassionate. He thought that if the Generation of the Revelation would doubt his role as the teacher of the Torah and the divine origin of the Torah, the experience of Sinai would be reduced to nothing more than *Anokhi Hashem*, "I am Hashem, your God" (Exodus 20:2), and *lo yihiyeh lekha*, "you shall not recognize the gods of others in My presence" (Exodus 20:3).[4] What this implies for obligations is an open question. Each generation would come up with its own interpretations.

Yes, there is plenty of reason for Moses to be livid because the future of the Jewish people is put to question, threatening a total emasculation and perversion of the mitzvot. Therefore, Moses wished for every means of bludgeoning the opposition, to eradicate the doubt as best he could. No residue should remain. A contest was not enough. Hashem created a new form of death. The earth opened its mouth and swallowed the assembly.[5] Then a fire descended and consumed the

---

2. *Rashi* to Numbers 16:1, s.v "*ve-Datam va-Aviram*." Kohath, the son of Levi, had four sons: Amram, Izhor, Hebron, and Uzziel. Exodus 6:18. Moses and Aaron were sons of Amram, and Korach was the first-born son of Izhor. Exodus 6:20–21. Moses was the leader of the Jewish people and Aaron was the High Priest. Korach thought that the next position of honor, the Kohathite Princehood, should have been conferred upon him because he was the eldest son of the second son of Amram. Instead, Moses appointed Elizaphan, the son of Kohath's youngest son, Uzziel, as the Kohathite Prince. Numbers 3:30.
3. Numbers 16:28.
4. The text refers to the first two of the Ten Commandments, which the Children of Israel heard directly from Hashem. *Makkot* 24a; *Horayot* 8a; *Rashi* to Exodus 19:19, s.v. "*Mosheh yidabber*."
5. Numbers 16:30–33.

men who brought *ketoret*.[6] And then finally is the blossoming of the Staff of Aaron.[7]

But the last sign, I would submit, was not just icing on the cake. No, it was a sign for the generations. And how? What testifies to the divine nature of the Torah? It is *periḥah,* blossoming. What grows and flowers? What produces the vital life force of the people? It will always be the belief that the Torah is from heaven. "The righteous person shall live through his faith" (Habakkuk 2:4).

And this sign has two other parallels to the word *yiphraḥ*. First, "I will be to Israel like the dew, and he will blossom like a rosebush" (*yiphraḥ ka-shoshanah*) (Hosea 14:6). *Klal Yisrael* is compared to a rose. It retains its beauty and form, despite being surrounded by thorns.[8] And also, *tzaddik ka-tamar yiphraḥ,* "a righteous man will flourish like a date palm" (Psalms 92:13). When the Torah expands and lights up, finding new relevance to life, it resembles the palm tree, of which every part is useful.[9]

6. Numbers 16:35.
7. Numbers 17:23.
8. Song of Songs 2:2; *Rashi* ad loc.
9. Genesis Rabbah 41:1. The Midrash explains that just as the date-palm has no waste, as its fruits are eaten, its heart (i.e., the *lulav*) is used for praise of Hashem during the *Hallel* prayer, its branches are used for *sekhakh* (i.e., the covering of the *sukkah*), its fiber is used for ropes, its boughs are used for measure (i.e., as a sieve), and its rafts are used as beams for a house, similarly there is no waste in Israel. Some are masters of Scriptures, others of Mishnah, others of Talmud, and others of Haggadah.

Blossoms before Leaves

June 19, 2004

Three days after the miracle of the Splitting of the Sea of Reeds, we, the Jewish people, found ourselves in a crisis of faith. We had journeyed in the Wilderness for three days and our water supply ran out. We complained disrespectfully and boisterously, "What will we drink?" (Exodus 15:24). But how could we ask "What will we drink?" a mere three days after the Splitting of the Sea of Reeds?

This leads R. Shimon Schwab to propose that a miracle, no matter how gripping, has a limited shelf life.[1] Yes, it is very gripping when it occurs and makes an impact on us. We marvel at it and are amazed. But since a miracle does not engage the mind or captivate the heart, it eventually wears off.

Well, R. Shimon Schwab's thesis gets quite a workout in today's *sidrah*. Korach and his assembly challenged Moses and Aaron's leadership, and Hashem created a new form of death. The earth opened its mouth

1. R. Shimon Schwab (New York, 1908–1995), *Ma'ayan Beit ha-Sho'evah: Al Parshiyyot ha-Shavua ve-al Inyanin Shonim* (Brooklyn, NY: Mesorah, 1994), 172, Exodus 15:22.

and swallowed up the rebels.[2] And Hashem sent a fire from heaven to kill the rebels.[3] So now everyone knows who the chosen ones are.

But what happens? The miracle does not even convince. Instead, the people complain to Moses and Aaron, "You have killed the people of Hashem" (Numbers 17:6). Another miracle is necessary. As the *Ḥatam Sofer* explains, the Children of Israel saw that the fire-pans that Korach's assembly had used to offer *ketoret* were consecrated for holy use, as a covering for the Altar.[4] They took this to mean that the assembly did not deserve to die, because if they deserved to die, the pans should have been buried.[5] This led them to believe that it was not the test of the *ketoret* that resulted in the death of the sinners, but that Moses and Aaron had killed them.[6]

"He stood between the dead and the living" (Numbers 17:13). Did the people not see the living personification of the teaching that one should be an *ohev shalom ve-rodef shalom*?[7] Aaron risked his life for the Jewish people by running through the camp with *ketoret* to save them from the plague.[8] But instead, the people understood only part of the message that "*lo ha-sam memit ela ha-ḥet memit,*" it is not the *ketoret* that causes death, but sin that causes death.[9]

In the end, it is another miracle that, once and for all, ends all the murmurings and all the rebellious spirit. It takes a miracle that is a catalyst. It revisits a prior slice of life. It revisits what is familiar and

2. Numbers 16:32.
3. Numbers 16:35.
4. Numbers 17:2–3.
5. See *Avodah Zarah* 62b and *Sanhedrin* 45b (stating that the stone with which a person was stoned, the tree upon which he was hanged, the sword with which he was decapitated, and the cloth with which he was strangled are buried with him).
6. R. Moses Sofer (*Ḥatam Sofer*, Hungary, 1762–1839), *Torat Mosheh, Koraḥ*, Numbers 17:6.
7. Mishnah, *Avot* 1:12.
8. See *Yalkut Shimoni, Tzav* 514 (recording that Aaron risked his life to save the people from the plague by burning the *ketoret* outside the Tabernacle).
9. Cf. *Berakhot* 33a ("It is not the lizard that kills, but sin that kills."). The plague was stopped through *ketoret* because the Children of Israel thought that *ketoret* brought about death after observing that Nadab and Abihu, as well as Korach and his assembly, died while bringing *ketoret*. *Rashi* to Numbers 17:13.

known but was taken for granted. Now there will be a new perspective on the events. It is *peraḥ* before the *titz*; the Staff of Aaron produces blossoms before leaves.[10]

"Moses stood at the gateway of the camp and said, 'Whoever is for Hashem, join me!' And all the Levites gathered around him" (Exodus 32:26). Blossoms before leaves. But revisit what happened a moment ago. Do you not realize that Aaron risked his life for you? "He stood between the dead and the living" (Numbers 17:13).

And then blossoms before leaves – "Behold, he is going out to meet you, and when he sees you, he will rejoice in his heart" (Exodus 4:14).

Leadership in Jewish life is not about power, authority, and honor. It is about being the first citizen of Hashem's Torah and the exemplar of loving and pursuing peace. Because Aaron is the blossom before the leaves, his leadership does not diminish anyone. Just the opposite, the passion, single-mindedness, and sense of mission that he brings with him elevate the moral climate of society, uplifting everyone in the process.

10. See Numbers 17:23.

Ḥukkat

Because You Did Not Believe in Me to Sanctify Me

June 30, 1984

We are all familiar with the concept that the divine scales of judgment treat the minor infraction of the great as strictly as the egregious errors of ordinary people.[1] Perhaps the most famous example of this principle is the stern punishment meted out to Moses and Aaron when they failed to obey the divine command to only speak to the rock at the Wilderness of Zin and instead Moses hit the stone twice.[2] For this, Moses and Aaron were punished – "You will not bring this congregation to the Land that I have given them" (Numbers 20:12). They would no longer be the leaders of the Jewish people.

1. See *Yevamot* 121b ("The Holy One, Blessed is He, deals strictly with the righteous even to a hair's breadth.").
2. Numbers 20:7–11.

Now, Moses was able to be such an extraordinary intercessor for the Jewish people, annulling the harshest decrees. But for himself, all his entreaties and beseeching were to no avail. Moreover, we know that divine justice works *middah ke-neged middah*.[3] How is this attribute of divine justice manifest in the incident of the Wilderness of Zin?

I would submit that a minor infraction can never merit such a severe punishment if it did not embody a dangerous philosophy that people could read into the action. *Rashi* tells us that Moses missed sanctifying the Divine Name because his obedience would have generated a shocking challenge to the Children of Israel. What would have been the challenge? If a stone, which cannot hear or see, and which does not require sustenance, obeys the divine command, how much more so should we, who are capable of comprehension and need sustenance.[4]

Well, if Moses did not convey the *kal ve-ḥomer*, then, as *Likkutei Yehoshua* points out, he must have been at least subliminally apprehensive of it.[5] He was, after all, an *ohev Yisrael* and was fearful that if, God forbid, the Children of Israel would not be up to the challenge, a *ḥillul ha-Shem* would result. It was perhaps this philosophy, this fear of failure, that was responsible for irrevocably removing the leadership reins from Moses. A leader who continuously witnesses the failure of his people eventually fears new challenges because of possible failure.

But to lead the Children of Israel into the Land of Israel, into the new way of life, the type of leadership required was precisely the one that welcomed challenge head-on. Material striving had to be sanctified when the society of *leḥem avirim* ended. Only the leader and expansive Torah personality who was prepared for these challenges would be successful.

---

3. *Sanhedrin* 90a. Cf. *Sotah* 8b. The doctrine of *middah ke-neged middah* is expressed in the maxim of Hillel, "He saw a skull floating on the water and said, 'Because you drowned someone, you were drowned, and the one who drowned you will eventually be drowned'" (Mishnah, *Avot* 2:6).
4. *Rashi* to Numbers 20:12, s.v. "*le-hakddisheni.*"
5. R. Yehoshua Shaynfeld, *Likkutei Yehoshua* (New York: Hadar, 1957), 129.

It was Joshua who would succeed Moses. He was not the most brilliant Torah student.[6] Moses himself thought that his own sons would succeed him.[7] But Joshua did instead because "the guardian of his master shall be honored" (Proverbs 27:18). He was "his servant, Joshua b. Nun, a lad, who would not depart from within the Tent" (Exodus 33:11). He observed Moses in every aspect of the life experience to see how the great Torah luminary applied the Torah to his daily life. "Greater is the service of Torah than the learning of Torah."[8] He wanted to catch even Moses' first reaction and emotion to every experience. Joshua stood at the foot of Mount Sinai to wait for Moses' return.[9] His portion of manna fell there the entire forty days, signifying that he belonged there.[10] He was Moses' closest companion. He wanted to observe Moses as soon as he would come down and see his first reaction, catch his first words. It would be the exemplar par excellence of applying the Torah to everyday living who would be fit to be the leader of the new generation.

When the insular Torah personality clashes with some form of evil, he is very vulnerable. The encounter with the unfamiliar might well fill him with self-doubt and a secret desire to emulate the enemy itself. But the man who is preoccupied with the application of the Torah to every sphere of life has already anticipated the evil that he faces and has already shaped an attitude of contempt toward the evil, whether it is the power of the sword or crude materialism, and is therefore well prepared to do battle. He does not face the unfamiliar, but what he knows well. The encounter will not disarm him or overwhelm him.

When the Children of Israel were faced with the threat of Amalek, whom did Moses send? Joshua. Amalek represents the threat of demoralization. After the Children of Israel had witnessed one miracle after another, and were filled with a dizzying sense of invincibility, Amalek attacked them, as if to say, "I am not impressed with anything, with the

---

6. See Nahmanides to Numbers 13:4 (noting that the Spies were listed in the order of their importance, and Joshua was listed fifth).
7. *Rashi* to Numbers 27:16, s.v. "*yifkod Hashem.*"
8. *Berakhot* 7b.
9. *Rashi* to Exodus 24:13.
10. *Rashi* to *Yoma* 76a, s.v. "*zeh Yehoshua.*"

Exodus from Egypt, with the Splitting of the Sea of Reeds."[11] The insular personality could not wage the battle. He might be overwhelmed by the glamour of power. But the expansive personality of Joshua would have been thoroughly familiar with this cult and would have already formed an attitude of contempt toward it, and therefore would be victorious.

Joshua instituted ten conditions when he divided the Land of Israel.[12] He realized in advance that the new way of life would be characterized by conflict between the interests of the individual and those of society. He had the prescience to legislate all these matters, not applications of the Torah, but legislation in the spirit of the Torah.

The individual who wants to apply the Torah to every life experience can potentially exert a much greater influence on society than the insular personality. Joseph's brothers first said "indeed we are guilty concerning our brother" (Genesis 42:21) only after they heard the Viceroy of Egypt pronounce "I fear God" (Genesis 42:18). Joseph accused them of being spies. He put them to the test. First he said, "I will divide you up and let only one of you return."[13] Then, three days later, Joseph tells them, in essence, "I will not subject you to unnecessary torment and anguish, for perhaps what you claim is true, that you are Canaanites, that is, *ba'alei battim*. I will subject you only to a torment that is necessary."[14] "I fear God."

This really hit home, this pronouncement of a fear of God in the squalor of a paganistic culture by a Viceroy who had absolute power. Fear of God proceeding from such a source had a much more powerful impact than could be possible from Jacob himself. No torment by Jacob himself, the departure of the Divine Presence,[15] all the discord within the family, could bring Joseph's brothers to cry out "indeed we are guilty."

---

11. *Rashi* to Deuteronomy 25:18; Nahmanides to Exodus 17:16.
12. *Bava Kamma* 80b–81a. Among the conditions were that the people may pasture their animals in privately-owned forests without the objection of the owners of the forests, and may gather wood from their neighbors' fields.
13. See Genesis 42:16.
14. See Genesis 42:18–20. Joseph allowed all the brothers except Simeon to leave Egypt on the condition that they return with Benjamin.
15. *Midrash Tanḥuma, Va-Yeshev* 2; *Pirkei de-Rabbi Eliezer* 38.

Perhaps we need a little dose of Joshua in all our institutions of contemporary Jewish life, especially in our educational institutions, which emphasize too much the insular personality. Let us remember that Joshua started out being called "a servant of Moses"[16] but ended his life being called "a servant of Hashem."[17]

16. Joshua 1:1.
17. Joshua 24:29.

Let Them Hatch Plots

June 30, 1990

One dimension of the kindness that Hashem showers upon us is expressed in the verse *utzu etzah ve-sufar*, "let the nations hatch evil plots against us, but they will be annulled," *dabbe'ru davar ve-lo yakum*, "let them adopt resolutions against us, but nothing will come of them," *ki immanu Kel*, "for God is with us" (Isaiah 8:10). Hashem intervenes in history to ensure our destiny.

A classical instance of this variety of kindness is recorded in today's portion. After the Children of Israel were denied access to the land of the Amorite, they were forced to take a route that would make them pass through the narrow river valley of Arnon. Two mountainous ranges facing each other overhung this narrow valley. The Amorites saw an opportunity to annihilate the Jewish people by hiding in the caves in the mountainous range on the Moabite side. They planned to hurl themselves at the Children of Israel when they passed through the valley.

But their plans were foiled. Before the Children of Israel passed through, Hashem made a miracle occur. The mountains on the side of the land of the Amorite, which contained jagged projections, smashed against the mountainous range on the Moabite side, and all the soldiers stationed in the caves were crushed and pulverized.

Unaware of the death trap, the Children of Israel blithefully passed through. Then Hashem decided that He would show the Children of Israel the miracle that he had wrought for them. Another miracle occurs and the mountains retreat to their original positions. Now the Well of Miriam ascends and the water that flows from the well carries down the limbs of the enemy soldiers to the site of the Children of Israel. Upon seeing the evidence of the miracle, the Children of Israel burst out in song, the Song of the Well of Miriam.[1]

According to Tradition, the *shirah* was not just to commemorate the miracle of the moment, but was a parting song to the Well of Miriam, as it was now perched on the high plane "overlooking the surface of the wilderness" (Numbers 21:20), and would no longer be needed.[2]

But the Song of the Well of Miriam is introduced, as is the Song of the Sea of Reeds, in the future tense, *az yashir Yisrael*.[3] So the song has an eternal message. Today, there is no Well of Miriam, but there is another mechanism that proclaims on a daily basis *utzu etzah ve-sufar*. This is our beloved State of Israel. Despite the concerted efforts of twenty million Arabs, Israel exists and prospers.[4]

For the secular historian, powerful economic, sociological, and political forces determine world events; Jewish history is at a periphery and is a byproduct of these forces. But for the believing Jew, antecedent events do not push Jewish history. Instead, we are pulled by magnetic

1. Numbers Rabbah 19:25; *Rashi* to Numbers 21:15, s.v. "*ve-eshed ha-neḥalim*."
2. R. Naphtali Tzvi Yehudah Berlin (*Netziv*, Russia, 1816–1893), *Ha'amek Davar*, Numbers 21:16.
3. Numbers 21:17.
4. Within hours of Israel's declaration of independence on May 14, 1948, Egypt, Syria, Trans-Jordan, Iraq, and Lebanon invaded Israel. Reginald Seigel, "Arab Nations Attack Israel," *UPI NewsTrack*, May 15, 1948. The combined population of those countries then was at least twenty million. See Department of Economic Affairs, Statistical Office of the United Nations, *Demographic Yearbook, 1949–1950* (New York, 1950), 71, 77 (estimating the population of Egypt, Syria, Jordan, and Lebanon in 1948 to be approximately 19.5 million, 3.1 million, 0.4 million, and 1.2 million, respectively; estimating the population of Iraq in 1947 to be 4.8 million).

forces towards our destiny. "The life of eternity He implanted in us."[5] World history represents the various scenarios that Hashem generates to ensure that we march on to our destiny. The abrupt change from an acute shortage to a glut in the oil market is not just the manifestation of the forces of supply and demand in the marketplace, but a *ḥesed Elyon* to relieve tension for us in Israel.[6] So, too, the Iran-Iraq war and the crumbling of Communism all over the world.

But if we are to read history and find the kindness of Hashem of *utzu etzah ve-sufar,* we must have a very delicate sensitivity. One who has no sensitivity to the subtle manifestation of Hashem's kindness may react with a muteness to even bold manifestations of Hashem's kindness.

Perhaps a realization of this, that the Well of Miriam was an eternal and timeless message and that there would be other vehicles to reveal Hashem's kindness of *utzu etzah ve-sufar,* the Children of Israel did not mention Miriam's name. Instead, they recalled "the well that the princes dug" (Numbers 21:18). Why? Because producing a Miriam with her colossal *ḥesed* of defying the decree of Pharaoh and keeping the male children alive[7] could not have been done in a vacuum. There had to have been a foundation that would inspire and further cultivate this.

The foundation was Abraham.[8] "Let some water be brought and wash your feet" (Genesis 18:4). There first had to be an Abraham to drive away the dust from their feet, the notion of "my strength and the might of my hand made me all this wealth" (Deuteronomy 8:17), as the more one runs, the more dust accumulates on one's feet.[9] There then

---

5. *Birkhat ha-Torah* (blessing recited by the person called to the Torah after his portion has been read).
6. See Elizabeth Eder, "OPEC: Demise of a Cartel?," *Harvard International Review* 6, no. 1 (September/October 1983): 33–34; David Toufic Mizrahi, "If Oil Isn't Important, Who in the Middle East Is?," *Washington Post,* November 3, 1985, C1.
7. Exodus 1:17.
8. *Mekhilta, Be-Shallaḥ, Hakdamah.* The Midrash records that the Well of Miriam was given to the Children of Israel in the merit of Abraham, who served water to the three angels that visited him. See also *Rashi* to Genesis 18:4, s.v. "*yukkaḥ na.*"
9. R. Chaim Mosheh Gostynski, *Naḥalat Ḥamishah: Al Ḥamishah Ḥumshei Torah,* vol. 1 (New York: Moinester, 1949), 54; R. Shraga Tzvi Altman (Hungary, 1902–1944), *Ateret Tzvi: Al Ḥamishah Ḥumshei Torah, Nakh, Mo'adim, Derashot le-Yamim Nora'im,*

could be a Miriam and the midwives who feared of God.[10] And there also had to be a man who would summon all means of resourcefulness to place the emphasis on *khabdehu*, "honor him," instead of *ḥashdehu*, "be suspicious of him."[11] Only one who has a delicate sensitivity to *ḥesed* can be expected to develop a grand *ḥesed* of *mesirut nefesh*.

Both the Song at the Sea of Reeds and the Song of the Well of Miriam were triggered by spoils.[12] Perhaps it is only when these two songs become integrated, when "Hashem shall reign for all eternity" (Exodus 15:18) will be pronounced by reading history, just as it was pronounced when we witnessed open miracles, that we will be closer to "Sing to Hashem a new song!" (Psalms 98:1).

---

u-Pirkei Avot ve-Sugyot ha-Shas, eds. R. Shlomo Friedman and R. Yaakov Levi (Benei Berak: Eshel, 1968), 244.

10. Exodus 1:17.
11. *Kallah Rabbati* 9 ("Others should always be considered in your eyes as robbers, but honor them as if they were Rabban Gamliel."); *Derekh Eretz Rabbah* 3 (same). See also R. Aharon Levine (*Reisha Rav*, Poland, 1879–1941), *She'elot u-Teshuvot Avnei Ḥefetz* 29:12 (Munich: Vaad ha-Hatzalah, 1948), 55, and *Ha-Derash ve-ha-Iyyun*, vol. 2 (Biłgoraj: N. Kronenberg, 1931), *ma'amar* 34, p. 33 (noting that the concept of "*khabdehu ve-ḥashdehu*" is similar to the statement in *Derekh Eretz Rabbah*, loc. cit., but he has searched for and not found the source of that exact phrase).
12. See Exodus 14:30–15:1; *Rashi* to Numbers 21:16.

Balak

How Goodly Are Your Tents, O Jacob

July 7, 1984

It has always been a source of disturbance for us that of all the beautiful and lofty blessings bestowed on the Jewish people through the agency of the great Prophets, it would be the blessing of Balaam, our arch enemy and the personification of evil itself, that would make its way to the beginning of our prayers, *mah tovu ohalekha Yaakov*, "how goodly are your tents, O Jacob" (Numbers 24:5).

Moreover, a blessing has value only when it is uttered with a feeling of purity and sincerity. But Balaam never meant to bless the Jewish people, as our Sages tell us, "from the blessing of that evil one, we learn what was in his heart."[1] He observed the encampment of the Jewish people in the desert and saw that the opening of their tents did not face one another. He wanted to curse the Children of Israel that they should

1. *Sanhedrin* 105b (statement of R. Yohanan); *Rashi* to Numbers 24:6, s.v. "*ke-neḥalim nittayu.*"

not have houses of worship or houses of study. In this vein, our Sages interpret the rest of the discourse of *mah tovu*.[2]

Finally, we may ask another question. What compels or at least indicates that Balaam's real intention was to curse the Jewish people? And what connection do tents have with houses of worship and houses of study? How does his observation of the modesty of the Jewish people lead to an indication that he wished that they would not have houses of worship or houses of study?

I would submit that an enemy is incapable of authentic praise. His praise will always be faint, parsimonious, and suffused with double entendres. In his most generous moment, he will invoke a compliment that speaks of a virtue that he hopes will be but fleeting. His grand vision will be such that the natural course of events will never bring it about, but rather it will come to fruition only through the supernatural struggle and striving of the one for whom the vision is professed.

This is the type of praise that runs through Balaam's *mah tovu* discourse. He speaks of character traits that are not absolute virtues. The phrase "as gardens by a river" (Numbers 24:6) symbolizes diversity.[3] But diversity is not an absolute virtue. It must be cultivated properly, within the framework of harmony and unity. If not, the diversity is a source of discord and dissension, threatening the social fabric. By praising diversity, which is not an absolute virtue, Balaam was hoping that it would develop

---

2. The Talmud at *Sanhedrin* 105b continues: Balaam desired that the Divine Presence should not rest upon them. Instead he said "your dwelling places, O Israel" (Numbers 24:5). He wished to say that their kingdom should not endure. Instead he said "as the valleys are they spread forth" (Numbers 24:6). He wished to say that they should have no olive trees or vineyards. Instead he said "as gardens by the river's side" (ibid.). He wished to say that their odor should not be fragrant. Instead he said "as aloes that Hashem planted" (ibid.). He wished to say that they should not have kings of stature. Instead he said "as cedar trees beside the waters" (ibid). He wished to say that they should not have a king the son of a king. Instead he said, "Water shall flow from his buckets" (Numbers 24:7). He wished to say that their kingdom should not rule over other nations. Instead he said, "His seed shall be by abundant waters" (ibid.). He wished to say that their kingdom should not be strong. Instead he said, "His king shall be higher than Agag" (ibid.). He wished to say that their kingdom should not be awe-inspiring. Instead he said, "His kingdom shall be exalted" (ibid.).
3. *Yalkut Shimoni, Balak* 771.

in its most deteriorated form, that their kingdom should not endure, that is, in a way that unity and royalty would not be possible.[4]

He then praises the wealth of the Jewish people, "like gardens by a river" (Numbers 24:6). Now, if he really rejoiced in the wealth of the Jewish people, should he not have spoken of the symbols of national prosperity in an overflowing manner by referring to olives and grapes? Since he spoke of gardens, he seemed to want to limit the wealth to vegetables. We therefore infer that he wanted to say that they should have no olives or vineyards.[5]

Then he looked at the source of the success of the nation. He decided to ascribe the success to something ephemeral, "like aloes planted by Hashem" (Numbers 24:6), rather than something concrete. Because he chose to ascribe the success of the nation to something ephemeral, we can infer that what he really wanted was that "their odor should not be fragrant," that they should not have a good reputation.[6]

He then speaks of the assertiveness of the Jewish people. Now, assertiveness is also not an absolute virtue. If a nation makes its presence known through its moral principles, its assertiveness is a virtue. But if the assertiveness is manifested in a self-serving manner, this character trait only invites hatred. So Balaam says that the Children of Israel are "like cedars" (Numbers 24:6). What he really wanted to say was that they should not have kings of stature.[7]

Finally, he speaks of the industry of the people. He ascribes success to their handiwork and secretly hopes that lethargy will set in and the success will collapse. "Water shall flow from his wells" (Numbers 24:7).

Our Sages remark on the verse "Hashem, your God, reversed the curse to a blessing" (Deuteronomy 23:6) that all Balaam's blessings were only temporary and returned to being curses as he intended, except for one blessing, the blessing of *mah tovu*.[8] Now, I submit that it had to be

---

4. *Sanhedrin* 105b.
5. Ibid.
6. *Maharsha, Ḥiddushei Halakhot ve-Aggadot, Sanhedrin* 105b, s.v. "*reiḥan nodef.*"
7. *Sanhedrin* 105b.
8. Ibid.

this way, because a nation that finds satisfaction in complements that constitute praise only if praise is read into them is a nation that has failed. It is symptomatic of finding justification and complacency in whatever standard they have achieved. It is only *mah tovu* that is lasting. This blessing represents the only behavioral characteristic described by Balaam instead of a character trait that is sometimes a virtue and sometimes a vice. In his perverseness, he gloated and snickered that the Jewish people jealously guard their privacy. Each family unit is an entity unto itself. He foolishly thought that this would be the basis of permanent disunity and therefore houses of worship and houses of study would never be formed.

But how wrong he was. The integrity of the family unit is an absolute good. Standing at its base are loyalty and a sense of responsibility. These two traits are the cement and the building blocks for developing the highest level of unity, harmony, and love in the Jewish nation. The marital relationship is capable of the highest intensity of love and selfless devotion, serving as a model for children and the basis for the permanence and constructive purpose of houses of worship and houses of study. Since *mah tovu ohalekha* describes the essence of the Jew, it cannot be converted into a curse. It is not a blessing, but a description of reality.

How appropriate it is to recite this as the opening verse for the Morning Prayer. The *Magen Avraham* says that before the Morning Prayer, we must accept upon ourselves the commandment "love your fellow as yourself" (Leviticus 19:18).[9] By doing this, we make our prayer not merely a dialogue between an individual and the *Ribbono shel Olam*, but rather we thereby connect ourselves to *Kenesset Yisrael* and make it a dialogue between the Jewish nation and the *Ribbono shel Olam*.

What are the basic building blocks for love of our fellow Jew? It is nothing less than loyalty and a sense of responsibility to both Hashem and the Jewish people. These virtues are nurtured in the marital relationship. Careful cultivation of these virtues within the marital relationship is capable of expanding and intensifying these virtues in society at large and engendering true harmony and unity in the Jewish people.

---

9. R. Abraham Abele Gombiner (*Magen Avraham*, Poland, ca. 1635–1682), *Magen Avraham* to *Shulḥan Arukh, Oraḥ Ḥayyim* 46.

Mah tovu is the secret for the proper development and boundaries of diversity, the proper use of wealth and the direction and purpose of assertiveness and industry, as well as the true basis for charm and a good reputation.

In the beginning of our prayers, we draw attention to the essence of the Jew and dedicate ourselves to the intensification and further development of the traits of loyalty and responsibility, which are the true bases of authentic *ahavat Yisrael.*

Pinḥas

One Nation under God

June 29, 2002

Several days ago, the U.S. Court of Appeals for the Ninth Circuit ruled that the recital of the phrase "one nation under God" in the Pledge of Allegiance violates the doctrine of separation of church and state.[1] The ruling evoked outrage along the entire political spectrum, from the President on down.[2] In addition, some commentators felt that given that the country is beset with major crises such as a possible terrorist attack of various horrific forms and scandals in

1. Newdow v. U.S. Cong., 292 F.3d 597, 612 (9th Cir. 2002), *amended by* 328 F.3d 466 (9th Cir. 2003), *rev'd on other grounds sub nom.* Elk Grove Unified Sch. Dist. v. Newdow, 542 U.S. 1 (2004).
2. Linda P. McKenzie, "The Pledge of Allegiance: One Nation Under God?," *Arizona Law Review* 46 (2004): 381 (noting that President George W. Bush called the ruling "ridiculous"); Carl Hulse, "Lawmakers Vow to Fight Judges' Ruling on the Pledge," *New York Times*, June 27, 2002, A20; Charles Lane, "U.S. Court Votes to Bar Pledge of Allegiance: Use of 'God' Called Unconstitutional," *Washington Post*, June 27, 2002, A1.

major corporations, the taking up of this trivial issue is an insult to the American people.[3]

I agree with the first statement that the ruling is an outrage, but I disagree with the second. It serves well as a catalyst to challenge us and ask ourselves, what does it take to make a religious man?

America is a country with a definite ideology. Americans cherish their liberties and glorify material striving. The land of equal opportunity makes the dream of leaping "from rags to riches" accessible to all. There can be no doubt that the ideology has produced a good country. R. Mosheh Feinstein referred to America as a *medinat ḥesed*.[4]

Permit me to suggest that such expressions as "in God we trust" on our coinage, "God bless America" in our patriotic song, and "one nation under God" in the Pledge of Allegiance are all saying nothing more than "Dear God, please protect, preserve, and bless an ideology that we like and is good." It is "Please, Hashem, save now!" (Psalms 118:25). But according to U.S. law, it does not rise to that level because the judges have continually said that an expression repeated by rote loses its religious significance.[5]

Permit me to suggest that if our relationship with Hashem begins and ends with "Please, Hashem, save now," this is not religion. We must proceed to the next step, "Please, Hashem, for I am Your servant" (Psalms 116:16). Tell me what You want me to do, and I'll do it.

The American ideal of liberty is enshrined in the Liberty Bell in Philadelphia. Inscribed in the Liberty Bell is the biblical verse "You shall proclaim freedom (*deror*) throughout the land for all its inhabitants" (Leviticus 25:10). In Hebrew, we have two words for freedom:

---

3. See, e.g., "The Pledge Distraction," *Star-Ledger* (Newark, NJ), June 28, 2002, 22 (editorial).
4. See R. Moshe Feinstein (New York, 1895–1986), *Iggerot Mosheh, Oraḥ Ḥayyim* 2:24, p. 197, and *Ḥoshen Mishpat* 3:5, p. 253.
5. Lynch v. Donnelly, 465 U.S. 668, 716 (1984) (Brennan, J., dissenting) ("I would suggest that such practices as the designation of 'In God We Trust' as our national motto, or the references to God contained in the Pledge of Allegiance to the flag can best be understood, in Dean Rostow's apt phrase, as a form a 'ceremonial deism,' protected from Establishment Clause scrutiny chiefly because they have lost through rote repetition any significant religious content" [internal citation omitted]; Marsh v. Chambers, 463 U.S. 783, 818 (1983) (Brennan, J., dissenting) (similar).

deror and *ḥerut*. What is the difference? *Ḥerut,* in the understanding of our Sages, is freedom from the Evil Inclination.[6] "There is no freer man (*ben ḥorin*) than one who engages in the study of the Torah."[7] The true man of freedom is the one who occupies himself in Torah. It is not the man of liberty but the man of discipline who submits to the authority of the Torah. The one who does this will not feel choked, having no space. The more the person adheres to the Torah, the more he will feel liberated as well.

The Liberty Bell has a crack in it, for the Liberty Bell represents *deror*. This is liberty with no mention of the constraints on liberty. It is left undefined. We must fill the crack in the Liberty Bell with *ḥerut*. This will define the contours of liberty for us within the framework of our Torah.

I would suggest that the next time that we take the Pledge of Allegiance, we should request that we should be grateful for the religious freedom that the country gives us and relate to the pledge on the level of what the words mean to us as a Jewish people. One nation under God. Then, "Please, Hashem, I am Your servant." Tell me what You want and I'll do it. "Indivisible" – *Yisrael ve-Oraisa ve-Kudesha berikh Hu, ḥad hu,* "Israel, the Torah, and the Holy One, Blessed is He, are one."[8] And with liberty, i.e., *ḥerut,* and justice for all.

---

6. The Torah describes the script of the Tablets as *ḥarut* (etched) on the Tablets. Exodus 32:16. Commenting on this description, the Mishnah states that one should read the word *ḥarut* as *ḥerut* (freedom), because there is no freer man than one who occupies himself with the study of Torah. Mishnah, *Avot* 6:2. In R. Nehemiah's view, *ḥerut* in this context means freedom from the Angel of Death. See Exodus Rabbah 32:1. The Evil Inclination is considered to be the Angel of Death. See *Bava Batra* 16a. Thus, *ḥerut* signifies freedom from the Evil Inclination. See R. Judah Loew b. Bezalel (*Maharal,* Prague, ca. 1525–1609), *Derekh ha-Ḥayyim* to Mishnah, *Avot,* ch. 3.
7. Mishnah, *Avot* 6:2.
8. See *Zohar* 3:73a.

The Two *Temidim*

(Undated)

When the author of a halakhic work distinguished by its economy of expression and absence of homiletical digressions chooses to embellish his work with apparently irrelevant Aggadic material in the beginning and at the end, this evokes mystery. Thus, our *posek*, R. Moses Isserles, begins his monumental work of *Oraḥ Ḥayyim* with the verse *shivviti Hashem le-neggdi tamid*, "I set Hashem before me always" (Psalms 16:8), and ends with *tov-lev mishteh tamid*, "a good-hearted person feasts perpetually" (Proverbs 15:15).

What we have here is that everything that is precious in Jewish tradition in the path of life is sandwiched between the two *temidim*. Perhaps the introduction to *Oraḥ Ḥayyim* includes a veiled reference to the two *temidim* that we offered in the Tabernacle and the Temple, "the one lamb shall you make in the morning and the second lamb shall you make in the afternoon" (Numbers 28:4).

Historically, the *tamid* offered in the afternoon corresponds to the momentous event of the offering of the *korban pesaḥ*, which transpired in the afternoon, *bein ha-arbayim*.[1] The *korban pesaḥ* symbolizes Jewish communal identity and responsibility.[2] Every aspect of the service of the *korban pesaḥ* indicates this. The lamb is a very delicate, sensitive animal. If one limb is injured, the entire lamb suffers egregiously.[3] The *korban* is slaughtered in a group[4] and is eaten in a group.[5] But the lamb also represents the deity of the Egyptians.[6] Taken together, these laws indicate that the *korban pesaḥ* represents the erosion of alien beliefs through our group identity. Our collective identity leads to our awareness of the presence of Hashem, and hence, "I set Hashem before me always" (Psalms 16:8).

The second *tamid*, the one offered in the morning, corresponds to the momentous event of *Mattan Torah*, which occurred in the morning.[7] How appropriate is the phrase "a good-hearted person feasts perpetually" (Proverbs 15:15) to accompany *talmud Torah*, as "the orders of Hashem are upright, gladdening the heart" (Psalms 19:9).

The Torah understood how to preserve the importance of the *temidim*. First, to impress upon us the importance of *temidim*, there must be universal participation on a coercive basis.[8] There is a furious debate between the Sadducees and the Sages. The Sadducees claimed that *yaḥid misnadev*, i.e., an individual could fund the *korban tamid*, but the Sages said that the *temidim* must be financed through the Temple funds.[9] Now, the victory was so important that during the first eight days of Nisan, we cannot establish fast days because to preserve the viability of the *temidim*, everyone must participate.[10] If it is only on a voluntary basis, the institution is subject to erosion and neglect.

---

1. Exodus 12:6.
2. See R. Samson Raphael Hirsch, Exodus 12:43.
3. Leviticus Rabbah 4:6.
4. *Rashi* to Exodus 12:6, s.v. "*kehal adat Yisrael*"; *Pesaḥim* 64a–b, 91a.
5. *Rashi* to Exodus 12:46, s.v. "*be-bayit eḥad ye'akhel*"; *Tosefta, Pesaḥim* 6:9; *Mekhilta, Bo* 15.
6. Exodus 8:22; *Rashi* ad loc., s.v. "*to'avat Mitzrayim*"; Exodus Rabbah 16:3.
7. See Numbers 28:6; *Rashi* ad loc.; Exodus 19:16.
8. *Menaḥot* 65a; Nahmanides (*Ramban*, Spain, 1194–1270) to Numbers 28:2; *Yalkut Shimoni, Pinḥas* 777.
9. *Menaḥot* 65a.
10. Ibid.

Another aspect of this universality is that everyone must participate either directly or indirectly through *ma'amadot*.[11]

Also, something important always requires preparation. The Torah was given "on the third day when it was morning" (Exodus 19:16).[12] If *talmud Torah* is important to us, then before we go to a *shiur* or learn with a *ḥavruta*, we must prepare. Before we go to a communal meeting, we must think through things clearly, just as we would do for an important business meeting. The latter is not a spontaneous event.

Moreover, the *temidim* denote constancy; they were brought even on the Sabbath and even in the case of ritual impurity.[13] This tells us that no excuse is accepted for failure to learn Torah.

Finally, there are the *gizrei etzim* that are required both for the morning *tamid* and the afternoon *tamid*.[14] These pieces of wood were entirely unnecessary, as the Heavenly fire descended, so the twigs were not fuel for the *ma'arakhah* (Altar pyre).[15] This teaches us that for the *temidim* to be important to us, we must develop an attitude of generosity and magnanimity of spirit. We cannot say, "Well, if the institutions begin to teeter and become desperate, then we will rush in to support them." No. We need a magnanimous attitude that we lend support, even if the institution is not in dire need. This elevates the institutions to higher stations.

---

11. Mishnah, *Ta'anit* 4:2; *Ta'anit* 26a. One who brings an offering to the Temple is required to stand by the offering and watch over it. *Sotah* 8a; *Rashi* ad loc., s.v. "*akurbinyyehu*" (citing *Sifrei* to Numbers 142). Because everyone must participate in the *tamid* offering, theoretically every Jew must be present in the Temple Court during the offering. To enable all to satisfy the requirement that they be physically present when the *tamid* is offered, the Early Prophets established the *ma'amadot* (lit., "stations"). Each *ma'amad* consisted of Priests, Levites, and Israelites who would stand by the offering, acting as emissaries for the people. The Priests and Levites serving in the Temple were divided into twenty-four groups (*mishmarot*), and a *ma'amad* was assigned to each *mishmar*. Each *mishmar* served in the Temple one week at a time, on a rotating basis.
12. The Children of Israel were instructed to prepare themselves three days in advance of the giving of the Torah on Mount Sinai. Exodus 19:15.
13. *Pesaḥim* 77a; *Menaḥot* 72b.
14. Leviticus 1:7; *Yoma* 26b.
15. *Rashi* to Leviticus 1:7.

If we take the *temidim* seriously, we can accomplish the "continual burnt-offering that was brought at Mount Sinai" (Numbers 28:6). We can achieve the ecstasy with the routine and the ordinary, just as with the burnt offering that we brought at Mount Sinai, at the singular event in our history.

Matot

According to Whatever Comes from His Mouth Shall He Do

July 21, 1984

It is rare when the opening portion of a *sidrah* not only strikes us as disconnected from what is recorded before and after it, but in addition takes on a floater character, i.e., our curiosity would not be aroused in the slightest if the *parashah* were written many other places in the Torah. Such is the dilemma that we are faced with in today's reading, in which the *parashah* of *Matot* begins with the passage of *nedarim*.

While the *parashah* of *nedarim* may very well appear disjointed and isolated in terms of the thrust of the development of an idea or a theme, it fits very well into a historical context. *Matot* is always read during *bein ha-metzarim,* the three-week period between the Seventeenth of Tamuz and the Ninth of Av. We are all familiar with our Sages' dictum that the First Temple was destroyed because of the violation of the three cardinal sins, i.e., idolatry, immorality, and bloodshed, but the Second Temple was destroyed on account of the sin of *sin'at ḥinnam*, "unwarranted hatred," to teach us that *sin'at ḥinnam* is equivalent to the three cardinal sins.[16]

Perhaps the coinciding of *Matot* with the Three Weeks is to give us a message that the *parashah* of *nedarim* is the key to understanding the genesis of *sin'at ḥinnam* and its possible remediation. Four features are striking in the *parashah* of *nedarim*. First, "according to whatever comes from his mouth shall he do" (Numbers 30:3). How often are we careless regarding what we say? We do not remember what we said, what we committed ourselves to do. We might forget, but others do not. The beneficiaries of our commitments sure do remember. And is there any wonder why there is hatred in the world? It is not baseless hatred for the promisee. It is baseless only from the standpoint of the careless and forgetful promisor.

Second, "it will be on the day that he hears."[17] We are impressed with the element of timing. Only on the day that a man hears the vow of his wife or daughter does he have the chance to void it. How many times are we asked a favor and we hesitate? We do not respond with spontaneous urgency or enthusiasm. Because we do the favor eventually, we forget about the hesitation and the uncertainty that we caused the beneficiary. Then we wonder, why all this hatred, this *sin'at ḥinnam*?

Third, we are impressed with the jurisdictional aspect of *hattarat nedarim*. Vows that pertain to the personal relationship between a man and his wife are in the jurisdiction of the husband to void.[18] If, however, they do not pertain to his personal relationship with her, only vows of affliction, regarding *innui nefesh*, are permitted to be voided by him.[19] But what if the woman is betrothed and she has a father and a fiancé? Then she is under the jurisdiction of both.[20]

---

16. *Yoma* 9b.

17. See Numbers 30:6, 30:8–9, 30:13, 30:15.

18. *Nedarim* 68a; Maimonides, *Mishneh Torah, Nedarim* 12:1.

19. Numbers 30:14; *Rashi* ad loc.; *Nedarim* 79a; Maimonides, *Mishneh Torah, Nedarim* 12:1.

20. *Rashi* to Numbers 30:9; R. Shabbetai b. Joseph Bass (*Siftei Ḥakhamim*, Prague, 1641–1718), *Siftei Ḥakhamim* ad loc., n. 2; *Nedarim* 66b–67a. To annul the vow in that case, both the father and the fiancé must annul the vow. If one of them annuls the vow and the other does not, the vow is binding. If one confirms the vow, the other cannot annul it.

This appreciation of jurisdiction leads us to thinking that everything that we say and do entails some boundary of jurisdiction. We may choose to consult one group and ignore or exclude another, causing ill feeling in the process. Our actions may generate side effects to third parties, and we never take the jurisdiction and boundaries that we face into account.

Fourth, "if on the day of her husband's hearing, he shall restrain her and he shall revoke the vow that is upon the utterance of her lips by which she had prohibited something upon herself, then Hashem will forgive her" (Numbers 30:9). This speaks of the case when the husband voided the wife's vow not in her presence.[21] Not knowing of her husband's action, thinking the vow was fully operative, she violated the vow. In reality, she did nothing wrong, but she thought that she was doing wrong at the time. We are told that she requires forgiveness. "Hashem will forgive her" (ibid.).

When we relate this to interpersonal relationships, we begin to think perhaps into our own experience. Perhaps we once pursued a course of action, believing that we were right, and we made no reference at all to Halakhah, even harboring an amorphous feeling that whatever Halakhah had to say was irrelevant. Then, after fighting our battle, we bungle into a knowledge of the halakhic point of view. Jubilantly, we wave the *Shulḥan Arukh* in front of our adversary and shout gleefully that Halakhah supports and vindicates our position. Does this conduct generate respect for Halakhah? I submit that it generates the opposite, ridicule. The adversary will hate Torah scholars and say, "Until now, no mention of Halakhah. Well, Halakhah is only a self-serving vehicle, to be invoked out of expediency and convenience."

When we reflect upon the *parashah* of *nedarim*, we are immediately impressed that there is no other area in the Torah where the subjective is given such free rein and where the potential for abuse of the free rein is so large. For a vow to take effect, we need consistency between speech and intention, *piv ve-libbo shavvin*.[22] Without consistency, there is no vow.

---

21. *Rashi* to Numbers 30:6.

22. *Mishneh Torah, Nedarim* 2:2; *Tur, Yoreh De'ah* 210; *Shulḥan Arukh, Yoreh De'ah* 210:1.

Well, a person can always claim that what he said was merely a slip of the tongue. Now, there is no area in human relationships where man is more capable of complete honesty than in the realm of *beino le-vein atzmo* (i.e., with himself), for only we know what we really feel. We may not have the courage to admit our feelings, though, and we may need some assistance to draw them out. Here is where the *Ḥakham* comes in. He must find the *pesaḥ* or *ḥaratah.*[23] The one who makes the vow cannot use the *Ḥakham* as a rubber stamp. But the opportunity for abuse is wide open, as in the story of Zedekiah.[24]

The first step of honesty is the honesty that man can achieve with himself. With this, he can proceed to achieve honesty between himself and his fellow man, and between himself and God, eliminating the *sin'at ḥinnam* from the face of the earth.

We are reminded of the story of R. Joshua b. Levi. When the Angel of Death came to take his life, he asked the Angel to show him his place in the Garden of Eden. The Angel of Death agreed. R. Joshua b. Levi then demanded, "Give me your knife; you might frighten me on the way." The Angel of Death gave R. Joshua b. Levi his knife. When

23. See *Nedarim* 21b. A Sage annuls a vow by finding a *pesaḥ* (opening), a circumstance that would have prevented the vower from making the vow had he fully considered the circumstance at the time of making the vow. Another basis for the Sage to annul a vow is *ḥaratah* (regret), when the vower subsequently regrets making the vow even though no circumstance is found that would have caused the vower to refrain from making the vow at the outset. Instead, he states that the vow was made in anger or in haste.

24. *Nedarim* 65a. Zedekiah once discovered Nebuchadnezzar eating a live hare. Nebuchadnezzar said to Zedekiah, "Swear to me that you will not reveal my deed." Zedekiah swore to him that he would not reveal the incident. Ultimately, Zedekiah became physically ill as a result of the constraint that he had placed upon himself through his vow and petitioned Sanhedrin to release him from his vow. The Sanhedrin granted his request.

When Nebuchadnezzar heard that people were ridiculing him, he knew that Zedekiah had revealed the incident. He summoned the members of the Sanhedrin and asked them, "Have you seen what Zedekiah has done? Did he not swear in the name of Heaven not to reveal my secret?" They explained that Zedekiah had asked to be released from his vow and they granted his request. "Do you permit people to petition for release from an oath?" asked Nebuchadnezzar. "Yes," they replied. Nebuchadnezzar then asked, "Is it permissible to release someone from a vow

they reached the Garden of Eden, R. Joshua jumped into the Garden alive and swore that he would not come out.

What decided R. Joshua b. Levi's fate was that he never went to the *Ḥakham* to annul his oath. This means that he never abused the process of *hattarat nedarim*. He never used the *Ḥakham* as a rubber stamp to shut out his true feelings. He was honest with himself, so he deserved that this last oath should create the impact that he desired.[25]

The story tells us that the man of integrity lives in the Garden of Eden in This World. He can steal the sword of the Angel of Death, meaning that he can eliminate fear. Such a man is a gentle and soothing influence in the world, bringing cheer, confidence, and stability wherever he goes.

---

only in the presence of the one to whom the vow was made, or even not in his presence?" "It is permissible only in the other one's presence," they answered. "Why then did you not tell Zedekiah that you could not release him from his vow except in my presence?" said Nebuchadnezzar. Immediately, Nebuchadnezzar showed his displeasure with the members of the Sanhedrin by forcing them to sit on the ground.

According to some authorities, although ideally an annulment of a vow made for the benefit of another person should be made in the presence of the other person, an annulment that is not made in the presence of the other person is valid *be-di'eved* (after the fact). See R. Nissim b. Reuben Gerondi (*Ran*, Spain, 1320–1376), *Ran* to *Nedarim* 65a, s.v. "*tanya ha-muddar hana'ah me-ḥavero*"; R. Asher b. Jehiel (*Rosh*, Germany, ca. 1250–1327), *Rosh*, *Gittin* 4:9; *Tosafot* to *Gittin* 35b, s.v. "*liḥush*."

25. *Ketubbot* 77b.

Deuteronomy

Ekev

What Is One Born of a Woman Doing among Us?

August 18, 1984

Anyone who experiences great adventure will not fail to recount repeatedly the most exciting aspects of the experience. Yet, Moses, who experienced the most magnificent of all human experiences, ascending the heavens as a mortal to receive the Torah, selected for recounting only part of his experience, leaving out, apparently, the most exciting part.

Yes, he tells us of his diligence as a student of Torah: "I remained on the mountain for forty days and forty nights; bread I did not eat, and water I did not drink" (Deuteronomy 9:9). He tells us of his total faithfulness as an intercessor, again punctuating his remarks with the phrase "forty days and forty nights; bread I did not eat and water I did not drink" (Deuteronomy 9:18). He tells us how he beseeched the Master of the Universe to reconcile Himself with

His people to the highest level possible, to restore them to their previous status.[1]

But a great drama unfolded in the firmament when Moses ascended to receive the Torah, and of this drama, Moses makes no mention. When Moses arrived, the angels did not want to release the Torah. They proclaimed, "What is one born of a woman doing among us?" They protested that the Torah, which resided in the heavens for 974 generations before the world was created, should remain there. Thereupon, Hashem tells Moses that he must provide an answer to the angels.[2]

Moses displays his ingenuity. He goes through the Ten Commandments and shows that the Torah is only an abstract doctrine as far as the angels are concerned. But for him, a mortal, and for the Children of Israel, it is a live and relevant doctrine.[3]

At that point, the angels concede defeat and release the Torah. Such excitement and drama, and Moses never even intimates to this incident.

Moreover, we are now standing at *mishneh Torah* at the end of Moses' reign as leader of a people for forty years, a people sometimes brutal in their cynicism toward him, reading malice into his actions. Was Moses not fearful of ridicule and scorn when he told the Jewish nation again and again the phrase "bread I did not eat and water I did not drink"? Was this a verifiable fact?

I would submit that when Moses ascended to the heavens to receive the Torah, he came both as the leader of the Jewish people and as a representative of the nation. He assumed two distinct roles. In his role as a leader, he was the exemplary student and teacher of the Torah. All the forty-eight *kinyanin* of Torah[4] were his, in the most exemplary manner, *kinyanei Torah* divided into the attitudinal framework of

1. Deuteronomy 19:18–19. After the Sin of the Golden Calf, Moses demanded that Hashem rather than an angel should lead the Children of Israel in the Wilderness, thus restoring the Children of Israel to their prior relationship with Hashem. See Exodus 33:15; R. Solomon b. Isaac (*Rashi*, France, 1040–1105), *Rashi* ad loc.; Nahmanides (*Ramban*, Spain, 1194–1270) to Exodus 23:20.
2. *Shabbat* 88b–89a.
3. Ibid.
4. Mishnah, *Avot* 6:6.

be-eimah, be-yir'ah, u-be-anavah (with trepidation, fear, and humility), the perseverance, concentration, and dedication of total commitment for a student and teacher, and finally, the necessary empathetic attachment to the Jewish nation.

Moses' extraordinary success in this regard is summed up with the phrase "bread I did not eat and water I did not drink," in his three-fold role as student, teacher, and intercessor. These were not empty words. The conduct of his everyday life provided eloquent testimony to his fulfilling his role with such symbolic single-mindedness and monomaniacal persistence. The words that Moses spoke did not represent to anyone something that they did not fully know and appreciate.

But when it came to his secret mission in the heavens as the representative of the people, Moses, with all his forty-eight *kinyanin*, could not impart an aura of status to the Torah. That accomplishment could be achieved only if the drama in heaven would be re-enacted in each generation. Moses' demonstration of the relevancy of the Torah at its most basic level, that the Torah belongs to humans and not to angels, represented the first push toward producing the glow for the Torah. Relevancy imparts centrality to Torah, and this is the essence of status.

Moses was given gifts by the angels when they conceded defeat. One of these gifts was the *ketoret*.[5] How appropriate a gift. Just as the *ketoret* amalgamates disparate herbs into a harmonious whole, even drawing in the *ḥelbbenah*, producing the most aromatic fragrance,[6] so, too, the quest to impart the spark of Torah into the darkest corners brings out the sweet fragrance of Torah and hence elevates its status.

The angels realized that Moses' show of relevancy amounted not to wresting the Torah from them, but rather imparting a level of magnificence to it that they could never impart to it. Moses was therefore their beloved friend, worthy of the gift of *ketoret*.

Now, the fragrance of Torah is found in many ways. The fragrant herbs can seek out the *ḥelbbenah*, but often the herbs exult in their singularity. It is when the *ḥelbbenah* makes the leap to the fragrant herbs

5. *Shabbat* 89a. The Talmud *ad locum* records that the Angel of Death gave the secret of *ketoret* to Moses.
6. Exodus 30:34; *Rashi* ad loc., s.v. "*ve-ḥelbbenah*"; *Keritot* 6b.

that the greatest impact of status of the Torah is made. We never realize the profound significance of this until we observe a lost opportunity of the *ḥelbbenah* to join the fragrant herbs.

Reb Meir's One Hundred Club

August 23, 1986

We are living in a society that greatly values membership in exclusive clubs. We, the Jewish people, have an exclusive club too, called Reb Meir's One Hundred Club. "R. Meir used to say, 'One is required to say one hundred blessings each day'" (*Menaḥot* 43b). Indicative of the prestige attached to membership is the fact that Hashem, Himself, in today's portion, bids us to be members. "Now, O Israel, what (*mah*) does Hashem, your God, ask of you? Only to fear Hashem, your God, to go in all His ways and to love Him, and to serve Hashem, your God, with all your heart and will all your soul" (Deuteronomy 10:12). *Mah*, "what," can be read as *me'ah*, "one hundred," and hence one hundred is what Hashem requires of us.[1]

1. *Menaḥot* 43b; *Rashi* ad loc., s.v. "*mah Hashem Elokekha.*" See also *Midrash Tanḥuma, Koraḥ* 12 (stating that King David instituted the recitation of one

In what lies the mystique of membership? It is that we were forced to hear ninety-eight curses on Mount Ebal, so we must recite ninety-nine blessings to neutralize the curses. Moreover, we really heard ninety-nine curses because one was a curse that was not written in the Torah, so we need the hundredth blessing, which is the one blessing that *is* written in the Torah, to counteract it.[2]

Now, we face a crisis every Sabbath. The *Shemoneh Esrei* is curtailed to seven blessings and we are therefore missing quite a number of blessings. But we dare not allow our membership to lapse. We must remain members in good standing.

For those who take a minimalist approach, seeking only nominal membership in the society, there is a simple way of maintaining membership. We need only refrain from speaking during *ḥazarat ha-shatz* and other strategic places during *tefillah* and we acquire the requisite hundred, just by answering *amen* to someone else's blessings.[3] To these people we say, "*Barukh Hashem asher natan menuḥah be-yom ha-Shabbat*."[4] Thank

---

hundred blessings each day because a hundred men were dying every day in Jerusalem); See *Ba'al ha-Turim* to Deuteronomy 6:7, s.v. "*u-ve-kumekha*" (expounding upon the *tagin* (decorative crown) above the letter *kuf* in the word *u-ve-kumekha*, which letter has the numerical equivalence of a hundred, as a source for the recitation of one hundred blessings each day); *Ba'al ha-Turim* to Deuteronomy 4:4, s.v. "*ve-atem ha-devekim*" (similar exposition of the *tagin* above the *kuf* in the word "*ha-devekim*").

2. R. Eleazar b. Judah of Worms (*Roke'aḥ*, Germany, ca. 1176–1238), *Sefer ha-Roke'aḥ, Hilkhot Berakhot* 320. The ninety-eight curses are enumerated at Deuteronomy 28:16–69. A ninety-ninth curse is mentioned at Deuteronomy 28:61, "Also any illness and any blow that is not written in this Book of the Torah." All the blessings are of rabbinic origin except one blessing that is written in the Torah at Deuteronomy 8:10, "You will eat and you will be satisfied, and bless Hashem, your God, for the good Land that He gave you."
3. See R. Asher b. Jehiel (*Rosh*, Germany, ca. 1250–1327), *Rosh, Berakhot* 9:24; R. Joseph Caro, *Shulḥan Arukh, Oraḥ Ḥayyim* 284:3; R. Israel Meir ha-Kohen Kagan (*Ḥafetz Ḥayyim*, Radin, 1838–1933), *Mishnah Berurah* 46:14.
4. See Compensatory Blessings for Grace after Meals on the Sabbath ("Blessed are You Hashem... Who gave Sabbaths for rest to His people, Israel, with love for a sign and for a covenant.").

God that He associated blessing with rest so that there is a painless way to retain our membership.

But there is an activist approach to completing the hundred blessings. We gleefully pursue *birkhot ha-nehenin* by enjoying all types of delicacies.[5] To these people we say "*gam barukh yihiyeh*" ("he shall remain blessed") (Genesis 27:33).

There is also an insidious method to pursue blessing for the sake of securing honor and recognition, reminiscent of the story of the man who was very slighted when the *gabbai* offered him the honor of taking the Torah scroll out of the Ark and returning it to the Ark because this meant that the greater honor of *aliyyah le-Torah* would be forestalled. But the reason the ruffled man claims he is insulted is because he desperately wants to retain his membership in the One Hundred Club. To him we say, "*Ha-verakhah aḥat hi lekha, Avi*?" ("Have you but one blessing, Father?") (Genesis 27:38).

There is, however, a high road, a path of the noble spirit. To meet the demands of the membership committee, he will of course follow the dictates of the *Shulḥan Arukh* and look for *birkhot ha-nehenin* not found in his daily routine. But the noble spirit seeks not only nominal membership. The elevated spirit seeks not to recite blessings but rather to transform himself into the essence of blessing, to achieve "by you shall Israel bless" (Genesis 48:20) and "may Hashem turn His countenance to you" (Numbers 6:26).

Such a man evokes the spirit of *ve-akhalta ve-savata u-verakhta*, "You shall eat and be satisfied and bless Hashem" (Deuteronomy 8:10). The Ministering Angels said before the Holy One, Blessed is He: "Master of the Universe, it is written in Your law, 'Who does not show favor and Who does not accept a bribe' (Deuteronomy 10:17), but do You not show favor to the Jewish people, as it is written, 'May Hashem lift His countenance to you?' (Numbers 6:26)?" Hashem replied to them,

5. See *Menaḥot* 43b (noting that R. Hiyya b. R. Avya would complete the hundred blessings on the Sabbath by reciting blessings over fragrant spices and delicacies).

"Shall I not lift up My countenance for Israel, for I wrote for them in the Torah, 'You shall eat and be satisfied and bless Hashem your God' (Deuteronomy 8:10), and they are particular to recite *birkhat ha-mazon* even if the quantity consumed was the size of only an olive (*ke-zayit*) or an egg (*ke-veitzah*)."[6]

6. *Berakhot* 20b. The Vilna Gaon questions why *ke-zayit,* the equivalence of the size of an olive, is mentioned before *ke-veitzah,* the equivalence of the size of an egg. An olive is smaller than an egg. If one is stringent to make a blessing after consuming a quantity of food equivalent to the size of an olive, surely one is stringent to say a blessing after consuming a quantity equivalent to the size of an egg. The Vilna Gaon explains that the order signifies that Jews are praiseworthy for seeking an opportunity to recite the after-blessing in a group of ten (a *minyan*) or at least three (a *mezuman*). A quantity of food equivalent to the volume of three eggs is sufficient to satiate one person. In addition, three eggs have a volume equivalent to that of ten olives. If a Jew has a meal with a volume of three eggs, he seeks to divide the meal among another nine people so that each has a *ke-zayit,* and then the group of ten may say the after-blessing. If he cannot find a sufficient number of people to form a *minyan,* he at least seeks to divide his meal with two other people so that each has a *ke-veitzah* and the after-blessing can be recited in a *mezuman.* *Be'ur ha-Gra* to Proverbs 22:9.

Re'eh

Charity

(Undated)

Halakhah presents us with a striking contrast between a business and a charitable commitment. In the commercial arena, four different levels of obligation are identified. In the weakest category is the resolve of the heart, as for example, when a seller makes up his mind to accept a customer's bid. Since the commitment was not verbalized, no legal or even moral obligation to actuate the commitment exists.[1] In the second category falls the case of a verbal commitment. Retraction here brands the retractor "untrustworthy."[2] If the transaction advanced to the stage where money exchanged hands but legal title was not acquired, as for example where a proper *kinyan* was not made, retraction requires the reneging party to accept an official judicial censure called a "*mi*

1. R. Jehiel Michal Epstein (Belorus, 1829–1908), *Arukh ha-Shulḥan, Yoreh De'ah* 258:39.
2. R. Yohanan, *Bava Metzia* 49a; R. Isaac b. Jacob Alfasi (*Rif,* Algeria, 1013–1103), *Rif, Bava Metzia* 49a; *Mishneh Torah, Mekhirah* 7:8–9; R. Asher b. Jehiel (*Rosh,* Germany, ca. 1250–1327), *Bava Metzia* 4:12; R. Jacob b. Asher (*Tur,* Spain, 1270–1343), *Tur, Ḥoshen Mishpat* 204; *Shulḥan Arukh, Ḥoshen Mishpat* 204:7–8; *Arukh ha-Shulḥan, Ḥoshen Mishpat* 204:8–9.

she-para," a sort of reverse *mi she-berakh.*[3] Finally, if the transaction was consummated by means of a *kinyan,* the Jewish court will generally enforce compliance.[4]

But with respect to *tzedakah,* the *Shulḥan Arukh* rules that even a resolve of the heart must be actuated.[5] This is based on the phrase in the Torah of *nediv lev,* "generous of heart."[6] Why this stringency?

Perhaps the answer lies in the *Sifrei*'s interpretation of the prohibition of *lo se'ammetz et livav'kha,* "you should not harden your heart" (Deuteronomy 15:7). This is taken not only as an act of omission, the refusal to give charity, but also an act of commission, that is, taking action to thwart the inclination to give charity, to desensitize ourselves with respect to the suffering of our fellow Jew.[7]

If the negative commandment of *lo se'ammetz* is thus interpreted, it seems to us that the positive commandment *pato'aḥ tiftaḥ et yade'kha,* "you shall surely open your hand to him" (Deuteronomy 15:8), should also be given this broader meaning. Not only should we open our hand and give charity, but we should expand our capacity to be sensitized to the needs and suffering of our fellow Jew.

We are living in an era of big government and a proliferation of Jewish social welfare organizations. We may very well imagine that the needs of our fellow Jew are well taken care of and do not require our personal attention. How much must we expand our capacity to feel suffering today!

The story is told of a *ḥasid* who boasted to his *rebbe* that although he was very wealthy, he imposed upon himself a frugal standard of living,

---

3. See *Bava Metzia* 49a; *Mishneh Torah, Mekhirah* 7:1–6; *Rosh, Bava Metzia* 4:13; *Tur,* op. cit.; *Shulḥan Arukh,* op. cit., 204:1; *Arukh ha-Shulḥan,* op. cit., 204:1.
4. See Maimonides (*Rambam,* Egypt, 1135–1204), *Mishneh Torah, Mekhirah* 1–9; *Shulḥan Arukh, Ḥoshen Mishpat* 189–203. *Kinyan* is the acquisition of legal rights by the performance of a symbolic act. For a discussion of the different means of effecting *kinyan* and cases when *kinyan* alone is not sufficient to create a legally binding obligation, see R. Aaron Levine, *Free Enterprise and Jewish Law: Aspects of Jewish Business Ethics* (New York: Ktav, 1980), 34–36.
5. *Rema* to *Shulḥan Arukh, Yoreh De'ah* 258:13; *Shulḥan Arukh, Ḥoshen Mishpat* 212:8.
6. Exodus 35:22. See also II Chronicles 29:31; *Shevuot* 26b.
7. *Sifrei,* Deuteronomy 116, as interpreted by R. Eliezer b. Samuel of Metz (France, ca. 1115–ca. 1198), *Sefer Yere'im* 202.

sufficing himself with bread and water. The *rebbe* became enraged. "Not only can I not voice approval, but I must be very critical," he said. "If bread and water are good enough for you and your family, you will imagine that stones are good enough for the poor!"[8]

There are three levels of giving symbolized by *zahav* (gold), *kesef* (silver), and *neḥoshet* (copper).[9] *Zahav* stands for "*zeh ha-noten bari.*" This is the gift to charity when we are healthy and prosperous. Then there is the gift of *kesef*, which stands for *ke-she-yesh sakkanat paḥad*. It is the gift that we give when we are threatened with some danger. It is the gift that is tendered when man naturally has more compassion, a more noble perspective and vision. Then finally, there is the *neḥoshet* gift, *netinat ḥoleh she-omer tenu*. This is the gift of the man who is on his deathbed and says "*tenu*" (give). The man is at the threshold of *olam ha-emet*. Such a man is naturally attuned to righteousness and nobility.

Would it only be that the profundity of the nobility of the *neḥoshet* Jew were transferred to the healthy donor. That would produce, I submit, *zahov tahor*, the purest gold of all.

Rabbot maḥashavot be-lev ish, "man has many sentiments" (Proverbs 19:21). We ascribe many of them simply to fad. But when someone expresses a beautiful sentiment, he resolves to give money to charity, can we allow this sentiment to fade away, to disintegrate? No! The beautiful sentiment must be elevated to the height of a beautiful action.

There are many ways to sensitize ourselves to the needs of our fellow Jew. But perhaps there is no better way than the method imposed on the legendary philanthropist R. Mayer Amschel Rothschild (1744–1812). As he was deluged with requests, an eager petitioner asked to have but

---

8. The story is recorded in the name of R. Dov Ber of Mezhirich (*Maggid mi-Mezritch*, ca. 1704–1772). See R. Elazar Dov b. Aaron, *Sifron shel Tzaddikim* (Benei Berak: Makhon Mitzvah, 1998), 54; Ellen Frankel, *The Classic Tales: 4,000 Years of Jewish Lore* (Northvale, NJ: Jason Aronson, 1993), 506.
9. R. Hayyim Loew b. Bezalel (Friedberg, ca. 1520–1588), *Iggeret ha-Tiyyul* (Lemberg: Lewin, 1864), *ḥelek ha-remez, ot* 7; R. Zalman Sorotzkin (*Lutzker Rav*, Ukraine, 1881–1966), *Oznayyim la-Torah*, vol. 2 (Jerusalem: Makhon ha-De'ah ve-ha-Dibbur, 2005), *Terumah* 25, p. 242; R. Menachem Mendel Kasher (Israel, 1895–1983), *Torah Shelemah, ḥelek* 20 (Jerusalem: Beit Torah Shelemah, 1992), Exodus 25:50, *ot* 38. See also *Da'at Zekenim* to Exodus 25:3.

one word with him. When given the opportunity to speak, the petitioner said, "*Gemara.*" "What do you mean?" asked R. Amschel. "*Gemara* means *Gut morgen* (good morning), *Reb Anshel,*" replied the petitioner. "Does it mean anything else?" asked R. Amschel. "Yes," said the petitioner. "*Gib me'os* (give money), *Reb Anshel.*" R. Amschel then gave him some money. The petitioner accepted the donation but lingered, looking a bit dissatisfied. "What's wrong?" inquired R. Amschel. "*Gemara*!" repeated the petitioner. "I already gave. What does *Gemara* mean now?" asked R. Amschel. "*Gib mer* (give more), *Reb Anshel.*" [10]

Gib mer, Rabboisai.

10. In one version of this story, the petitioner is R. Hayyim of Volozhin (Poland, 1749–1821), collecting funds for Yeshivat Etz Hayyim. See Eliezer Leoni, ed., *Voloz'in: Sifrah shel ha-Ir ve-shel Yeshivat "Etz Ḥayyim"* (Tel Aviv: Ha-Irgunim shel Benei Voloz'in, 1970), 263. For other versions of the story, see Abraham Englisher, *Der Yiddisher Otzer* (Yiddish), 124, ¶ 441; Immanuel Olsvanger, *Rosinkess mit Mandlen: Aus der Volksliteratur des Ostjuden; Schwänke, Erzählungen, Sprichtwörter, und Rätsel* (transliterated Yiddish) (Basel: Verlag, 1931), 43–44; Israel Folktale Archives, "A Verbal Play in Donation Solicitation," Eastern Europe, IFA 2912 (Haifa: University of Haifa); Israel Folktale Archives, "One Word," Poland, IFA 9447 (Haifa: University of Haifa); Israel Folktale Archives, "Rabbi Meyer Amschel Rothschild and the Gemara," Poland, IFA 10961 (Haifa: University of Haifa); Israel Folktale Archives, "Gemara," Poland, IFA 13816 (Haifa: University of Haifa).

Shoftim

Social Outrage

September 1, 1984

Social outrage can be either spontaneous or artificially aroused. The spontaneous form is, of course, very effective in uplifting the moral climate of society. But spontaneous outrage against an evil is a rare event in human history. Society is often content to continue its agenda of everyday life while the shrieks and wretched cries of the victim are directed toward heaven. But if the leaders of society are to react with passion to every evil they behold, their fulminations will after a while be regarded as rantings.

It has been the challenge of civilization for many centuries to devise a plan for arousing social outrage. The treatment by the Torah of the case of the murdered victim found in an open space and whose assailant is unknown provides a model for arousing social outrage.

What is selected is a crime that is at once heinous and contemptible, but at the same time one for which no one will accept blame. The murdered victim is such a case. Talmudic explication of the crime establishes that the ritual of *eglah arufah* is not operative unless the crime was in open disdain of the law.[1] This is evidenced when the murderer makes no attempt to cover up his crime. If the victim is found buried in a rubble or if the victim was alive when found, the crime may have been one of passion and accompanied by a tinge of guilt. Paradoxically, this heinous crime is one that everyone could comfortably rationalize by imagining that the victim was a highwayman himself and his would-be victim turned on him. It is precisely under these circumstances where society must be shaken out of its complacency and driven to self-scrutiny.

Well, everyone is made to feel a bit guilty for the crime. Three or five members of the Supreme Court do the measuring to find the closest city to the victim.[2] The Elders of the city take a heifer not yet three years old to a dry valley of craggy terrain, wash their hands in a river, and pronounce, "Our hands have not spilled this blood, and our eyes did not see" (Deuteronomy 21:7). Our Sages interpret this to mean that the Elders are saying that they had no indirect responsibility for the murder.[3] We did not create the conditions to drive a man to crime, nor were we soft on crime, to encourage crime.

But the greatest drama is reserved to arouse the conscience of society to the heinousness of the crime. We surely get the impression that the heifer represents the victim. We behead the heifer that cannot bear fruit on craggy, rocky terrain. This encapsulates the nature of the crime. By killing someone, the victim is deprived of an opportunity to bear fruit, to perform dutiful deeds.[4]

But the heifer also clearly represents the murderer. All murderers receive *hereg*, as they are compared to the *eglah arufah*.[5] What symbolism is there here, making the killing of the heifer the execution of the murderer in effigy? We are making a statement that as long as the crime goes unnoticed, nothing the murderer will do in his future life will be regarded by us as bearing fruit. Society today all too frequently is willing

1. See *Sotah* 45b.
2. Deuteronomy 21:2; *Rashi* ad loc.; *Sotah* 44b.
3. *Sotah* 45b; *Rashi* to Deuteronomy 21:7.
4. *Sotah* 46a; *Rashi* to Deuteronomy 21:4.
5. *Sanhedrin* 52b. Just as the death of the *eglah arufah* is effected with a sword and from the neck (Deuteronomy 21:4), so, too, the execution of a murderer is performed with a sword and from the neck.

to tolerate murderers based on what they do with their lives in the future, despite the fact that no atonement was ever made for the crime! We look at the total life experience of the murderer. That is wrong. There must be outrage regarding the seriousness of the crime. We can never forgive or forget unless there is atonement for the crime itself.

Well, there was once a statesman in Jewish history who really internalized the meaning of the *eglah arufah*. He was Yosef *ha-Tzaddik*. After Jacob had been separated from Joseph for twenty-two years, he did not believe that Joseph was still alive until he saw the wagons that Joseph had sent to transport him. "Then the spirit of their father Jacob was revived" (Genesis 45:27). Our Sages tell us that the last lesson Joseph received from Jacob was the lesson of *eglah arufah*.[6] Joseph now showed Jacob that he really internalized the message. If the State can produce social outrage, it certainly can produce goodness. A famine has the potential to bring out the very worst in human nature, the jungle mentality. The only hope that this could be prevented is for the State to show a model of extraordinary magnanimity. This will prevent brutality from developing.

Joseph did precisely that by offering to sell food to all the surrounding lands that were affected by the famine.[7] This is indeed extraordinary. In bad times, a country will jealously hold whatever it has for itself. Witness the "beggar thy neighbor" policies of the 1930s.[8]

---

6. *Rashi* to Genesis 45:27, s.v. "*et kol diveri Yosef*"; Genesis Rabbah 94:3, 95:3. The Hebrew word for wagons, *agalot*, is similar to the word *eglah*, heifer. This signaled to Jacob that Joseph remembered that the last lesson that Joseph had received from Jacob was that of *eglah arufah*.
7. Genesis Rabbah 91:5; R. Enoch Zundel b. Joseph (Białystock, d. 1867), *Etz Yosef* ad loc., s.v. "*ke-Yosef she-zan ha-olam.*"
8. "Beggar-thy-neighbor" is an economic policy of protectionism, competitive devaluation of the national currency, and similar devices designed to restore a country's benefits from trade at the expense of competitor nations. For example, a deliberate devaluation of a country's currency would make exports from that country cheaper and imports more expensive. According to economist Joan Robinson, beggar-thy-neighbor policies were widely adopted by major economies during the Great Depression of the 1930s. See Dietmar Rothermund, *The Global Impact of the Great Depression, 1929–1939* (London: Routledge, 1996), 6–7.

We find ourselves now in the season of the Days of Awe. We are told by our Sages that a single act on our part can tip the scales of justice for merit or disaster.[9] Each person is an entire world.[10] Let us not allow ourselves to be overtaken by indifference. Indifference sanctions evil and dissipates goodness before it has a chance to grow.

9. See *Kiddushin* 40b.
10. *Sanhedrin* 37a ("Whoever preserves a single life from Israel is considered by Scripture as if he had preserved an entire world.").

Ki Tetze

I Have Strayed Like a Lost Sheep; Seek Out Your Servant

September 8, 1984

The Jew is engaged in a lifelong search for his spiritual essence. The spiritual essence of man, his *neshamah*, is called an *avedah*, a "lost object."[1] As the *Shem mi-Shemuel* points out, King David cries out, "I have strayed like a lost sheep; seek out your servant" (Psalms 119:176).[2]

As we near Rosh Ha-Shanah and our level of self-scrutiny increases and intensifies, the *parashah* of *Ki Tetze* unfolds in front of

1. On the eve of the Sabbath, Hashem gives man a *neshamah yeterah*, an "additional soul," which departs at the conclusion of the Sabbath. When the additional soul departs, it is referred to as "lost." See *Beitzah* 16a; *Ta'anit* 27b.
2. R. Shmuel Bornsztain (*Shem mi-Shemuel*, Poland, 1855–1926), *Shem mi-Shemuel: Al Seder Parshiyyot ha-Torah u-Mo'adei Kodesh*, 9th ed., vol. 4 (Jerusalem, 1992), *Pinḥas* (5673/ July 1913), p. 363.

our eyes and we read the law of *hashavat avedah,* the "restoration of lost property."[3] We can use this as a model for self-restoration.

First, we encounter that an *avedah* must be returned with two *simanim.*[4] So, too, the soul can be identified with two signs. These are the sign of *tefillin* and the sign of *berit milah.*[5] Now, unlike a lost article, for which the presentation of the identification marks signifies the end of the search, finding the two signs of the soul is only the beginning of the search. The sign of *tefillin* is said in connection with the *tefillin shel yad,*[6] which are placed on the arm opposite the heart, *ke-neged ha-lev.*[7] Unlike the other parts of the body in *Nishmat,* for which appropriate imagery is found to describe them, the heart is not described in *Nishmat.* The Jewish heart escapes a finite description, as the Jewish heart can leap into infinity. The heart is the personal commitment to the mitzvot.

The second sign is the *berit milah.*[8] Here we connect ourselves in our communal identity to the future, our destiny; the past of our Tradition; and the present. This is timeless, boundless. This is also infinity.

Now, with regard to the search for the *avedah,* we are told that if retrieving and returning the lost object would cause a financial loss to the finder that is greater than the benefit to the owner, the finder is exempt from retrieving and returning the lost object to the owner.[9] But this can emasculate the obligation completely, as all remote losses and imaginary losses could be included. "May there be no destitute among you" (Deuteronomy 15:4). We are bidden to do nothing that could have the effect of impoverishing ourselves.[10]

3. Deuteronomy 22:1–3.
4. *Bava Metzia* 27b–28a.
5. *Shem mi-Shemuel, Pinḥas,* loc. cit.
6. Exodus 13:16; Deuteronomy 6:8.
7. *Menaḥot* 37b; *Rashi* to *Berakhot* 13b, s.v. "*she-tehe simah ke-neged ha-lev*"; Maimonides (*Rambam,* Egypt, 1135–1204), *Mishneh Torah, Tefillin* 4:2.
8. Genesis 17:11 ("You shall circumcise the flesh of your foreskin, and that shall be the sign of the covenant between Me and you.").
9. *Bava Metzia* 30a.
10. *Bava Metzia* 33a.

And we are told of other exemptions from the law of *hashavat avedah*. One is a "*zaken ve-eino le-fi kevodo*," a Sage for whom it is not befitting his honor to pick up the lost object. Another is a *Kohen* who sees a lost object in a cemetery.[11]

Now, the ambit of *zaken ve-eino le-fi kevodo* appears to be constantly expanding; if there is no status involved in the activity, we do not pursue it. Then, similar to the *Kohen* who finds a lost object in a cemetery, we are afraid to search in certain areas because our spirituality will become tainted; we will defile ourselves. Taking hold of the *avedah* therefore becomes very elusive. But we are told, "Return; you shall return them" (Deuteronomy 22:1), even one hundred times.[12]

But once the *avedah* is caught, there is a dispute if the finder is a *shomer ḥinnam*, an "unpaid custodian," or a *shomer sakhar*, a "paid custodian."[13] A *shomer ḥinnam* is not responsible for *geneivah ve-avedah*, but a *shomer sakhar* is.[14] But who paid the finder that he would become a *shomer sakhar*? The *Gemara* tells us "*perutah de-Rav Yosef*" (lit., "R. Joseph's coin").[15] In R. Joseph's view, the finder is considered to be compensated with the money that he would have otherwise been required to give to a poor man who appeared at his door while he was engaged in the mitzvah of returning the lost object.[16] But this is rare; it is unlikely that a

11. Ibid. The exemptions from the obligation to restore lost property are derived from the word "*ve-hit'allamta*" (lit., "you shall hide from them") at Deuteronomy 22:1, "You shall not see the ox of your brother or his sheep wandering and hide from them (*ve-hit'allamta*); you shall return them to your brother." The simple interpretation of the verse is that one may not ignore a lost object. That concept, however, is explicitly stated subsequently in Deuteronomy 22:3, "*lo tukhal le-hit'allem*," "you shall not hide yourself." Consequently, the Sages interpreted the word *ve-hit'allamta* in Deuteronomy 22:1 to indicate that there are times when one is permitted to ignore a lost object. *Rashi* to Deuteronomy 22:1, s.v. "*lo sir'eh ve-hit'allamta*."
12. *Bava Metzia* 31a.
13. *Bava Kamma* 56b; *Bava Metzia* 29a.
14. Exodus 22:6–12; *Rashi* to Exodus 22:9; *Bava Metzia* 94b.
15. *Bava Kamma* 56b; *Tosafot* to *Bava Metzia* 29a; *Nedarim* 33b.
16. R. Joseph's position is based on the principle, recorded at *Sukkah* 25a, that one who is engaged in the performance of one mitzvah is generally exempt from performing another mitzvah at the same time. *Rashi* to *Bava Metzia* 29a, s.v. "*ke-shomer sakhar*."

poor man will knock on his door precisely when he is engaged in the mitzvah of returning the lost object.[17] This is the challenge that we face once we achieve some spiritual accomplishment. The danger is that we become selfish, preoccupied with the mitzvah, and have no time for anyone else.

But the biggest challenge arises when the *avedah* is already found. To which *neshamah* should we turn? *So'ne le-t'on kodem ohev le-ferok*. The obligation to assist an enemy load his animal takes precedence over the obligation to help one's friend unload his animal.[18] Unlike the physical *avedah,* which can possibly remain hidden from the owner forever, this cannot be the case with the *neshamah,* as the *Sefat Emet* explains the verse "the righteous man, being meritorious, takes his own portion and his fellow's portion in the Garden of Eden" (*Ḥagigah* 15a).[19] In the thinking of the *Sefat Emet,* when the righteous man experiences divine assistance that he cannot attribute to his own efforts but rather to the portion of the wicked man that the wicked man lost on account of his sins, the righteous man repents. The righteous man's repentance, in turn, inspires the wicked man to repent. When the wicked man repents, he regains his lost portion from the righteous man. Then, in the Next World, the righteous man is rewarded for having "returned" the merits of the wicked. Let us now grab this for ourselves.

17. *Tosafot* to *Bava Metzia* 29a. Because of the unlikelihood of this case, Rabbah is of the opinion that the custodian of the lost object is considered an unpaid custodian.
18. *Bava Metzia* 32b. The *Beraita* cited by the Talmud *ad locum* explains that assisting one's enemy in this case takes precedence in order to subdue one's Evil Inclination.
19. R. Yehudah Aryeh Leib Alter (*Sefat Emet,* Poland, 1847–1905), *Sefat Emet, helek* 5, *Ki Tetze* (5635/September 1875), s.v. "*lo sir'eh khulei, hashev tishivem.*"

One Mitzvah Leads to Another

August 31, 1985

We are all familiar with the dictum *mitzvah goreret mitzvah,* the performance of one commandment brings in its wake the opportunity to perform another commandment.[1] The principle, as *Rashi* points out, is derived from today's reading by the sequence of mitzvot presented. We start off with the mitzvah of *kan tzippor*. Then we proceed to *ma'akeh,* followed by three laws relating to the prohibition of combining different species, *kil'ayim*. Finally, the panorama ends with the mitzvah of *tzitzit.*[2]

What a spectacular assortment of mitzvot. We are almost tempted to say that it represents a random selection. But this cannot be. I would

1. Mishnah, *Avot* 4:2 (statement of Ben Azzai).
2. *Rashi* to Deuteronomy 22:8. *Rashi* explains that one who fulfills the mitzvah of sending away the mother bird will merit building a new home and thus will fulfill the mitzvah of building a protective fence. He will also merit owning a vineyard, a field, and fine clothing, and will thus observe the commandments of *kil'ayim* and *tzitzit.*

suggest that *mitzvah goreret mitzvah* enunciates the principle that moral sensitivity to perform mitzvot is a character trait that requires cultivation and hard work before we perfect it.

Moral sensitivity to mitzvot begins with internalizing the lesson of *kan tzippor*. R. Samson Raphael Hirsch explains the rationale behind *kan tzippor*. If we witness in nature a pristine act of compassion, the mother bird performing the function of a mother bird, hovering over her nestling, we must stand in admiration of the act. We grab the mother bird, as if to say, "I can take her for myself." And then we release her. Her actions of motherhood earn for her independence and freedom. If we recognize a pristine act of compassion, we ourselves develop the ability to become compassionate.[3]

But this is not enough. We now go to the next mitzvah. The homeowner is bidden to construct a parapet for his home. But for whom? For the "*nofel*," one who falls, as the verse states, "If you build a new house, you shall make a fence for your roof, so that you will not place blood in your house if one who falls (*ha-nofel*) falls from it" (Deuteronomy 22:8). This is a person who will fall anyway; he is destined to fall since the Six Days of Creation.[4] Yes, we must develop a sense of compassion and responsibility, even for the dregs of society. And only then are we ready to enter the *parashah* of *kil'ayim*, the area of the prohibition of mixing different species.

When we look today at the contemporary Jewish scene, both here and in Israel, we are saddened to find the extreme strain between the right and the left. We ask, what is the source of this polarization? Is it a product of compassion or is it the result of hatred, skipping the lesson of *kan tzippor* and *ma'akeh*?

Moreover, if we study the three laws of *kilyaim*, we can plainly see that the laws of *kil'ayim* are not monolithic. There are different spheres in life that are involved. Let us take *kil'ei ha-kerem*. Here, what is involved is the planting of a vineyard. This is symbolic of being engaged

---

3. R. Samson Raphael Hirsch, Deuteronomy 22:7.
4. *Shabbat* 32a; *Rashi* to Deuteronomy 22:8, s.v. "*ki yippol ha-nofel*"; *Sifrei*, Deuteronomy 229. The person whom the fence is intended to protect is referred to at Deuteronomy 22:8 as "one who falls" (*ha-nofel*) before he actually falls, indicating that he was destined to fall.

in an activity that "gladdens God and man" (Judges 9:13). When we are involved in Torah idealism, we must be concerned with not drawing sustenance from alien elements and also with *marit ayin*.[5] But when it comes to the combining of the pure and impure animals for plowing, it is only the intimate association of the animals that is prohibited. This is the economic sphere.

Then we proceed to the *shaatnez* of a garment. What is a garment but our shield against the elements in the winter and the summer, physical survival? The type of union or bond we may have with the forbidden mixture here is even a closer association. Wool can press hard against linen, only they should not be woven together.[6] In a broader sense, this means that when a secular Jew takes the lead in being concerned with the physical survival of our people, we should follow and recognize what he does. We can work closely together for the goal.

We are nothing less than amazed when we come to the culmination of the sequence. And what is it? It is *tzitzit*. And here, *kil'ayim* is actually permitted.[7] What do *tzitzit* symbolize? It is the manner in which we display our Jewishness. When it comes to Jewish identity, we should reserve our most strenuous efforts to reach out to uncommitted Jews, to form a bond with them to prevent their Jewishness from disappearing. This means that the religious Jew should take a very profound interest

5. *Marit ayin* is the prohibition against behaving in a manner that may raise suspicion that one is violating Jewish law. For example, officials who entered the Temple treasury were required to be barefoot and wear garments with no hemmed parts or wide sleeves to prevent any suspicion of theft. Mishnah, *Shekalim* 3:2. The biblical source for this practice cited by the Mishnah is the verse "you shall be clean in the eyes of Hashem and Israel" (Numbers 32:22). See also *Shabbat* 146b (discussing prohibition of hanging wet clothing in public on the Sabbath, giving the appearance that the clothing was washed on the Sabbath); *Yoma* 38a (noting that fine bread was never found in the hands of the children of the House of Garmu, which baked the Showbread for the Temple, so that no one should say that the bakers profited from the preparation of the Showbread).
6. *Rashi* to Deuteronomy 22:11 and Leviticus 19:19; *Sifrei*, Deuteronomy 232; Mishnah, *Kil'ayim* 9:8; *Niddah* 61b. *Rashi* explains that *shaatnez* is a contraction for the phrase "*shua tavvoi ve-nuz*," carded, spun, and woven.
7. Deuteronomy 22:12; *Rashi* ad loc.; *Yevamot* 4a.

in doing what he can to prevent intermarriage, to show a concern for the spiritual survival of every Jew.

Now, it is the Jew who wears a *tallit* who plants a vineyard. Instead of putting the *tallit* over his head, the planter of the vineyard should construct a *ḥuppah* as we do on *Simhat Torah*. When the secular Jew feels that the religious Jew cares with a passion about his spiritual survival – his identity – and the religious Jew cares about his physical wellbeing, when he feels the presence of both the *ma'akeh* and the chirping of the *kan tzippor* from above, then real meaning is infused into the words of our Sages that "the left hand pushes away and the right hand draws near."[8] This will produce the *aguddah aḥat,* which will hastily bring *Meshiaḥ Tzidkenu.*

8. *Sotah* 47a.

The Work of Amalek Today

September 13, 1986

In today's portion, we are presented with a striking contrast. On the one hand, the Torah goes to extraordinary lengths to evoke within us a feeling of admiration for certain actions. It does this by departing from the usual practice of not recording the reward of a precept, and does so in two instances. In connection with the mitzvah of *shiluaḥ ha-ken*, the Torah states "so that it will be good for you and will prolong your days" (Deuteronomy 22:7), and in connection with the prohibition of using false weights and measures it says "so that your days shall be lengthened on the Land that Hashem, your God, gives you" (Deuteronomy 25:15). On the other hand, the Torah goes to the other extreme trying to work us into a frenzy against Amalek by saying: "Wipe out the memory of Amalek from under the heaven. You shall not forget!" (Deuteronomy 25:19). Even the memory of Amalek must be blotted out.

Well, the juxtaposition of precepts is no coincidence. Perhaps the Torah wants us to focus and reflect upon what it regards as noble and admirable and make us infer that the opposite is ignoble and abhorrent.

Only with this approach can we begin to understand why the Torah directs us to harbor such a profound hatred toward Amalek.

What is noble and admirable? It is the performance of the mitzvah of *shiluaḥ ha-ken*. If we chance upon a bird's nest and find the mother bird sitting on her fledglings, we may not take the mother bird. But rather, we must send her away. Why? R. Samson Raphael Hirsch suggests that the Torah is telling us that since we found the mother bird performing her maternal duties, this guarantees her freedom and independence. We have no right to take away the mother bird. When we witness an act of nobility, we must admire it.[9]

Well, if taking notice of nobility and admiring it constitutes *arikhut yamim*, then holding an act of nobility in utter contempt is Amalek.

Another act of nobility is the observance of the precept of false weights and measures. What is so special about this precept? Are there not many other precepts that deal with dishonesty and deceit? What is special is that the use of false weights and measures constitutes invisible fraud.[10] Someone who has a deep sensitivity to evil and is revolted even by evil that cannot be detected will not be tempted by it. Moreover, he will not be able to bear even the possibility of holding false weights and measures in his possession. He cannot tolerate the notion that he may in some way be responsible for the mere existence of the tools of evil, the tools of invisible fraud, when they might cause harm.

If a deep sensitivity to invisible fraud wrenches the conscience of the noble man and constitutes *arikhut yamim*, then the open practice of evil, which offends not only higher morality but assaults humanity itself, is Amalek.

Last Sabbath, the world Jewish community was shocked beyond description when two Arabs perpetrated a massacre of twenty-one Jews while they were engaged in prayer in their newly renovated synagogue in Istanbul, Turkey.[11] Many regard it as the single most brutal act against

9. R. Samson Raphael Hirsch, Deuteronomy 22:7.

10. *Bava Metzia* 61b.

11. Henry Kamm, "Terror in Istanbul: 2 Gunmen Kill 21 in Synagogue; Bar Doors and Then Open Fire at Sabbath Service in Istanbul," *New York Times*, September 7, 1986, A1.

our people since the Holocaust.[12] It is the work of Amalek, the brutal contempt for nobility.

Three different groups claimed credit for the carnage, the open practice of evil, which assaults humanity itself, and boasted of it.[13] It is the work of Amalek. "He struck those of you who were hindmost, all the weaklings at your rear" (Deuteronomy 25:18). It was a fearless attack against the weak and laggard. "That he happened upon you on the way" (ibid.). By no stretch of the imagination did the act constitute a prize for the perpetrator or a threat to anyone. And it was also the chilling of what was boiling within us,[14] the desecration of the gift of the Jew to the world, the gift of holiness. There is nothing sacred to the terrorists. They profaned our holiness.

Yes, it was the work of Amalek, but did it evoke the response "Wipe out the memory of Amalek"? No! Was the conscience of the international community aroused? Was the Security Council of the United Nations convened? Did the superpowers meet with urgency and desperation and commit themselves to blot out this plague from the face of the earth, to hunt down the Abu Nidal group like mad dogs threatening humanity? Did the press respond with the ferocity and resoluteness that the situation required? No! No! No!

Instead, the Amalek act evoked at best a moderate response. Civilization condemned the act by proclaiming, "*lo yavo be-kehal Hashem,*"

---

12. See "Slaughter in Turkey Stuns Jewish World," *Jewish Advocate*, September 11, 1986, 1, 17.
13. Groups claiming credit for the attack included the Muslim fundamentalist group Islamic Holy War; a pro-Iranian organization called Islamic Resistance; and a group in Nicosia, Cyprus, Palestinian Revenge Organization. Kamm, "Terror in Istanbul."
14. Cf. *Midrash Tanḥuma, Ki Tetze* 9; *Rashi* to Deuteronomy 25:18, s.v. "*asher kar'kha ba-derekh*" (third interpretation). Amalek is described as "*asher kar'kha ba-derekh*" (lit., "he happened upon you on the way") (Deuteronomy 25:18). Associating the word *kar'kha* with *kar*, "cold," the Midrash explains that Amalek cooled off the fear of the other nations for the Children of Israel when they left Egypt by being the first one to instigate a battle with them after they appeared invincible as a result of the miracles that Hashem had wrought for them. The Midrash offers a parable of a boiling hot bath into which no one could descend. One scoundrel jumped into the bath. Although he was scalded, he cooled off the bath for others.

"he shall not enter the congregation of Hashem."[15] Such treacherous murderers do not belong in the community of God. *Ve-gam dor asiri lo yavo,* even the tenth generation of them.[16]

But there was Jimmy Carter who said, "Do not reject an Egyptian" (Deuteronomy 23:8). Yes, he condemns the act of murderers, but says, unfortunately, such acts of brutality will continue until we give serious attention to the aspiration of the Palestinians for a homeland.[17] Then others use the incident as a platform to inveigh against various evils in the world, equating all of them with this heinous incident. Where is their sense of proportion?

But as far as we are concerned, we know that divine compassion works in mysterious ways. The Midrash tells us that when the mitzvah of *shiluaḥ ha-ken* is performed as it should be, that is, we assure the freedom and independence of the mother bird, the heavenly hosts take up the cause of the mother bird and protest to Hashem, "Master of the Universe, what about the mother bird? Think of all the suffering that the separation from her offspring causes her. How can You, Hashem, allow this separation?" Whereupon Hashem replies, "Yes, my ministering angels, the pity for the mother bird is well spoken and she merits your pity, but why do you not take up the cause of My children, separated from Me by means of the Exile? I see that there is no one to take up their cause. I will have to do it Myself. '*Le-ma'ani le-ma'ani e'eseh*' ('for My own sake, for My own sake, I will do it') (Isaiah 48:11)."[18]

Ve-halo devarim kal ve-ḥomer. If Hashem's pity and compassion for the Jewish people are aroused when everyone takes up the cause of the mother bird, which deserves pity and compassion, but everyone is neglecting the cause of the Children of Israel, *a fortiori,* when the whole world is either reacting in a muted tone or using the evidence of carnage for their own political agenda, diverting attention away from the

15. Cf. Deuteronomy 23:3–4.
16. Ibid.
17. Crystal Nix, "Terror in Istanbul: Reaction from Far and Wide; Clerics and Leaders Condemn the Raid," *New York Times,* September 8, 1986, A8.
18. *Tikkunei Zohar, tikkun* 6.

enormity of the treachery and evil involved, Hashem's compassion for us will surely be aroused. *Le-ma'ani, le-ma'ani e'eseh.*

The *Kaddish* to which the *siddur* of the *Shatz* was opened when the carnage took place surely is reverberating in the heavenly court – "*Yisggaddal ve-yiskaddash Shemeh Rabba,*" "May His name that is great grow exalted and be sanctified"... "*ba-agala u-ve-zeman kariv ve-im'ru amen,*" "swiftly and at a time that comes soon; now respond 'amen.'"

Ki Tavo

The Three Keys

September 7, 1985

Tonight, together with Jews all over the world, we will begin our preparation for the Days of Awe with the recitation of *Seliḥot*. Tradition has it that since the destruction of the Temple, all the gateways to Heaven are sealed and can be penetrated only by means of tears of contrition and sincerity.[1]

Gaining access to life, health, and fulfillment by means of tears strikes the modern man as peculiar. Rather, our instinct tells us to reach for the three master keys: the key of rain, the key of childbirth, and key of *teḥiyyat ha-metim*. We are well aware of the teachings of our Sages that the Master of the Universe, Himself, controls these keys and does not entrust their stewardship to a mortal.[2] But these

1. *Bava Metzia* 59a.
2. *Ta'anit* 2a. With respect to rain, the Torah states, "Hashem will open for you His good storehouse, the heaven" (Deuteronomy 28:12). With respect to childbirth, the Torah states, "God remembered Rachel; God listened to her, and He opened her womb" (Genesis 30:22). With respect to the resurrection of the dead, the Torah states, "You

same Sages tell us that on occasion, Hashem lent out the keys, one at a time.[3]

We find ourselves today in the position of a dwarf resting on the shoulders of giants. We identify with the cumulative human achievements of the past. We are under the delusion that we possess the key of rain. The key of rain symbolizes the control over natural phenomena to produce material wealth. Who is not dazzled by the prodigious production capacity of the modern industrial state along with the unprecedented standard of living it has brought in its wake? We would like to believe the claim of the technocrats that we know enough today to prevent a cataclysmic depression.

We also imagine that we are in full control of the key of childbirth. The tremendous advances of medical science have enormously reduced the infant mortality rate, to say nothing of test tube babies and genetic engineering.

And we even imagine that we control the key of *teḥiyyat ha-metim*. Resurrection is by no means a monolithic concept. In a broad sense, it means conferring a spark and a glittering to someone after all hope has been abandoned. In the second blessing of the *Shemoneh Esrei*, we indeed mention together with the *gevurah* of Hashem of *teḥiyyat ha-metim* the related *gevurot* of *somekh nofelim*, "supporting the fallen," *rofeh ḥolim*, "healing the sick," and *mattir asurim*, "releasing the confined." And when we look at society today, we may convince ourselves that, in a way, we also are controlling with respect to *teḥiyyat ha-metim*. How? The social safety net in fact is part of Western Civilization. And has medicine not had the effect of reducing pain and suffering for mankind, giving a person a second chance and a new lease on life?

Well, our Sages knew that one who subliminally is under the delusion that the three master keys are in his pocket will be convinced that he is in full control of his own destiny. Such a person will in fact be

---

will recognize that I am Hashem, when I open your graves and raise you up from your graves" (Ezekiel 37:13).

3. *Sanhedrin* 113a; *Tosafot* to *Ta'anit* 2a. Elijah was lent the key of rain and the key of the resurrection of the dead. *Sanhedrin* 113a (rain); I Kings 17 (resurrection of the dead). In addition, Elisha was lent the key of the resurrection of the dead. See II Kings 4:24–35.

overwhelmed with a feeling of omnipotence and will never be moved to tears to break down the barrier between us and Hashem. In their wisdom, the Sages understood that the easiest delusion to shatter is the delusion that mankind controls the key of *teḥiyyat ha-metim*. So, in principle, for the Days of Awe, we focus on repentance, which is in a real sense the kindness of Hashem to allow us a second chance, *teḥiyyat ha-metim*.[4] And we focus on the *gevurot* of Hashem with respect to all aspects of *teḥiyyat ha-metim*.

In all the *Seliḥot*, we emphasize different things, but there is a common denominator that we always mention. And what is that? It is the *Anenu* prayer. Here we are given a panorama of Jewish history, a collection of instances where Hashem provides us with the dazzle of his key of *teḥiyyat ha-metim*, in all its profound dimensions.

We start the *Anenu* prayer with "He Who answered Abraham on Mount Moriah, may He answer us. He Who answered his son Isaac when he was bound atop the altar, may He answer us."

I ask: Where do we see that Abraham or Isaac, let alone both, made requests at the *Akedah*? But I would submit that what we are saying here is: Who is like Hashem, who penetrates the deep recesses of the heart and knows our fondest wish, a wish of desperation that we dare not even articulate? Was it not the wish of Abraham to be the perfectly loyal servant of Hashem, but not sacrifice his son? Was it not the fondest wish of Isaac to be an *olah temimah* but remain alive to serve Hashem?

Hashem understood the inarticulate cry of anguish and answered their prayers. We truly understand why we say "He Who revivifies the dead with abundant mercy."[5] Only Hashem gives the second chance with abundant mercy. This is not the *meḥayeh ha-metim* of man.

Now we can move to shatter the second delusion. What is the second delusion? It is that we hold the key of life. So we focus on the dazzle of Hashem's key of life on Rosh Ha-Shanah with the birth of

4. See *Midrash Shoḥer Tov*, Pslams 102:19; R. Nissim Solomon b. Abraham Algazi (Smyrna, ca. 1610–1683), *Shema Shelomoh*, *Va-Yera*, s.v. "*ve-nashuvah*;" R. Jonathan Eybeschuetz (Prague, 1690–1764), *Ya'arot Devash* 1:1, s.v. "*berakhah sheniyah*"; R. Eliezer Papo (*Pele Yo'etz*, Bulgaria, 1785–1828), *Beit Tefillah*, Blessing of *Meḥayeh ha-Metim*.

5. *Shemoneh Esrei* Prayer.

Isaac, such an inauspicious beginning with no expectation of carrying forward the message of Hashem. We merely have to look at ourselves and see the dazzle of the key of childbirth, the miracle of our own survival and development, that despite all the concerted attempts throughout history to annihilate us through pogroms, crematoria, and the force of assimilation, we are still here.

Now we are prepared to shatter the last delusion of the key of rain. On Sukkot, we are utterly obsessed with the *gevurah* of Hashem. We take the Four Species, which require water for their survival more than other vegetation, and shake them in six directions, so as to say, "Master of the Universe, You, and You alone, control our existence. Please ward off the bad winds and the evil dew so as not to negate our blessing."[6] And we pray that Hashem should withhold his rain the first six days of Sukkot not to show displeasure with us – do not drive us out of the *sukkah*![7]

Then we realize that our so-called sophistication can be the very means of our downfall. The more sophisticated the economic system, the more it rests on our confidence in it. Given the electronic transfers that are possible today, it might take only the nervousness of one portfolio manager after becoming uncomfortable with the exposure of banks to Third World debt to trigger an international banking panic.

Let us acknowledge that Hashem controls the three keys. Let us watch carefully how he turns them and uses them as our model for emulation in our interpersonal lives. With this, we will merit a year of blessing, salvation, *hatzlaḥah*, and *neḥamot*.

---

6. *Sukkah* 37b–38a.
7. *Ta'anit* 2a; *Rashi* ad loc.; *Sukkah* 28b.

The Reproof

(Undated)

The reading of the chapter of the Reproof is accompanied by trepidation and anxiety. Paradoxically, our Sages found hidden blessings in the litany of imprecations. Moreover, the very secret of our survival is found in the climax of the Reproof. Hashem will scatter us among the nations. "And among those nations you will not be tranquil. There will be no rest for the sole of your foot. There, Hashem will give you a trembling heart, longing of eyes, and suffering of soul" (Deuteronomy 28:65).

Yes, this is a harrowing mental state, but without it, our very survival would be in question. If we would be comfortable and in a state of peace of mind in the host country, we would be in danger of being swallowed up entirely, of losing our identity. It is only because we feel isolated and alienated that we remain together as a people and maintain our faith.

Throughout the millennia, all too often, this dreadful mental state was a product of persecution. We are therefore indeed blessed that in the present Diaspora, in the United States, we enjoy unprecedented religious freedom and economic opportunity. But our survival depends on "there will be no rest for the sole of your foot." And its manifestation of "a trembling heart, longing of eyes, and suffering of soul," I would submit, is the very manner in which we express the intensity of our Jewishness. Without it, we are reduced to mechanical robots. The ideal for us is to manufacture the nervous energy for our survival and spiritual growth in the Diaspora.

And who personified this more than Joseph? Finding himself in an alien culture, his trembling heart is what stood him in his trial of Lady Potiphar. It is what made him renowned as a *navon ve-ḥakham*, "discerning and wise" (Genesis 41:39), in times of unparalleled prosperity to prepare for the famine. It was Joseph who felt the profound sense of loss, the "suffering of soul," when he was separated from his roots, his father. It was Joseph who was the idealist, never being satisfied with the quality of human relationships, always striving higher – "He comforted them and spoke to their heart" (Genesis 50:21). And it was Joseph who let everyone know in the most dramatic terms that he did not regard the luxurious life in Egypt as in any way the ideal. He says, "When God will indeed remember you, then you must bring my bones up out of here" (Genesis 50:25). This is a "longing of the eyes," always longing for something better, something more noble and perfect.

We face today two unparalleled challenges in the golden *galut* of America. On the one hand, we face the threat of the diversion of a nervous energy away from what is precious to us to peripheral areas of insignificance. It is supposed to be a cause of cheer that observant Jews are making inroads into professions that they never dared to enter in the past, such as advertising and moviemaking. Well, there is the danger that all the energy of a "trembling heart" will be directed toward worrying about how we can succeed in a strange and unknown environment. And the "suffering of soul" will relate to losing contracts or recognition from people in the work environment, with the consequence that the trembling heart will not be attuned to the spiritual pitfalls in the work environment itself, i.e., to the ethical problems of treading the fine line between deception and persuasion.

And the moviemaker faces the challenge of corrupting the moral climate of society. For him, much more so, what will be left of the trembling heart? Often, it is too drained to be attuned to threats against our people. And the *da'avon nefesh* energy amounts to be worried only about losing the interest of people, importance, and prestige in the world environment, while caring nothing about losing contact with our roots. Then what happens to the "longing of the eyes"? It just evaporates into very superficial goods and externalities and is directed almost entirely toward career advancement.

The second threat is another paradox. The American Jewish community has built up an impressive array of institutions, so for everything that happens, from a problem in *kashrut*, to an incident of vile anti-Semitism, to international terror, we fully expect a Jewish institutional response. Institutions have a trembling heart, a longing of the eyes, and a suffering of the soul, but what about the heart of the individual?

If hidden blessings can be read into the Reproof, then, I submit, this can be done with respect to the very climax of the Reproof, the very last verse. We will be returned by means of vessels to Egypt.[1] This is symbolic of a return to the golden *galut*, the beginning of the Exile in Egypt, to the height of the Pharaoh of Joseph, when the Egyptians were overjoyed to see Joseph's brothers. And all of us will return – women, children, and the elderly – by means of ships, and the Egyptians will view us in the most glowing terms.

Why? Because we will be returning on the road of which Hashem said "you shall never again see it!" (Deuteronomy 28:68), so the nations of the world cannot say that the Jews are not under any special Divine Providence, as Hashem has abandoned His promise. And also we will be viewed not as parasites but as great benefactors of society. We will be using our great talents for the benefit of society. We will be looked upon as useful servants, even for our enemies. But with all the *menuḥah* that the host country gives us, *ve-ein koneh*, "there will be no buyer" (ibid.), we will not be swallowed up. We will not be acquired. Why? Because we will take on the personality of Joseph, the man who could not be enslaved.

1. Deuteronomy 28:68.

Nitzavim-Va-Yelekh

Producing Fear of Heaven in Public

September 15, 1990

The longest sermon recorded in Jewish history was delivered by Moses. It lasted all of thirty-seven consecutive days.[1] In painful and biting words, ranging from subtle reproof to shocking and open blasting, the sermon, spanning the entire *mishneh Torah*, was a description of how we fell short of "What does Hashem, your God, ask of you? Only to fear Hashem, your God, to go in all His ways and to love Him, and to serve Hashem, your God, with all your heart and with all your soul" (Deuteronomy 10:12).

But there was a happy moment. On the last day of his life, Moses wrote a *sefer Torah* and handed it over to the sons of Levi,[2] whereupon, the Children of Israel complained why they were not also given a *sefer*

1. The review began on the first day of the month of *Shevat* (Deuteronomy 1:3), and ended on the seventh day of Adar, the last day of Moses' life.
2. Deuteronomy 31:9.

Torah. Tomorrow, the Tribe of Levi would possibly claim that the Torah was given only to them. When Moses heard this, he proclaimed that in the forty years of his leadership, the Children of Israel witnessed so many wonders and signs but they did not really understand their significance. But today, "this day, you have become a people to Hashem, your God" (Deuteronomy 27:9).[3]

What do we have here? Moses observed jealousy and envy in the spiritual realm, and he did not attack it, but actually cherished it and regarded it as a virtue.

What a striking contrast is presented to us. In the material realm, envy, jealousy, and invidious comparison stand at the very fundamental basis of our high standard of living. Madison Avenue devotes considerable creative energy to cultivating in ordinary man a prodigious appetite for material goods, a desire to adopt nothing less than the lifestyle of the very wealthy. Once ordinary man is transformed into a hedonistic creature by means of persuasive advertising, we dangle a plastic card in front of him and pronounce to him that his wildest dreams are within reach. If a *pas be-melaḥ*[4] cult would suddenly appear and the ordinary man would adopt only a puny ambition in the material realm, the entire prosperity would precipitously collapse.

In sharp contrast, in the spiritual realm, we become purist and idealist. Here, we regard jealousy and envy as part of the dark side of human nature. We expect the *yeshivah* to eradicate these bad traits in our children. And when it comes to our own conduct as adults, we are hung up that our Torah and mitzvot should be only *le-shemah.*

Permit me to suggest that the role of envy in the spiritual realm needs serious reevaluation. First, let us point out that our Sages declared, "One should always (*le-olam*) occupy himself with Torah and good deeds, though it is not for their own sake, for out of doing good with an ulterior motive comes doing good for its own sake."[5] The great *ba'al musar,* the

3. *Rashi* to Deuteronomy 29:3, s.v. "*ad ha-yom ha-zeh.*"
4. See Mishnah, *Avot* 6:4 ("This is the way of the Torah: Eat bread with salt (*pat be-melaḥ*), drink water in small measure, sleep on the ground, live a life of deprivation – but toil in the Torah.").
5. *Pesaḥim* 50b; *Sotah* 22b.

Mikhtav me-Eliyahu, points out that with the word "*le-olam,*" our Sages are telling us that starting with *lo le-shemah* is the route for everyone.[6] It is pure delusion to imagine that we can immediately leap to *le-shemah. Lo le-shemah* must be accepted as a fact of life.

Moreover, the well-known dictum of our Sages of *kin'at soferim tarbeh ḥokhmah,* "jealousy between scholars increases wisdom," is not merely an Aggadic statement.[7] No, a whole edifice of halakhah is built on it, making encroachment easier in the sphere of Torah and *kelei kodesh.*[8]

If it takes the hedonistic person to catapult us to such high levels of material wellbeing, it takes his or her counterpart to catapult us to high levels of the spiritual domain. We must be transported on the wings of Hillel, who had such a prodigious appetite for Torah to hear *divrei Elokim ḥayyim* from Shemayah and Abtalyon that on the wintry day when he did not have the tuition to pay, he climbed up on the skylight and became a human icicle. He put his life in mortal danger because he was desperate to learn Torah.[9]

Mayor Dinkins was recently criticized for not expressing sufficient outrage against crime.[10] In essence, we were telling him, if you cannot produce the outrage spontaneously, then give the matter utmost priority with your speechwriters and, if necessary, take acting lessons, because outrage must come from the Mayor.

Well, this is not a new idea. It is an old one. The fourteenth century author *Menorat ha-Ma'or* provided us with a formula for *ḥinnukh* for parents. When parents observe disgraceful conduct, they must express outrage in the presence of their children so they will learn to distance themselves from the conduct. And when parents observe meritorious

6. R. Eliyahu Eliezer Dessler (Lithuania, England, and Benei Berak, 1892–1953), *Mikhtav me-Eliyahu,* eds. R. Aryeh Carmell and R. Alter Halperin, 5th ed., vol. 1 (Benei Berak: Hever Talmidav, 1964), 24–25.
7. *Bava Batra* 21a.
8. *Bava Batra* 21b–22a. For a discussion of Halakhah's approach to competition in the Torah educational sphere, see R. Aaron Levine, *Economic Morality and Jewish Law* (New York: Oxford University Press, 2012), 138–141.
9. *Yoma* 35b.
10. See Todd S. Purdum, "Crime and Mayor's Anger; Dinkins Hopes Reasoned but Tough Stance Will Combat Fears about Rising Violence," *New York Times,* September 8, 1990, A1.

conduct, they must exude praise for the conduct in the presence of their children so they can learn to emulate the conduct.[11]

If the great Rebbe, the Berdichever Rav (Ukraine, 1740–1809), would come down now from heaven, I am sure he would find much merit in the American custom of making testimonial dinners that recognize princes of *ḥesed* and those who are extraordinarily devoted to the community. Yes, one must elevate heroes of the spirit to produce fear of Heaven, attaching prestige to the exemplars of Torah and mitzvot. As the hasidic master R. Hayyim Meir Yehiel Shapira explains the verse "the hidden [sins] are for Hashem, but the revealed [sins] are for us and for our children forever, to carry out all the words of this Torah" (Deuteronomy 29:28), if everyone would be a *tzaddik nistar*, from whom would our children and grandchildren learn to be righteous?[12]

We say every day in our prayers "always should a person be fearing of Heaven in private and in public."[13] Perhaps we need to display a prodigious amount of fear of Heaven in public to produce fear of Heaven in private.

11. R. Israel b. Joseph ibn Al-Nakawa (Spain, d. 1391), *Menorat ha-Ma'or*, ed. Hillel G. Enelow, vol. 4 (New York: Bloch, 1932), 145.
12. R. Hayyim Meir Yehiel Shapira (*Sorof* of Moglenitz, Mogielnica, Poland, 1789–1849), *Tiferet Ḥayyim* (Warsaw: Kleiman, 1920), 32.
13. Morning Prayer, *Birkhot ha-Shaḥar*.

Ha'azinu

Full Containers and Leaking Buckets

September 28, 1985

The story is told of a world traveler who journeyed to a remote village in the interior of Australia. In accordance with local custom, he was invited to lecture a large gathering of natives. He graciously accepted with the proviso that an interpreter periodically interrupt his speech to translate and summarize the gist of his remarks.

Well, after the first hour of discourse, the interpreter jumped up on the stage and said, "Ping." At the end of the second hour, the interpreter said just two words, "Ping hang." At the conclusion of the lecture, at the end of the third hour, the interpreter said, "Ping hang chang." The crowd then broke out in thunderous ovation. Curious as to what these words meant, the speaker asked the translator to explain. The translator said, "'Ping' means 'nonsense,' 'ping hang' means 'more nonsense,' and 'ping hang chang' means 'the nonsense is over.'"

Speaking of nonsense, we are given a very bold statement in today's portion: "For it is not an empty thing for you, for it is your life"

(Deuteronomy 32:47). There is not a single word of the Torah that is empty or irrelevant. Each word relates to the very essence of our lives. And if we do find an empty word, the fault is ours.

In almost any sphere of our existence in the contemporary society, we encounter progress, advancement, and increased sophistication. The products and services that we consume embody the newer and better technology. Even the toys that our children play with reflect ever-increasing imagination and suitability for adults. We benefit from sophisticated political commentary and news analysis. The professional finds his office lined with journals, and is hard-put to keep up with his field.

Well, if everything about us is advancing in a sophisticated and scintillating manner, we run the grave risk of having the Torah appear to us as a *davar rek*, an "empty thing."

We are in a reversal from older times. Historians tell us that in the dark Middle Ages, there were no scientific or technical advances. The dark and monotonous daily existence was interrupted by the tragedy of plague and famine. It was against this backdrop that the most explosive elucidation of our Talmud took place, in the form of *Rashi* and the *ba'alei ha-Tosafot*. The Jew living then, facing a constant threat to his life, felt that the Torah was his life and source of support.

Today, we are in danger of viewing the word of the Torah as a *davar rek*. It was this type of realization that led our Rabbis in relatively recent times, beginning with the sainted *Ḥafetz Ḥayyim*, to say that R. Eliezer's statement that "whoever teaches his daughter Torah teaches her *tiflut*" (*Sotah* 21b) cannot possibly apply today.[1] Why? If a woman will be conversant in Western culture, compulsory education, and even graduate education, if she will know the Protestant Ethic, but nothing of the Jewish ideal, what will become of the creation of the Jewish home? This implies that to prevent the danger of the Torah becoming an empty doctrine, we must all be exposed to the profundity of the Torah. The profundity of the Torah is not just for the elite. It is for everyone.

If we are faced with the challenge of stretching our minds to draw out the profundity of the Torah to the best of our ability, we are faced also with perhaps the diametrically opposite challenge of believing that

1. R. Israel Meir ha-Kohen Kagan, *Likkutei Halakhot*, *Sotah* 21b (Warsaw, 1922).

the Torah has the mystical power to refine and perfect our nature, even if we understand only little of it and see no entertainment value in it. This idea is conveyed by a story in the Midrash of a king who visited a little hamlet. The King came with a gigantic wagon with a container and buckets and asked the villagers to draw water from the river with the buckets and pour water into the container.[2] The buckets were all found to have holes in them. Most villagers regarded the effort as futile, but one persisted, thinking that whatever could be accomplished should be done. But when the King realized this, he said angrily, "Why assume that I want to fill up the container? I only want to have the buckets rinsed out."[3]

Both the one who enervates himself to fill the container and to rinse out the buckets deserves our deepest admiration, but who stands greater? I submit it is the carrier of the bucket. He assumes the form of the *ba'al ha-bayit* who gets up extra early to come to a *shiur*. He is exhausted. He is fighting sleep. Yet he perseveres and listens to words of Torah.

Such *ahavat Torah* is the catalyst that sets the moral tone for society, igniting the desire to draw out the profundity of the Torah and bring about the day when throngs of people listen to magnificent words of Torah, to torrents of words of Torah, and no one says "ping hang chang."

---

2. Leviticus Rabbah 19:2.
3. This interpretation of the *midrash* is attributed to the *Gra*. See R. Tzvi Dravkin, *Ateret Ḥen*, vol. 2 (Benei Brak: Yeshivat Grodna, 2007), 198; R. Michel Shurkin, *Harerei Kedem*, vol. 1 (Jerusalem, 2000), 343.

Epilogue

Kaddish Gadol

2004 or 2005

There is a uniqueness of *kaddish gadol*. It is recited on only two occasions: at burial and *siyyum mesekhta*. What connection could there be?

Kaddish gadol speaks of a new world that Hashem will make *de-asid le-ischaddasa,* that will hereafter be renewed.[1] Yes, it is a world of *teḥiyyat ha-metim*. But what is the world like? It is one where idolatry will be uprooted from the land and replaced with the City of Jerusalem, and crowned with the building of the Temple. This is a place of spiritual force.

Recall Jerusalem of the times of the Temple. Ten miracles were performed for our forefathers in the Temple.[2] One of these miracles that we all experienced together was "*omdim tzefufim u-meshtaḥavim revaḥim,*" we stood crowded together yet we prostrated ourselves in ample space. It was a great dosage of fear of Heaven.

---

1. *Kaddish Gadol.* Cf. *Targum Onkelos* to Deuteronomy 32:12.
2. Mishnah, *Avot* 5:5.

I would ask you: Who longs for *Yerushalayim shel or*, the "Jerusalem of light"?[3] It is certainly not the people attached to This World. And it is not the people of Ronald Reagan's "shining city on a hill."[4] In the secular city, jealousy, lust, and glory reign supreme.[5] Not in the crude manner of Ham. No, but in the refined manner of Japheth. It is a place where the American dream becomes accessible to all. But what is the American dream all about? It is how far someone can go with "my strength and the might of my hand" (Deuteronomy 8:17).

Who longs for *Yerushalayim shel or*? It is those who learn Torah, those who believe in its teachings, and those who practice its teachings. It is the people who make the world of Abbaye and Rava their real world.

In the idyllic society of *talmud Torah*, *ḥesed* and simple virtue become the reality. We yearn for the renewal of this world. This is the world of *teḥiyyat ha-metim*.

3. See Genesis Rabbah 59:5 (stating that Jerusalem will be the light of the world, based on the prophecy "nations will walk by your light" [Isaiah 60:3]).
4. Ronald Reagan, "Election Eve Address: 'A Vision for America,'" November 3, 1980.
5. See Mishnah, *Avot* 4:21.

Glossary

ADDERABBA. Aramaic for "greater than this." On the contrary.

AGGADAH, (ADJ.) AGGADIC. A genre of rabbinic literature consisting primarily of biblical exegesis.

AGUDDAH AḤAT. One unit.

AHAVAT ḤINNAM. Unwarranted love.

AKEDAH. The Binding of Isaac.

ALEPH. First letter of the Hebrew alphabet.

ALIYYAH. Ascent, particularly of a spiritual nature. Also denotes the immigration of Jews to the Land of Israel.

ALIYYAH LE-TORAH. The calling of a member of a Jewish congregation to an elevated platform in the synagogue for a portion of the reading from the Torah. The person who is called recites a blessing before and after the portion of the Torah reading.

ANAV. A humble person.

ANAVAH. Humility.

ANNINUT. Status of a bereaved person during the period between the death and the burial of a close relative. The bereaved person is exempt from fulfilling certain religious obligations such as reciting the daily prayers, except during the Sabbath and the Festivals.

ARAVOT. Highest heavens.

ARIKHUT YAMIM. Long life.

AVEDAH. An object lost by its owner without his knowledge. One who finds such an object is required under Jewish law to return it to its owner.

AVODAH. Service.

AVODAT HA-KASEF. Lit., "service of the shoulder." Service of carrying the Ark on one's shoulders performed by the Levites from the family of Kohath.

BA'AL HA-BAYIT. Householder.

BEIN ADAM LA-MAKOM. Lit., "between man and God." Refers to the obligations between man and God.

BEIN ADAM LE-ḤAVERO. Lit., "between man and his fellow." Refers to the obligations governing interpersonal conduct.

BEIN HA-METZARIM. Lit., "between the straits." Three-week period of mourning beginning on the seventeenth day of Tammuz and ending on the ninth day of Av, established to commemorate the destruction of the First and Second Temples.

BEIT DIN. Jewish court of law.

BEIT MIDRASH. Torah study hall.

BEIT OLAMIM. Permanent Temple.

BEKHOR. Firstborn.

BERIT MILAH. Circumcision.

BIKKURIM. Offering of the first fruits to the Priests in the Temple, prescribed at Exodus 23:19 and Deuteronomy 26:1-11.

BIRKHAT HA-MAZON. Grace after Meals.

BIRKHOT HA-NEHENIN. Blessings recited over things that provide pleasure, such as food and drink.

BITTAḤON. Faith.

DERASH. Homiletical interpretation.

DERASHAH, (PL.) DERASHOT. Exposition. May also refer to a rabbinic sermon.

DEROR. Freedom.

EGLAH ARUFAH. Lit., "decapitated calf." Refers to a ritual prescribed by the Torah for a case when a victim of murder is found and the identity of the murderer is unknown. The elders of the town closest to the location where the corpse was found bring a calf to an untilled valley and decapitate it. The elders then wash their hands over the dead calf and proclaim that they are not responsible for the murdered individual.

EIVAH. Lit., "animosity." Halakhic principle that takes into consideration the emotional impact that one's actions have on others and aims to prevent feelings of animosity.

EMET. Truth.

EMUNAH. Faith.

ERETZ YISRAEL. Hebrew name of the Land of Israel. The term is biblical, although its meaning varies, designating both the territory actually inhabited by the Israelites (I Samuel 13:19) and the Northern Kingdom (II Kings 5:2). Only from the Second Temple period onward, however, was the term used to denote the Promised Land. It was the official Hebrew designation of the area governed by the British mandate in Palestine after World War I until 1948.

FOUR SPECIES. The four articles of plant life that a Jew is commanded to hold in his hand on the Festival of Sukkot, consisting of a branch of the date palm, a citron, willow branches, and myrtle branches.

GALUT. Exile. Dispersion of Jews from the Land of Israel.

GEDOLEI TORAH. Rabbinic leaders. Outstanding Torah scholars.

GEMARA. Aramaic for "completion" or "tradition." This term is popularly applied to the Talmud as a whole, or more particularly to the discussions and elaborations by the *Amoraim* on the Mishnah.

GEMATRIA. Exegetical method by which a word or phrase is associated with another word or phrase with the same numerical value.

GEMILUT ḤASADIM. Lit., "bestowal of loving kindness." The duty that encompasses the whole range of the responsibilities of sympathetic consideration toward one's fellow man.

GEVURAH. Strength. One of the ten *Sefirot*.

GOZEL VE-NISHBA. One who stole property worth at least a *perutah*, the modern-day equivalent of 0.025 grams of pure silver, and swore falsely that he did not steal it.

HAFTARAH. Selection from the Prophets that is read in the synagogue after the Torah reading on the Sabbath and the Festivals. The theme of the selection is usually related to the Torah reading that precedes it.

ḤAKHAM. Sage.

HAKKARAT HA-TOV. Gratitude.

HALAKHAH. Jewish law.

HALAKHAH LE-MOSHEH MI-SINAI. Lit., "it is the law given to Moses at Sinai." Laws regarded by the Talmud as having biblical authority although not explicitly mentioned in the Bible nor derived by hermeneutical principles. Examples of such laws include the laws of ritual slaughter, the feast of the water drawing on Sukkot, and certain details regarding the construction of *tefillin*.

ḤALAV YISRAEL. Milk and other dairy products produced under the supervision of a knowledgeable, Torah-observant Jew.

HALLEL. Praise. Recitation of Psalms 113 through 118 during the morning service on the first two days of Passover, Sukkot, Shavuot, and Hanukkah. On Rosh Ḥodesh and the last six days of Passover, Psalms 115:1-11 and 116:1-11 are omitted from the prayer.

HARAMAT KEREN. Uplifting of pride.

ḤARATAH. Remorse. One of the requirements for repentance in Jewish law.

HASHAVAT AVEDAH. Biblical commandment to return a lost object to its rightful owner.

ḤASID. A member of a hasidic branch of Orthodox Judaism.

HATTARAT NEDARIM. Absolution from the obligation of a personal vow granted by a Torah sage.

ḤATTAT. Offering that is required to be brought to atone for a sin committed inadvertently.

HATZLAḤAH. Success.

ḤAVRUTA. Study partner.

ḤAZARAT HA-SHATZ. Repetition of the *Shemoneh Esrei* by the cantor after a group of at least ten men have recited the prayer. "*Shatz*" is an acronym for "*Sheliaḥ tzibbur*," a messenger of the community.

HEFKER. Ownerless property.

HEKDESH. Consecrated property.

ḤELBBENAH. An herb with a putrid smell. One of the ingredients of the *ketoret*.

HEREG. Decapitation. One of the four types of capital punishment executed by a Jewish court.

ḤERUT. Freedom.

ḤESED. Kindness.

ḤESED ELYON. Divine kindness.

ḤILLUL HA-SHEM. Lit., "disgrace of the Name." Refers to an action that brings dishonor and disgrace to God.

HIN. Liquid measure equal to twelve *luggim.*

ḤINNUKH. Religious training.

HOD. Splendor. One of the ten *Sefirot.*

ḤOK, (PL.) ḤUKKIM. Divine decree for which the explanation is beyond human comprehension.

HORA'AT SHA'AH. Extraordinary procedure outside the framework of the law in cases of emergency.

ḤUKKIM. See "*Ḥok.*"

ḤUPPAH. Wedding canopy. May also refer to the Jewish wedding ceremony.

INNUI NEFESH. Deprivation of sensual pleasures.

KABBALAH. Esoteric and mystical teachings of Judaism.

KADDISH. Sanctification. Prayer that praises Hashem and expresses a yearning for the establishment of His Kingdom on Earth. The prayer is recited only with a *minyan* and has several forms. The mourner's *kaddish* is recited by a son for eleven months after the death of his parent. Other forms of the *kaddish* separate sections of the liturgy.

KAL VE-ḤOMER. *A fortiori.*

KARET. Excision. Death at the hands of Heaven as punishment for the intentional violation of certain sins.

KASHRUT. Jewish religious dietary laws.

KAVOD. Honor.

KEDUSHAH. Holiness. Also the name of the third section of the *Shemoneh Esrei.*

KELEI KODESH. Those involved in learning and teaching Torah.

KENESSET YISRAEL. The Jewish nation.

KETORET. A mixture of aromatic herbs burnt twice daily on the Golden Altar in the Temple and as part of the ritual performed by the High Priest in the Holy of Holies on Yom Kippur.

KETUBBAH. A woman's marriage contract in Jewish law.

KEVOD HA-TORAH. Honor of the Torah.

KIDDUSH HA-SHEM. Lit., "sanctification of the Name." An observable and noble action that brings glorification to God.

KIL'AYIM. Prohibition in Jewish law of mixing wool and linen, cross-breeding seeds, and cross-breeding animals.

KIN'AT SOFERIM TARBEH ḤOKHMAH. Lit., "jealousy between scribes increases wisdom." This dictum serves as a basis for allowing free entry of new teachers into a religious elementary school system.

KINYAN, (PL.) KINYANIM. Acquisition of legal rights by the performance of a symbolic act.

KINYAN HAGBAHAH. Mode of acquisition of movable objects involving the lifting of the subject article by the acquirer. The article may be raised merely by the force of the acquirer's body. Authorities differ as to whether it must be lifted by one handbreadth or three.

KIPPAH. Skullcap. Also known as a "yarmulke."

KLAL. Community.

KLAL YISRAEL. The Jewish nation.

KODASHIM. Portions of sacrificial offerings.

KODESH. Holy matters.

KOHEN. Priest. Principal functionary in the divine services. The special task of the Priests was to engage in rituals conducted mainly in the Temple. The post of the Priests is authorized by hereditary right, and they constitute a distinct class separate from the rest of the Jewish people.

KOL. A sound.

KORBAN, (PL.) KARBANOT. Sacrificial offerings prescribed by the Torah. The sacrifices were offered in the Tabernacle and the Temple at the hands of the Priests.

KORBAN PESAḤ. Paschal offering.

KULLAM ḤAYYAV PATUR. Judicial rule that if a Sanhedrin opens a capital case with a unanimous guilty verdict (*kullam ḥayyav*), the accused is exempt (*patur*) until some merit is found to acquit him.

LASHON HA-RA. Lit., "evil speech." Tale-bearing in which *A* delivers a damaging but truthful report regarding *B* to *C*, when *C* is neither the object of *B*'s mischief nor the intended target of *B*'s evil designs.

LEḤEM AVIRIM. Lit., "bread of angels." The manna.

LEKKET. Gleanings. Biblical commandment at Leviticus 19:9 that if one or two stalks of grain slip out of the reaper's hand while harvesting them, they must be left to the poor. If three stalks fall together, the owner may retrieve them.

LOG, (PL.) LUGGIM. A liquid measure equal to the volume of six eggs.

LUGGIM. See "*Log.*"

LULAV. One of the Four Species that the Torah requires the Jew to hold in his hand on the Festival of Sukkot. The obligation is based on Leviticus 23:42; the "branches of the palm tree" mentioned in the verse are identified as the *lulav*.

MA'AKEH. Parapet. Biblical requirement at Deuteronomy 22:8 to construct a parapet for a new house to prevent injury.

MA'AMAD, (PL.) MA'AMADOT. Lit., "stations." A group of Priests, Levites, and Israelites who would stand by the daily communal offering, acting as emissaries for the people to satisfy the requirement that one be physically present while one's offering is being brought.

MA'ASER. Tithe. During the time of the Temple, a portion of one's agricultural produce was required to be given to the Priests and Levites. First, *terumah* was set aside for the Priests. Next, *ma'aser rishon* (the first tithe), consisting of one tenth of the remainder, was given to the Levites. A second tithe was then given. In the first, second, fourth, and fifth years of the Sabbatical cycle, the second tithe was called "*ma'aser sheni,*" which was generally required to be eaten in Jerusalem. In the third and sixth years, the second tithe was called *ma'aser ani,* which was given to the poor.

MA'ASER ANI. Lit., "poor tithe." Tithe given to the Levites and the poor in the third and sixth year of the Sabbatical cycle. See also "*ma'aser.*"

MA'ASER RISHON. Lit., "first tithe." Tithe given to the Levites from agricultural produce after *terumah* was taken. See also "*ma'aser.*"

MA'ASER SHENI. Lit., "second tithe." Tithe of agricultural produce set aside during the first, second, fourth, and fifth years of the Sabbatical cycle after *terumah* and *ma'aser rishon* were taken. *Ma'aser sheni* was required to be eaten in Jerusalem. If it was too difficult to carry the produce to Jerusalem, the tithe could be redeemed for money, consisting of the value of the produce plus one-fifth. The money would then be taken to Jerusalem where the owner would spend it on food or peace offerings. See also "*ma'aser.*"

MAḤAR ḤODESH. Lit., "tomorrow is Rosh Ḥodesh." *Haftarah* for a Sabbath when Rosh Ḥodesh falls on the next day, Sunday, at I Samuel 20:18-42. The common name of the *haftarah* derives from its opening words, "Jonathan said to him, 'Tomorrow is the New Moon.'"

MALKHUT. Royalty.

MARIT AYIN. Concern for appearance of wrongdoing.

MAROR. Bitter herbs.

MASHGIAḤ. Supervisor. A title applied to one who is responsible for ensuring that the food products of a restaurant, factory, store, or hotel are kosher, also known as a *mashgiaḥ kashrut.* Alternatively, the term may refer to a spiritual supervisor in a *yeshivah,* known as a *mashgiaḥ ruḥani,* who is responsible for the spiritual development and well-being of the students.

MATTAN TORAH. The giving of the Torah to the Children of Israel on Mount Sinai.

MAYIM ḤAYYIM. Living water, such as spring water, used for ritual purification of the leper.

MAZZIK. A person or thing that causes damage or injury to another person.

MEDINAT ḤESED. A country of kindness.

MEGILLAH. Lit., "scroll." Most commonly refers to the Book of Esther, one of the Five Scrolls, but may refer to one of the other four scrolls. The Five Scrolls are a portion of the Hagiographa, each of which is read publicly on a different festival during the year. The other four scrolls are: Song of Songs; Ruth; Lamentations; and Ecclesiastes.

MEḤILAH. Forgiveness.

MELAKHOT. Lit., "activities." Typically refers to the thirty-nine categories of creative labor that were performed in the construction of the Tabernacle and that are prohibited on the Sabbath.

MESHIAḤ TZIDKENU. Lit., "the anointed one of our Righteousness." Messiah.

MESIRUT NEFESH. Self-sacrifice.

MET MITZVAH. A corpse found unattended. It is a positive commandment to bury the corpse. The commandment applies even to a priest, who would otherwise be forbidden from becoming ritually impure through contact with the dead.

MEZUZAH. Lit., "doorpost." Piece of parchment containing the verses at Deuteronomy 6:4-9 and 11:13-21, affixed to the doorposts of the house. The parchment is placed in a case and is affixed on the right-hand side of the doorpost.

MI SHE-BERAKH. Prayer recited during the reading of the Torah in the synagogue requesting God's blessing for each person called to the Torah.

MI SHE-PARA. Judicial imprecation imposed on a buyer or seller who retracts before a transaction is legally consummated but after the sales price has been paid. The formula for the imprecation is: "He who exacted punishment from the generation of the Flood and the generation of the Dispersion will exact punishment from one who does not stand by his word."

MIDDAH KE-NEGED MIDDAH. Measure for measure. Retributive justice.

MIDDOT. Lit., "measurements." Character traits.

MIDRASH. Hebrew designation of a particular genre of rabbinic literature consisting mainly of exegesis of specific books of the Bible.

MINYAN. A quorum of ten men necessary for public synagogue services and certain other religious ceremonies.

MISHMAR. Lit., "watch." One of the twenty-four watches of Priests and Levites who served in the Temple one week at a time on a rotating basis. The watches were subdivided into family groups, each of which served one day of the week.

MISHNAH. Designates the collection of rabbinic traditions redacted by R. Judah ha-Nasi at the beginning of the 3rd century. The purpose of the Mishnah is to elaborate, systematize, and concretize the commandments of the Torah.

MISHNEH TORAH. Lit., "repetition of the Torah." A name for Deuteronomy. Also a name for the code of Maimonides.

MITZVAH, (PL.) MITZVOT. A religious act or duty. The Bible contains 613 commandments, consisting of 248 positive commandments and 365 negative commandments.

MITZVAT ASEH. Positive biblical commandment. There are a total of 248 positive biblical commandments.

MITZVAT LO SA'ASEH. Biblical prohibition. There are a total of 365 biblical prohibitions.

MIZBE'AḤ HA-ḤITZON. Lit., "the outer altar." The sacrificial Altar that stood in the Temple Courtyard. Also called "*mizbe'aḥ ha-olah*" because the daily burnt offerings and other offerings were sacrificed on it, "*mizbe'aḥ ha-neḥoshet*" (altar of copper) because of its copper cover, or simply "*ha-mizbe'aḥ,*" the Altar.

MORA. Fear. One of the filial obligations toward one's parents.

MUSAF. Lit., "supplement." Additional sacrifice prescribed for the Sabbath and the Festivals. In the liturgy, it is the name for the additional prayer recited on the Sabbath, Rosh Ḥodesh, the Three Festivals, and Yom Kippur after *Shaḥarit*.

MUSAR. Jewish ethics or moral philosophy.

NAZIR. A person who voluntarily took the vow described at Numbers 6:1–21. The vow required one to abstain from drinking wine, refrain from cutting the hair on one's head, and avoid coming into contact with a corpse.

NEDARIM. Vows. See also "*hattarat nedarim.*"

NEGA. Affliction.

NESAKHIM. Libations. A libation of wine typically accompanied burnt offerings and peace offerings. The amount of the libation was one-fourth of a *hin* for a lamb, one-third for a ram, and one-half for a bull.

NESHAMAH YETERAH. Lit., "additional soul." An extra measure of spiritual energy. On the eve of the Sabbath, Hashem gives man an additional soul, which departs at the conclusion of the Sabbath. When the additional soul departs, it is referred to as "lost."

NETZAḤ. Eternity. One of the ten *Sefirot*.

OHEL MO'ED. Tent of Meeting. A tent pitched by Moses outside the camp of the Children of Israel in the Wilderness where Hashem spoke to Moses, as described at Exodus 33:7-11. The term may also refer to the Tabernacle.

OHEV SHALOM VE-RODEF SHALOM. One who loves and pursues peace. A description of Aaron.

OHEV YISRAEL. One who loves Jews.

OLAH. Burnt offering. An offering that is entirely consumed by the Altar fire.

OLAH TEMIMAH. Lit., "a perfect burnt-offering." The term is used to describe Isaac.

OLAM HA-EMET. The World of Truth.

ONA'AT MAMOM. Price fraud involving selling above or below the competitive norm.

PAR. Bullock.

PARASHAH, (PL.) PARSHIYYOT. Lit., "portion." Selection of a biblical book.

PARDES. Lit., "orchard." An acronym for *peshat, remez, derash,* and *sod. Peshat* is the literal interpretation of a verse; *remez* (lit., "hint") is a veiled reference, such as *gematria*; *derash* is homiletical interpretation; and *sod* (lit., "secret") is a mystical interpretation.

PAROKHET. Curtain of the Sanctuary that marked the division between the Holy and the Holy of the Holies.

PE'AH. Lit., "corner." Biblical commandment at Leviticus 19:9 that the corner of the field be left unharvested as a gift for the poor.

PESAḤ. Passover.

PESAḤ SHENI. Second Passover. A festival introduced for those who were unable to bring the paschal offering at its appointed time as a result of ritual impurity or an unavoidable absence from Jerusalem. In those circumstances, the offering could be brought one month later, on the fourteenth day of Iyyar.

PESHAT. Literal interpretation of a verse.

POSEK. A rabbinic scholar who renders practical halakhic decisions.

RABBOISAI. Yiddish for "gentlemen."

RAḤMANA LE-TZLAN. Lit., "God save us." God help us.

RASHA. Wicked person.

RAV. Rabbi.

RAV HA-ḤOVEL. Captain of a ship.

RE'AḤ NIḤO'AḤ. Pleasing fragrance. Description of the fragrance produced by the *ketoret*.

REBBE. Religious teacher.

REMEZ. Lit., "hint." Veiled reference.

RIBBONO SHEL OLAM. Master of the Universe.

RISHONIM. Early rabbinic authorities. The period of the *Rishonim* extended from the middle of the 11th century to the middle of the 15th century.

RODEF. Lit., "pursuer." According to Jewish law, if *A* pursues *B* with the manifest intent to kill him, everybody is under a duty to rescue *B*, even by means of killing *A*, if no lesser means are available to neutralize *A*.

ROSH AV. Head of a group of families of Priests and Levites serving in the Temple, which group constituted a subgroup of a *mishmar*.

ROSH ḤODESH. The first day of a Jewish month. Considered a minor Jewish festival on which fasting is prohibited but work may be done.

SAFEK SAKKANAH. Possibility of danger.

SA'IR HA-MISHTALE'AḤ. The he-goat that was sent off a cliff as part of the Yom Kippur service in the Temple. Also referred to as the "*Sa'ir la-Azazel*."

SA'IR LA-HASHEM. The he-goat that was offered as a sacrifice in the Temple on Yom Kippur.

SANHEDRIN. Assembly of ordained scholars that functioned both as the Supreme Court and Legislature before 70 C.E.

SEDER. Lit., "order." Ritual ceremony held on the night of Passover involving the recitation of the Haggadah.

SEFER TORAH. Torah scroll.

SEFIRAT HA-OMER. Counting of the forty-nine days between Passover and Shavuot, as prescribed at Leviticus 23:15-16.

SEFIROT. Ten creative forces that intervene between the infinite, unknowable God and our created world, as taught by the Kabbalah. The *Sefirot* are: *keter* (crown); *ḥokhmah* (wisdom); *binah* (understanding); *ḥesed* (loving-kindness); *gevurah* (power); *tiferet* (beauty); *netzaḥ* (eternity); *hod* (splendor); *yesod* (foundation); and *malkhut* (sovereignty).

SEKHAKH. Roof covering of a *sukkah*.

SELIḤOT. Prayers for pardon recited a few days before Rosh Ha-Shanah and during the days between Rosh Ha-Shanah and Yom Kippur.

SHAATNEZ. Forbidden mixture of wool and linen in a garment. Contraction of "*shua tavvoi ve-nuz*," "carded, spun, and woven."

SHALOM. Peace.

SHE'ELAH. A question regarding the application of Halakhah to a practical situation.

SHEḤITAH. Ritual slaughter.

SHELAMIM. Peace-offerings brought in the Temple.

SHEMA. Lit., "hear." Refers to the passage at Deuteronomy 6:4, "Hear, O Israel: The Lord is our God, the Lord is One." The term is used more generally to refer to the entire portion of the daily prayers that consist of Deuteronomy 6:4–9, Deuteronomy 11:13–21, and Numbers 15:37–41.

SHEMA YIGROM HA-ḤET. Lit., "lest some sin cause." Concern of the Patriarchs that perhaps some sin would cause Hashem's promises to them not to be fulfilled.

SHEMITTAH. Sabbatical year. Seventh year of a seven-year cycle, during which it is biblically prohibited to work the land and all loans are canceled.

SHEMONEH ESREI. Jewish prayer recited in the morning, afternoon, and evening services. Also referred to as the *Amidah,* the "standing prayer." The weekday formulation of the prayer consists of nineteen blessings, although it originally had eighteen. For the Sabbath and festivals, the middle thirteen blessings are replaced with blessings specific to the occasion.

SHERETZ. An animal that slithers along the ground or appears to do so because it has short legs and its movement is not readily noticeable.

SHEVI'IT. The Sabbatical Year.

SHIKHEḤAH. Forgotten sheaves. Biblical commandment at Deuteronomy 24:19 that if one or two bundles of wheat are forgotten in the field when other bundles are collected, the forgotten sheaves must be left to the poor.

SHILUAḤ HA-KEN. Biblical commandment at Deuteronomy 22:6–7 to send away the mother bird from her nest before taking her young or her eggs. A reward of long life is mentioned in connection with this commandment.

SHIRAH. Song. A triumphant hymn in praise of Hashem, such as the Song at the Sea of Reeds.

SHOFAR. Ram's horn sounded for memorial blowing on Rosh Ha-Shanah and other occasions.

SIDDUR. Prayer book.

SIDRAH, (PL.) SIDROT. Weekly Torah portion.

SIMAN, (PL.) SIMANIM. Sign; identification mark.

SIN'AT ḤINNAM. Baseless hatred.

SOD. Lit., "secret." Mystical interpretation.

SOTAH. A woman whose behavior has established her as a suspected adulteress.

SUKKAH. Temporary dwelling that the Torah instructs Jews to dwell in for the seven days of the Festival of Sukkot.

TA'AVOT. Desires.

TAḤANUN. Supplication. Petition for grace and forgiveness recited daily after the morning and afternoon *Shemoneh Esrei*, except on the Sabbath, Festivals, days of joy, and Tish'ah be-Av, and in a house of mourning during the week of mourning. Also called "*nefilat appayim*" (falling on the face).

TAHOR. Ritually pure.

TALLIT. Four-cornered cloth with fringes that is worn as a prayer shawl during the *Shaḥarit* and *Musaf* services.

TALMID. Student.

TALMUD. The record of discussions of scholars on the laws and teachings of the Mishnah. The Talmud consists of the Babylonian Talmud, codified in ca. 500 C.E., and the Palestinian Talmud, codified in ca. 400 C.E.

TALMUD TORAH. Learning of Torah.

TAMEI. Ritually impure.

TAMID, (PL.) TEMIDIM. Communal burnt offering, brought every day in the morning and the evening.

TAMIM. Pure.

TANNA, (PL.) TANNAIM. Aramaic *teni*, "hand down orally." The term designates a teacher dating from the Mishnaic times. The *Tannaic* period covers five generations of rabbinic authorities, spanning from 20 to 200 C.E.

TEFILLAH. Prayer.

TEFILLIN. Phylacteries. Two cube-shaped black leather boxes containing four biblical passages written by hand on parchment. The boxes are worn during the morning services. One box is worn on the head and the other on the arm, with leather straps affixed to the boxes for attaching the boxes to the head and the arm.

TEFILLIN SHEL ROSH. Phylacteries worn on the head. These phylacteries are constructed with four separate compartments, one for each of the four biblical passages that are required to be placed inside the phylacteries.

TEFILLIN SHEL YAD. Phylacteries worn on the hand. These phylacteries contain one compartment in which a single piece of parchment containing four biblical passages is placed.

TEḤIYYAT HA-METIM. Resurrection of the dead.

TEKHELET. Blue dye mentioned in the Bible that was used in the vestment of the High Priest, the tapestries of the Tabernacle, and *tzitzit.* The dye was derived from a sea creature, the *ḥilazon,* that appears on land only once in seventy years.

TEKIAH, (PL.) TEKIOT. Lit., "blowing." A long blast of the shofar.

TERAFIM. Idols worshipped by Laban.

TEREFAH. An animal or bird that possesses a specified defect that will certainly cause its death. Such a defect renders the animal or bird prohibited for consumption even if it was ritually slaughtered.

TERUAH. A series of nine staccato blasts of the shofar sounded on Rosh Ha-Shanah.

TERUMAH. Heave offering given to the Priests from agricultural produce before the first tithe was separated for the Levites.

TIFERET. Beauty. One of the ten *Sefirot.*

TINNOKOT SHEL BEIT RABBAN. School children.

TORAH. Lit., "instruction." Refers to the Bible as a whole.

TOSAFOT. French commentators on the Talmud who lived during the 12th to 14th centuries.

TUMAH. Ritual impurity.

TUMAT MET. State of ritual impurity from coming into contact with a human corpse.

TZA'AR BA'ALEI ḤAYYIM. Lit., "suffering of living creatures." Refers to the prohibition of causing pain to animals.

TZADDIK. Righteous person.

TZADDIK NISTAR. A hidden righteous person.

TZAHAL. Israeli Defense Forces. Acronym for "*tzeva ha-hagganah le-Yisrael*" (lit., "army of defense for Israel").

TZEDAKAH. Charity.

TZIBBUR. The collective; community.

TZITZIT. Knotted ritual fringes attached to the four corners of a *tallit*, in accordance with the biblical mandate at Numbers 15:38 and Deuteronomy 22:12.

URIM VE-THUMMIM. The oracles in the breastplate of the High Priest.

VADDAI SAKKANAH. Danger that is certain.

YEHAREG VE-AL YA'AVOR. Principle that one should allow himself to be killed rather than violate one of the three cardinal sins of idolatry, forbidden sexual relations, and murder.

YESHIVAH, (PL.) YESHIVOT. Institutes of Talmudic learning.

YOM TOV. Generic term for a Jewish holiday; a day of festival on which certain activities are prohibited.

Bibliography

Aaron b. Joseph ha-Levi, R. *Sefer ha-Ḥinnukh.* Edited by R. Yitzhak Yeshayah Weiss, R. David Zicherman, and R. Yitzhak Weinstein. Jerusalem: Makhon Yerushalayim, 1992.

Abrabanel, R. Isaac b. Judah. Commentary on the Torah.

Agency for Toxic Substances and Disease Registry. Toxicological Profile for Benzene, U.S. Public Health Service, U.S. Department of Health and Human Services, Atlanta, GA, August 2007, 1–2.

Ahai Gaon, R. *She'iltot de-Rav Aḥai Gaon.*

Al-Hakam, R. Joseph Hayyim b. Elijah. *Rav Pe'alim.*

———. *Torah le-Shemah.*

Al-Nakawa, R. Israel b. Joseph ibn. *Menorat ha-Ma'or.* Edited by Hillel G. Enelow. New York: Bloch, 1932.

Albo, R. Joseph. *Sefer ha-Ikkarim.*

Alfasi, R. Isaac b. Jacob. *Rif* to *Bava Metzia*; *Ḥullin.*

Algazi, R. Nissim Solomon b. Abraham. *Shema Shelomoh.*

Alter, R. Yehudah Aryeh Leib. *Sefat Emet.* Commentary on the Torah.

Alter, R. Yitzhak Meir. *Ḥiddushei ha-Rim al ha-Torah, Mo'adim ve-Likkutim.* Jerusalem: Mossad ha-Rim Levine, 1992.

Altman, R. Shraga Tzvi. *Ateret Tzvi: Al Ḥamishah Ḥumshei Torah, Nakh, Mo'adim, Derashot le-Yamim Nora'im, u-Pirkei Avot ve-Sugyot ha-Shas.* Edited by R. Shlomo Friedman and R. Yaakov Levi. Benei Berak: Eshel, 1968.

Altschuler, R. Jehiel Hillel b. David. *Metzudat David.*

Aly, Götz. *Hitler's Beneficiaries: Plunder, Racial War, and the Nazi Welfare State.* New York: Metropolitan Books, 2007.

Asher b. Jehiel, R. *Rosh* to *Bava Kamma*; *Bava Metzia*; *Berakhot*; *Gittin*; *Ḥullin.*

Bibliography

Azulai, R. Hayyim Joseph David. *Birkei Yosef* to *Shulḥan Arukh*.

———. *Ḥomat Anakh*.

———. *Tzavvarei Shalal: Perush al ha-Haftarot*.

Ba'al ha-Turim. Commentary on the Torah.

Bahya b. Asher, R. *Rabbeinu Beḥaye al ha-Torah*.

Baraita de-Rabbi Yishmael.

Bass, R. Shabbetai b. Joseph. *Siftei Ḥakhamim* to *Rashi*.

Batzri, R. Ezra. *Dinei Mamonot*. Vol. 4. Jerusalem: Haktav Institute, 1982.

Berlin, R. Naphtali Tzvi Yehudah. *Emek ha-Netziv*.

———. *Ha'amek Davar*.

———. *Ha'amek She'elah* on *She'iltot de-Rav Aḥai Gaon*.

Besdin, R. Abraham R. *Man of Faith in the Modern World*. Hoboken, NJ: Ktav, 1989.

Bornsztain, R. Shmuel. *Shem mi-Shemuel: Al Seder Parshiyyot ha-Torah u-Mo'adei Kodesh*. 9th ed. 6 vols. Jerusalem, 1992.

Broun, Kenneth S., ed. *McCormick on Evidence*. 7th ed. Eagan, MN: Thomson-Reuters, 2013.

Busch, Andrew E. *Ronald Reagan and the Politics of Freedom*. Lanham, MD: Rowman & Littlefield, 2001.

Buursma, Bruce. "Black Muslim Leader Sharing Jackson Limelight." *Chicago Tribune*, February 26, 1984, C1.

Caro, R. Joseph. *Beit Yosef* to *Tur*.

———. *Kesef Mishneh* to *Mishneh Torah*.

———. *Shulḥan Arukh*.

Carroll, Douglas. "How Accurate Is Polygraph Lie Detection?" In Anthony Gale, ed., *The Polygraph Test: Lies, Truth and Science*, 19–28. London: SAGE Publications, 1988.

Chesnoff, Richard Z. *Pack of Thieves: How Hitler and Europe Plundered the Jews and Committed the Greatest Theft in History*. New York: Doubleday, 1991.

Clairborne, William. "Israeli Jews Fight New Mormon Center; Brigham Young Presses Construction, Denies That It Intends to Seek Converts." *Washington Post*, December 24, 1985, A10.

Clemens, Richard G. "Poison Debt: The New Takeover Defense." *Business Lawyer* 42, no. 3 (May 1987): 747–760.

Cohen, R. J. Simcha. *How Does Jewish Law Work? Volume 2: A Rabbi Analyzes 119 More Contemporary Halachic Questions*. Northvale, NJ: Jason Aronson, 2000.

Colon b. Solomon Trabotto, R. Joseph. *She'elot u-Teshuvot ha-Maharik*.

Da'at Zekenim. Commentary on the Torah.

Danzig, R. Abraham. *Ḥayyei Adam*.

———. *Ḥokhmat Adam.*
Dean, Martin. *Robbing the Jews: The Confiscation of Jewish Property in the Holocaust, 1933–1945.* Cambridge: Cambridge University Press, 2010.
Denton, Herbert H. "Reagan Urges More Church Aid for Needy." *Washington Post,* April 14, 1982, A3.
Department of Economic Affairs, Statistical Office of the United Nations. *Demographic Yearbook, 1949–1950.* New York, 1950.
Derekh Eretz Rabbah.
Dessler, R. Eliyahu Eliezer. *Mikhtav me-Eliyahu.* Edited by R. Aryeh Carmell and R. Alter Halperin. 3 vols. Benei Berak: Hever Talmidav, 1964.
Dewar, Helen. "Senate Unanimously Rebuffs President on Social Security." *Washington Post,* May 21, 1981, A1.
Dinkel, Yaakov Chaim. *The Story of Shemittah.* Jerusalem, 2006.
Doron, Abraham and Ralph M. Kramer. *The Welfare State in Israel: The Evolution of Social Security Policy and Practice.* Boulder, CO: Westview Press, 1991.
Draper, Theodore. *A Very Thin Line: The Iran-Contra Affairs.* New York: Hill & Wang, 1991.
Dravkin, R. Tzvi. *Ateret Ḥen.* Vol. 2. Benei Brak: Yeshivat Grodna, 2007.
Edels, R. Samuel Eliezer b. Judah ha-Levi. *Ḥiddushei Halakhot ve-Aggadot.*
Eder, Elizabeth. "OPEC: Demise of a Cartel?" *Harvard International Review* 6, no. 1 (September/October 1983): 33–34.
Elazar Dov b. Aaron, R. *Sifron shel Tzaddikim.* Benei Berak: Makhon Mitzvah, 1998.
Eleazar b. Judah, R. *Sefer ha-Roke'aḥ.*
Eliezer b. Samuel of Metz, R. *Sefer Yere'im.*
Elijah b. Solomon Zalman, R. *Be'ur ha-Gra: Mishlei.* Edited by R. Meir Yehoshua Katzenellenbogen. Jerusalem: Mossad HaRav Kook, 2006.
———. *Haggahot ha-Gra* to *Megillah.*
Englisher, Abraham. *Der Yiddisher Otzer.*
Enoch Zundel b. Joseph, R. *Etz Yosef* to *Midrash Rabbah.*
Environmental Protection Agency. "Air Pollution and Operating Permit Program Update: Key Features and Benefits." February 1998.
Epstein, R. Baruch ha-Levi. *Torah Temimah.*
Epstein, R. Jehiel Michal. *Arukh ha-Shulḥan.*
Eybeschuetz, R. Jonathan. *Ya'arot Devash.* Vol. 2. Jerusalem: Makhon Or ha-Sefer, 1988.
Farnsworth, Clyde H. "Trade Bill Voted in Senate by 63–36 but Is Facing Veto." *New York Times,* April 28, 1988, A1.
Feinstein, R. Mosheh. *Iggerot Mosheh.*
Fiedler, Edgar R. "The Three Rs of Economic Forecasting—Irrational, Irrelevant and Irreverent." *Across the Board* 14 (June 1977): 62–63.

Frankel, Ellen. *The Classic Tales: 4,000 Years of Jewish Lore*. Northvale, NJ: Jason Aronson, 1993.

Frankl, Walter. "Sabbatical Year for the Soil." Gardener's Corner. *Jerusalem Post*, June 18, 1979, 7.

Friedman, Milton. *Capitalism and Freedom*. Chicago: University of Chicago Press, 1962.

———. "The Social Responsibility of Business Is to Increase Its Profits." *New York Times Magazine*, September 13, 1970, 32–33, 122–124.

Friedman, R. Alexander Zusha. *Ma'ayanah shel Torah*. Vol. 3. Tel Aviv: Pe'er, 1956.

Gelb, Leslie H. "Reagan's Military Budget Puts Emphasis on a Buildup of U.S. Global Power." *New York Times*, February 7, 1982, 28.

Gellis, R. Yaakov, ed. *Tosafot ha-Shalem: Otzar Perushei Ba'alei ha-Tosafot*. Jerusalem: Makhon Harry Fischel, 2009.

Gerondi, R. Nissim b. Reuben. *Ḥiddushei ha-Ran*.

Goldfield, David R. *Promised Land: The South Since 1945*. Arlington Heights, IL: Harlan Davidson, 1987.

Goldman, John J. "Could Boomerang at Reelection Time in '89; Koch Hurt by Attack on Jackson." *Los Angeles Times*, April 21, 1988, C20.

Gombiner, R. Abraham Abele b. Hayyim ha-Levi. *Magen Avraham* to *Shulḥan Arukh*.

Gostynski, R. Chaim Mosheh. *Naḥalat Ḥamishah: Al Ḥamishah Ḥumshei Torah*. New York: Moinester, 1949.

Greenberg, R. Aharon Yaakov. *Iturei Torah: Likkut, Nisaḥ u-Biur*. 6 vols. Tel Aviv: Yavneh, 1967–1970.

Greenberger, Robert S. "$100 Million Memorial to the Living... and the Dead." *Jewish Herald*, May 5, 1989, 4–5, 18.

Grodzinski, R. Hayyim Ozer. *Aḥiezer*.

Gunzberg, R. Aryeh Leib b. Asher. *Turei Even*.

Hananel b. Hushi'el, R. *Rabbeinu Ḥananel*. Commentary on Talmud.

Harris, Milton and Artur Raviv. "The Theory of Capital Structure." *Journal of Finance* 46, no. 1 (March 1991): 297–355.

Hartford Courant. "Jackson in Beirut, Declares Support for Palestinian Cause." September 30, 1979, 11.

Hermann, Donald H. J., III. "Privacy, the Prospective Employee, and Employment Testing: The Need to Restrict Polygraph and Personality Testing." *Washington Law Review* 47, no. 1 (1971): 73–154.

Hezekiah b. Manoah, R. *Ḥizkuni*. Commentary on the Torah.

Hirsch, R. Samson Raphael. Commentary on the Pentateuch.

Hulse, Carl. "Lawmakers Vow to Fight Judges' Ruling on the Pledge." *New York Times*, June 27, 2002, A20.

Ibn Abi Zimra, R. David b. Solomon. *Yekar Tiferet* to *Mishneh Torah.*
Ibn Attar, R. Hayyim b. Moses. *Or ha-Ḥayyim.* Commentary on the Pentateuch.
Ibn Habib, R. Jacob b. Solomon. *Ein Yaakov.*
Ibn Paquda, R. Bahya b. Joseph. *Ḥovot ha-Levavot.*
Ishbilli, R. Yom Tov. *Ḥiddushei ha-Ritva.*
Israel Folktale Archives. "A Verbal Play in Donation Solicitation." Eastern Europe, IFA 2912. Haifa: University of Haifa.
———. "Gemara." Poland, IFA 13816. Haifa: University of Haifa.
———. "One Word." Poland, IFA 9447. Haifa: University of Haifa.
———. "Rabbi Meyer Amschel Rothschild and the Gemara." Poland, IFA 10961. Haifa: University of Haifa.
Isserles, R. Moses. *Rema* to *Shulḥan Arukh.*
———. *Torat ha-Olah.*
Ivashina, Victoria and David Scharfstein. "Loan Syndication and Credit Cycles." *American Economic Review: Papers and Proceedings of the One Hundred Twenty Second Annual Meeting of the American Economic Association* 100, no. 2 (May 2010): 57–61.
Jacob b. Asher, R. *Perush ha-Tur al ha-Torah le-Rav Yaakov ben Ha-Rosh.* Jerusalem: Feldheim, 2006.
Jewish Advocate. "Slaughter in Turkey Stuns Jewish World." September 11, 1986, 1, 17.
Kagan, R. Israel Meir ha-Kohen. *Likkutei Halakhot.*
———. *Sefer Ḥafetz Ḥayyim.*
———. *Sefer Shemirat ha-Lashon.*
———. *She'elot u-Teshuvot le-Ḥafetz Ḥayyim.*
Kamenetsky, R. Yaakov. *Emet le-Yaakov: Sefer Iyyunim ba-Mikra al ha-Torah.* 3rd ed. New York, 2007.
Kamm, Henry. "Terror in Istanbul: 2 Gunmen Kill 21 in Synagogue; Bar Doors and Then Open Fire at Sabbath Service in Istanbul." *New York Times,* September 7, 1986, A1.
Karelitz, R. Abraham Isaiah. *Ḥazon Ish.*
Kasher, R. Menachem Mendel. *Torah Shelemah.* Jerusalem: Beit Torah Shelemah, 1992.
Katz, R. Reuben Hoeshke b. Hoeshke. *Yalkut Re'uveni.*
Keller, Bill. "Surge in Spending on Space Weapons Sought by Reagan." *New York Times,* February 2, 1985, 1.1.
Kimhi, R. David. *Radak.* Commentary on the Prophets.
Kook, R. Abraham Isaac. *Ma'amarei ha-Re'iyah: Kovetz Ma'amarim me-et ha-Rav Avraham Yitzḥak ha-Kohen Kook.* Jerusalem: Keren Goldah Katz, 1988.
———. *Mishpat Kohen.* Jerusalem: Mossad HaRav Kook, 1993.

———. *Orot ha-Kodesh*. Edited by R. David Cohen, Part II, Vol. 3. Jerusalem: Aguddah le-Hotza'at Sifrei ha-Ra'iyah Kook, 1950.
———. *Shabbat ha-Aretz: Hilkhot Shevi'it*. Jerusalem: Mossad HaRav Kook, 1993.
Krohn, R. Paysach J. *The Maggid Speaks: Favorite Stories and Parables of Rabbi Shalom Schwadron Shlita, Maggid of Jerusalem*. New York: Mesorah, 1987.
Kurtz, Howard. "Koch May Be a Victim of His Brickbats." *Washington Post*, April 21, 1988, A17.
Labaton, Stephen. "2 New England Appellate Judges Are Finalists for High Court." *New York Times*, May 27, 1993, A1.
Lamm, R. Norman. *Faith and Doubt: Studies in Traditional Jewish Thought*. New York: Ktav, 1971.
———. *The Royal Reach: Discourses on the Jewish Tradition and the World Today*. New York: Feldheim, 1970.
Lane, Charles. "U.S. Court Votes to Bar Pledge of Allegiance: Use of 'God' Called Unconstitutional." *Washington Post*, June 27, 2002, A1.
Laniado, R. Samuel b. Abraham. *Keli Yakar*.
Leoni, Eliezer, ed. *Voloz'in: Sifrah shel ha-Ir ve-shel Yeshivat "Etz Ḥayyim."* Tel Aviv: Ha-Irgunim shel Benei Voloz'in, 1970.
Lessin, R. Jacob Moses ha-Kohen. *Ha-Ma'or she-ba-Torah: Siḥot, Be'urim ve-Iyyunim be-Divrei Ḥazal ha-Nog'im le-Inyanei Da'at Torah, ve-Derekh Eretz*. Vol. 3. Jerusalem: Hathiya, 1962.
Levine, R. Aaron. *Case Studies in Jewish Business Ethics*. Hoboken, NJ: Ktav, 2000.
———. *Economic Morality and Jewish Law*. New York: Oxford University Press, 2012.
———. *Economic Public Policy and Jewish Law*. Hoboken, NJ: Ktav, 1993.
———. *Economics and Jewish Law*. Hoboken, NJ: Ktav, 1987.
———. *Free Enterprise and Jewish: Aspects of Jewish Business Ethics*. New York: Ktav, 1980.
———. "*Onaa* and the Operation of the Modern Marketplace." *Jewish Law Annual* 14 (2003): 225–258.
Levine, R. Aharon. *Ha-Derash ve-ha-Iyyun*. Vol. 2. Biłgoraj: N. Kronenberg, 1931.
———. *She'elot u-Teshuvot Avnei Ḥefetz*. Munich: Vaad ha-Hatzalah, 1948.
Lipschutz, R. Israel b. Gedaliah. *Tiferet Yisrael*.
Lipstadt, Deborah E. *Denying the Holocaust: The Growing Assault on Truth and Memory. New York*: Free Press, 1993.
Loew b. Bezalel, R. Hayyim. *Iggeret ha-Tiyyul*. Lemberg: Lewin, 1864.
Loew b. Bezalel, R. Judah. *Derekh ha-Ḥayyim* to Mishnah, *Avot*.
———. *Gur Aryeh*.
Luntshits, R. Ephraim Solomon b. Aaron. *Keli Yakar*. Commentary on the Pentateuch.

Maimonides. *Mishneh Torah.*
———. *Perush ha-Mishnayot.*
———. *Sefer ha-Mitzvot.*
Malkiel, Burton G. *A Random Walk Down Wall Street: The Best Investment Advice for the New Century*. New York: W. W. Norton, 1999.
Mankiw, N. Gregory. *Principles of Economics*. 7th ed. Stamford, CT: Cengage Learning, 2014.
Marchant, R. Dovid. *Gateway to Shemittah: A Comprehensive and Practical Guide to the Halachos of Shemittah*. Rev. 3rd ed. Jerusalem: Feldheim, 2014.
Marineau, Robert J. and David P. Novello, eds. *The Clean Air Act Handbook*. 2nd ed. Chicago: American Bar Association, 2004.
McKenzie, Linda P. "The Pledge of Allegiance: One Nation Under God?" *Arizona Law Review* 46 (2004): 379–414.
Meir b. Barukh of Rothenburg, R. *Ta'amei Masoret ha-Mikra*. Reprinted in *Teshuvot, Pesakim u-Minhagim*. Edited by Isaac Z. Kahana. Vol. 1. Jerusalem: Mossad HaRav Kook, 1957.
Meir Simhah ha-Kohen of Dvinsk, R. *Meshekh Ḥokhmah.*
Mekhilta.
Melamed, M. Y. "Kosher Food Overpricing: The Problem, and $ome Solutions." *Kashrus Magazine*, March 1987, 20–21.
Midrash ha-Gadol.
Midrash Rabbah.
Midrash Shoḥer Tov.
Midrash Tanḥuma.
Mishnah. *Avot*; *Bava Batra*; *Bava Kamma*; *Bikkurim*; *Ediyot*; *Ḥagigah*; *Ḥallah*; *Kil'ayim*; *Ma'aser Sheni*; *Makkot*; *Middot*; *Nega'im*; *Pe'ah*; *Shabbat*; *Shekalim*; *Shevi'it*; *Sotah*; *Ta'anit*; *Terumot*; *Yadayim*; *Yoma*.
Mizrahi, David Toufic. "If Oil Isn't Important, Who in the Middle East Is?" *Washington Post*, November 3, 1985, C1.
Mizrahi, R. Elijah. *Sefer ha-Mizraḥi.*
Mordecai b. Hillel ha-Kohen, R. *Mordekhai.*
Morgensztern, R. Menahem Mendel. *Ohel Torah: Likkutei Amarot Tehorot*. Benei Berak: Slavita, 1959.
Morin, Richard. "Majority in Poll Says Tower Not Disqualified by Drinking." *Washington Post*, March 1, 1989, A11.
Moshav Zekenim al ha-Torah: Kovetz Peirushei Ba'alei ha-Tosafot. Jerusalem: Keren Hotza'at Sifrei Rabbanei Bavel, 1982.
Nahmanides. *Ramban*. Commentary on the Torah.
New York Times. "Jackson and Arafat Confer in Lebanon: Civil Rights Leader Later Suggests That He Serve as a Mediator between U.S. and P.L.O." September 30, 1979, 7.

———. "Reagan Proclaims He's in Good Shape: He Declares His Age or Health Will Not Become an Issue." March 31, 1984, 1.28.

Nix, Crystal. "Terror in Istanbul: Reaction from Far and Wide; Clerics and Leaders Condemn the Raid." *New York Times*, September 8, 1986, A8.

Norzi, R. Jedidah Solomon Raphael b. Abraham. *Minḥat Shai.*

Obadiah b. Abraham of Bertinoro, R. *Bartenura* to Mishnah.

Olsvanger, Immanuel. *Rosinkess mit Mandlen: Aus der Volksliteratur des Ostjuden; Schwänke, Erzählungen, Sprichtwörter, und Rätsel.* Transliterated Yiddish. Basel: Verlag, 1931.

Oratz, R. Ephraim. *And Nothing but the Truth: Insights, Stories, and Anecdotes of Rabbi Menachem Mendel of Kotzk.* New York: Judaica Press, 1990.

Oxford Dictionary of the Jewish Religion. Edited by Adele Berlin. 2nd ed. New York: Oxford University Press, 2011.

Palaggi, R. Hayyim. *Ammudei Ḥayyim.*

Papo, R. Eliezer. *Beit Tefillah.*

Pear, Robert. "Reagan Sends $1 Trillion Budget to Congress, and Battle Is Joined." *New York Times*, January 6, 1987, A1.

Perfet, R. Isaac b. Sheshet. *She'elot u-Teshuvot ha-Rivash.*

Philo. *The Special Laws.*

Pirkei de-Rabbi Eliezer.

Porter, Michael E. *Competitive Advantage of Nations.* New York: Free Press, 1990.

Purdum, Todd S. "Crime and Mayor's Anger; Dinkins Hopes Reasoned but Tough Stance Will Combat Fears about Rising Violence." *New York Times*, September 8, 1990, A1.

Rabinowitz, R. Zadok ha-Kohen. *Resisei Lailah.*

Reagan, Ronald. "Election Eve Address: 'A Vision for America.'" November 3, 1980.

Reinitz, R. Yaakov Koppel. *Shoham Yakar* to *Perush Ba'al ha-Turim al ha-Torah.* Jerusalem: Feldheim, 1996.

Rothermund, Dietmar. *The Global Impact of the Great Depression, 1929–1939.* London: Routledge, 1996.

Schachter, R. Hershel. *Nefesh ha-Rav.* Brooklyn, NY: Flatbush Beth Hamedrosh, 1994.

Schiff, Gary S. "The Politics of Fertility Policy in Israel." In Paul Ritterband, ed., *Modern Jewish Fertility*, 268–270. Leiden: Brill, 1981.

Schwab, R. Shimon. *Ma'ayan Beit ha-Sho'evah: Al Parshiyyot ha-Shavua ve-al Inyanin Shonim.* Brooklyn, NY: Mesorah, 1994.

Schwartz, Richard H. *Judaism and Vegetarianism.* Smithtown, NY: Exposition Press, 1982.

Seigel, Reginald. "Arab Nations Attack Israel." *UPI NewsTrack*, May 15, 1948.

Shabbetai b. Meir ha-Kohen, R. *Siftei Kohen* to *Shulhan Arukh.*

Shapira, R. Hayyim Meir Yehiel. *Tiferet Ḥayyim.* Warsaw: Kleiman, 1920.

Shapira, R. Nosson Nota. *Megaleh Amukot.*

Shaynfeld, R. Yehoshua. *Likkutei Yehoshua.* New York: Hadar, 1957.

Shimoff, R. Ephraim. *Rabbi Isaac Elchanan Spektor: Life and Letters*. Jerusalem: Sura Institute for Research. New York: Yeshiva University Press, 1959.

Shurkin, R. Michel. *Harerei Kedem*. Vol. 1. Jerusalem, 2000.

Sifrei to Numbers and Deuteronomy.

Sirkes, R. Joel. *Baḥ* to *Tur*.

Sofer, R. Abraham Samuel Benjamin. *Ketav Sofer*.

Sofer, R. Moses. *She'elot u-Teshuvot ha-Ḥatam Sofer*.

———. *Torat Mosheh*.

Solomon b. Isaac, R. *Rashi*. Commentary on the Torah and Talmud.

Soloveitchik, R. Aaron. "Israel's Day of Independence: Reflections in Halacha and Hashkafa." *Gesher: A Publication of Student Organization of Yeshiva Rabbi Isaac Elchanan Theological Seminary* 4, no. 1 (1966): 7–23.

Soloveitchik, R. Joseph B. *Ḥamesh Derashot*. Jerusalem: Makhon Tal Orot, 1974.

Soloveitchik, R. Yosef Dov. *Beit ha-Levi al Derush u-Milei de-Aggadata*. Jerusalem, 1985.

Sorotzkin, R. Zalman. *Oznayyim la-Torah*. Vol. 2. Jerusalem: Makhon ha-De'ah ve-ha-Dibbur, 2005.

Star-Ledger (Newark, NJ). "The Pledge Distraction." June 28, 2002, 22 (editorial).

Stern, Kenneth S. *Holocaust Denial*. New York: American Jewish Committee, 1993.

Strashun, R. Samuel b. Joseph. *Ḥiddushei ha-Rashash*.

Sussman, Barry. "By 3 to 2, Americans Disapprove of Reagan Plan for Social Security." *Washington Post*, May 16, 1981, A8.

Talmud (Babylonian). *Arakhin; Avodah Zarah; Bava Batra; Bava Kamma; Bava Metzia; Beitzah; Berakhot; Eruvin; Gittin; Ḥagigah; Ḥullin; Keritot; Ketubbot; Kiddushin; Megillah; Menaḥot; Nazir; Nedarim; Niddah; Pesaḥim; Rosh ha-Shanah; Sanhedrin; Shabbat; Shevuot; Sotah; Sukkah; Ta'anit; Tamid; Yevamot; Yoma; Zevaḥim.*

Talmud (Jerusalem). *Gittin; Ma'aser Sheni; Megillah; Sanhedrin.*

Targum Onkelos.

Targum Sheni to *Megillat Esther*.

Tikkunei Zohar.

Torat Ḥayyim: Ḥamishah Ḥumshei Torah. Edited by R. Mordecai Leib Katzenellenbogen. Jerusalem: Mossad HaRav Kook, 1993.

Torat Kohanim.

Tosafot. Commentary on Talmud. *Bava Batra; Bava Kamma; Bava Metzia; Eruvin; Gittin; Kiddushin; Makkot; Sanhedrin; Ta'anit.*

Tosefta. *Bava Kamma; Keritot; Pe'ah; Pesaḥim.*

Tykocinski, R. Yehiel Michel. *Sefer ha-Shemittah*. Pt. 2. Jerusalem: Mossad HaRav Kook, 2006.

van der Heide, Albert. "PARDES: Methodological Reflections on the Theory of the Four Senses." *Journal of Jewish Studies* 34 (1983): 147–159.

Vital, R. Hayyim b. Joseph. *Sha'ar Ru'aḥ ha-Kodesh*.

Wallfish, Asher. "Hillel Battling Shas over New 'Who's a Jew'-Type Bill." *Jerusalem Post,* March 6, 1986, 2.

———. "*Yeshivot Hesder* Head for Clash with Agency." *Jerusalem Post,* April 27, 1987, 2.

Weinraub, Bernard. "Gore Suspends Presidential Campaign: The Senator Says He Will Retain His Delegates." *New York Times,* April 22, 1988, A16.

Weisser, R. Meir Loeb b. Jehiel Michel. *Malbim.* Commentary on the Torah.

Weissman, R. Moshe. *The Midrash Says: The Book of Vayikra.* Brooklyn, NY: Benei Yaakov Publications, 1982.

Willowski, R. Jacob David. *Beit Ridvaz* (on R. Israel Shklov, *Pe'at ha-Shulḥan*).

Yalkut Shimoni.

Yashar, R. Mosheh Meir. *He-Ḥafetz Ḥayyim be-Netivot ha-Tefillah.* Jerusalem: Makhon Hatam Sofer, 1974.

———. *He-Ḥafetz Ḥayyim: Ḥayyav u-Po'alo.* Vol. 3. Tel Aviv: Netzah, 1961.

Zaretsky, David. *Mishlei he-Ḥafetz Ḥayyim.* 2nd ed. Tel Aviv: Abraham Ziyoni, 1958.

Zevin, R. Shlomo Yosef. *Le-Or ha-Halakhah: Ba'ayot u-Veirurim.* Jerusalem: Mossad HaRav Kook, 1946.

———. *La-Torah ve-la-Mo'adim.* Jerusalem, 2002.

Zohar.

Name Index

Aaron, 8, 17, 19–20, 33, 92n1, 130n17, 133n6, 154, 156, 161, 162, 165, 167, 169, 183, 189, 193, 196n2, 197, 198–200, 202
Aaron b. Joseph ha-Levi, R. (*Ra'ah*), 26n5, 37n7, 38n9, 57n20, 102n2, 103n8, 110n13, 128n9
Abbaye, 289
Abigail, 93n1
Abihu, 17, 19, 32–33, 162, 199n9
Abiram, 192
Abrabanel, R. Isaac b. Judah, 7n11, 143, 157n15
Abraham, 17, 24, 30, 55n6, 92n1, 187n4, 209, 272
Absalom, 12n11
Abtalyon, 280
Abulafia, R. Meir b. Todros ha-Levi (*Ramah*), 26n8, 71
Adam, 187n4
Ahab, 47–48
Ahai Gaon, R., 71n18, 119n6
Ahasuerus, 95
Ahijah the Shilonite, 92n1
Ahitophel, 12n11
Akiva, R., 97, 119–120
Alfasi, R. Isaac b. Jacob (*Rif*), 75n5, 244n2
Algazi, R. Nissim Solomon b. Abraham, 272n4
Al-Hakam, R. Joseph Hayyim b. Elijah (*Ben Ish Ḥai*), 170n13
Al-Nakawa, R. Israel b. Joseph ibn, 281n11
Alter, R. Yehudah Aryeh Leib (*Sefat Emet*), 19nn11–12, 152n12, 259
Alter, R. Yitzhak Meir (*Ḥiddushei ha-Rim*), 152
Altman, R. Shraga Tzvi, 209n9
Altschuler, R. Jehiel Hillel b. David (*Metzudat David*), 143n3
Aly, Götz, 102n4
Amalek, 204, 264–267
Amos, 92n1
Amotz, 92n1
Amram, 196n2

Name Index

Arafat, Yasser, 64
Ard, 112n22
Arukh ha-Shulhan. *See* Epstein, R. Jehiel Michal
Ashbel, 122n22
Asher b. Jehiel, R. (*Rosh*), 75n5, 119n7, 229n24, 230n24, 239n3, 244n2, 245n3
Assaf, 187n4
Azariah b. Oded, 92n1
Azulai, R. Hayyim Joseph David (*Hida*), 12n13, 110n14, 165n8

Baḥ. *See* Sirkes, R. Joel
Bahya b. Asher, R. (*Rabbeinu Beḥaye*), 7n11, 25
Balaam, 212–215
Bartenura. *See* Obadiah b. Abraham of Bertinoro, R.
Barukh, 92n1
Bass, R. Shabbetai b. Joseph (*Siftei Ḥakhamim*), 227n20
Batzri, R. Ezra, 75n6, 110n14
Beit ha-Levi. *See* Soloveitchik, R. Yosef Dov
Beit Yosef. *See* Caro, R. Joseph
Bekher, 112n22
Bela, 112n22
Ben Ish Ḥai. See Al-Hakam, R. Joseph Hayyim b. Elijah
ben Petura, 119
Benjamin, 12, 13n16, 111, 112n22, 205n14
Berdichever Rav. *See* Levi Yitzhak of Berdichev, R.
Berkowitz, David, 150n2
Berlin, Adele, 194n12
Berlin, R. Naphtali Tzvi Yehudah (*Netziv*)
  Emek ha-Netziv, 89n5
  Ha'amek Davar, 7n11, 19n14, 56n9, 208n2
  Ha'amek She'elah, 119n6
Besdin, R. Abraham R., 112n21
Birkei Yosef. *See* Azulai, R. Hayyim Joseph David
Bornsztain, R. Shmuel (*Shem mi-Shemuel*), 56, 161, 256, 257n5
Breyer, Stephen, 150
Broun, Kenneth S., 147n4
Busch, Andrew E., 10n1
Buursma, Bruce, 65n15

Caleb, 174–176, 178n1, 179–180, 183
Carmell, R. Aryeh, 280n6
Caro, R. Joseph
  Beit Yosef to *Tur*, 88n3
  Kesef Mishneh, 37n4
  Shulḥan Arukh, 12nn9–10, 26n8, 28n1, 45n11, 71n13, 71n16, 75nn5–6, 85n1, 86n6, 88nn3–4, 98n7, 108n2, 109n5, 110n14, 118n1, 119n7, 129n16, 148n9, 165n8, 177n10, 181n1, 215n9, 228n22, 239n3, 240, 244n2, 245nn3–5
Carroll, Douglas, 147n4
Carter, Jimmy, 267
Chesnoff, Richard Z., 102n4
Clairborne, William, 44n8
Clemens, Richard G., 85n2
Clinton, William J., 150
Cohen, R. David (*Rav ha-Nazir*), 58n22
Cohen, R. J. Simcha, 140n5
Colon b. Solomon Trabotto, R. Joseph (*Maharik*), 81, 82n2

Da'at Zekenim, 246n9
Danzig, R. Abraham
  Ḥayyei Adam, 71n16
  Ḥokhmat Adam, 109n5, 110n14
Dathan, 192
David, 12n11, 28, 30, 34, 90, 92n1, 154, 156, 187n4, 238n1, 256

Dean, Martin, 102n4
Deborah, 92n1
Delilah, 145
Denton, Herbert H., 10n2
Derekh ha-Ḥayyim. See Loew b. Bezalel, R. Judah
Dessler, R. Eliyahu Eliezer (*Mikhtav me-Eliyahu*), 280n6
Dewar, Helen, 126n3
Dinei Mamonot. See Batzri, R. Ezra
Dinkel, Yaakov Chaim, 114n3
Diskin, R. Moses Joshua Judah Leib (*Maharil Diskin*), 113n1
Doron, Abraham, 44n5
Draper, Theodore, 163n1
Dravkin, R. Tzvi, 286n3
Dushnitzer, R. Eliyahu ha-Kohen, 74

Edels, R. Samuel Eliezer b. Judah ha-Levi (*Maharsha*), 175n3, 214n6
Eder, Elizabeth, 209n6
Ehi, 112n22
Ein Yaakov. See ibn Habib, R. Jacob b. Solomon
Eldad, 168–169
Eleazar b. Aaron the Priest, 20, 92n1
Eleazar b. Harsom, R., 155n8
Eleazar b. Judah of Worms, R., 49n12, 239n2
Eleazar b. Pedat, R., 132
Eliezer, R., 285
Eliezer b. Dodavahu, 92n1
Eliezer b. Jacob, R., 33n5
Eliezer b. Samuel of Metz, R., 245n7
Elihu b. Berakhel the Buzite, 92n1
Elijah, 92n1, 271n3
Elijah b. Solomon Zalman, R. (Vilna Gaon or *Gra*), 93n1, 241n6
Elisha, 48–50, 92n1, 271n3
Elizaphan, 161, 162n9, 196n2
Elkanah, 92n1
Emek ha-Netziv. See Berlin, R. Naphtali Tzvi Yehudah
Emet le-Yaakov. See Kamenetsky, R. Yaakov
Enelow, Hillel G., 281n11
Englisher, Abraham, 247n10
Enoch Zundel b. Joseph, R. (*Etz Yosef*), 252n7
Ephraim Solomon b. Aaron of Luntshits, R. (*Keli Yakar*), 18n7, 60n5, 110n12, 155n7, 175n4, 193n10
Epstein, R. Baruch ha-Levi (*Torah Temimah*), 69n2
Epstein, R. Jehiel Michal (*Arukh ha-Shulḥan*), 26n8, 75n5, 85n1, 86n6, 88nn3–4, 98n7, 244nn1–2, 245n3
Esau, 112
Esther, 93n1
Etz Yosef. See Enoch Zundel b. Joseph, R.
Eybeschuetz, R. Jonathan, 272n4
Ezekiel b. Buzi, 92n1, 95
Ezra, 138–140

Farnsworth, Clyde H., 77n1
Farrakhan, Louis, 65
Feinstein, R. Mosheh, 26n6, 82, 111n19, 219
Fiedler, Edgar R., 23n14
Frankel, Ellen, 246n8
Frankl, Walter, 114n2
Friedman, R. Alexander Zusha, 49n12
Friedman, Milton, 88
Friedman, R. Shlomo, 210n9
Ford, Gerald, 23n14

Gad, 92n1
Gale, Anthony, 147n4

Gehazi, 50
Gelb, Leslie H., 10n3
Gellis, R. Yaakov, 49n10
Gera, 112n22
Gerondi, R. Nissim b. Reuben (*Ran*), 230n24
Gershom, 129, 133
Gog, 168
Goldfield, David R., 80n8
Goldman, John J., 62n3
Gombiner, R. Abraham Abele b. Hayyim ha-Levi (*Magen Avraham*), 215
Gostynski, R. Chaim Mosheh, 209n9
Gra. *See* Elijah b. Solomon Zalman, R.
Greenberg, R. Aharon Yaakov, 130n17
Greenberger, Robert S., 103n9
Grodzinski, R. Hayyim Ozer, 119n8
Gunzberg, R. Aryeh Leib b. Asher (*Sha'agat Aryeh*), 92n1
Gur Aryeh. *See* Loew b. Bezalel, R. Judah

Ha'amek Davar. *See* Berlin, R. Naphtali Tzvi Yehudah
Ha'amek She'elah. *See* Berlin, R. Naphtali Tzvi Yehudah
Habakkuk, 92n1
Ha-Derash ve-ha-Iyyun. *See* Levine, R. Aharon
Ḥafetz Ḥayyim. *See* Kagan, R. Israel Meir ha-Kohen
Haggai, 92n1
Halperin, R. Alter, 280n6
Ham, 289
Ha-Ma'or she-ba-Torah. *See* Lessin, R. Jacob Moses ha-Kohen
Ḥamesh Derashot. *See* Soloveitchik, R. Joseph B.
Hananel b. Hushi'el, R., 88n3, 149n13
Hanani the Seer, 93n1
Hannah, 93n1, 186
Harris, Milton, 85n2
Ḥatam Sofer. *See* Sofer, R. Moses
Hayyim of Volozhin, R., 247n10
Hayyei Adam. *See* Danzig, R. Abraham
Haziel the Levite, 92n1
Ḥazon Ish. *See* Karelitz, R. Abraham Isaiah
Hebron, 196n2
He-Ḥasid Yavetz. *See* Yavetz, R. Joseph b. Hayyim
Heiman, 187n4
Hermann, Donald H. J., III, 148n8
Hezekiah b. Manoah, R. (*Ḥizkuni*), 164
Ḥida. *See* Azulai, R. Hayyim Joseph David
Ḥiddushei Halakhot ve-Aggadot. See Edels, R. Samuel Eliezer b. Judah ha-Levi
Ḥiddushei ha-Rim. *See* Alter, R. Yitzhak Meir
Hillel, 73, 79, 156, 203n3, 280
Hirsch, R. Samson Raphael, 12n12, 17, 57, 152, 164, 169, 222n2, 261, 265
Hiyya b. R. Avya, R., 240n5
Ḥizkuni. *See* Hezekiah b. Manoah, R.
Ḥokhmat Adam. *See* Danzig, R. Abraham
Ḥomat Anakh. *See* Azulai, R. Hayyim Joseph David
Hosea, 92n1, 136
Ḥovot ha-Levavot. *See* Ibn Paquda, R. Bahya b. Joseph
Huldah, 93n1
Hulse, Carl, 218n2
Huppim, 112n22
Hur, 183

Ibn Abi Zimra, R. David b. Solomon (*Radbaz*), 12n8
Ibn Attar, R. Hayyim b. Moses (*Or ha-Ḥayyim*), 18n10, 135n2, 183

Ibn Habib, R. Jacob b. Solomon, 153n16
Ibn Paquda, R. Bahya b. Joseph, 89n7
Ido, 92n1
Iggeret ha-Tiyyul. *See* Loew b. Bezalel, R. Hayyim
Isaac, 24, 55n6, 92n1, 272–273
Isaac, R., 162n10
Isaiah, 92n1
Ishbili, R. Yom Tov (*Ritva*), 6n6, 39n13, 88n3
Ishmael b. Pavi, 155n8
Isserles, R. Moses (*Rema*), 12n9, 75n6, 81n1, 88n4, 114n4, 129n16, 221, 245n5
Ithamar, 20
Iturei Torah. *See* Greenberg, R. Aharon Yaakov
Ivashina, Victoria, 85n4
Izhor, 196n2

Jackson, Jesse, 62, 64–65
Jacob, 18, 24, 79n6, 86, 89n8, 92n1, 112nn22–23, 192, 205, 212, 252
Jacob b. Asher, R. (*Tur*), 26n8, 39n14, 71n15, 75n5, 85n1, 86n6, 88nn2–3, 98n7, 109n5, 109n7, 118n1, 119n7, 171n15, 181n1, 228n22, 244n2, 245n3
Japheth, 289
Jeremiah, 92n1
Jethro, 51
Joel, 92n1
Johanan the High Priest, 155n8
Jonah b. Amitai, 92n1
Joseph, 13n16, 86, 112, 161, 183, 205, 252, 275–276
Joseph, R., 258
Joshua, 92n1, 169, 174–176, 178n1, 183, 204–206
Joshua b. Levi, R., 229–230
Judah, 12, 157

Kagan, R. Israel Meir ha-Kohen (*Ḥafetz Ḥayyim*)
Mishnah Berurah, 239n3
Sefer Ḥafetz Ḥayyim, 55n5, 63nn6–10, 99n8
Kahana, Isaac Z., 193n9
Kamenetsky, R. Yaakov, 33
Kamm, Henry, 265n11
Karelitz, R. Abraham Isaiah (*Hazon Ish*), 26n6, 114n1, 119n9
Kasher, R. Menachem Mendel, 246n9
Katz, R. Reuben Hoeshke b. Hoeshke, 171n16
Katzenellenbogen, R. Mordecai Leib, 193n9
Keli Yakar (of R. Samuel b. Abraham Laniado). *See* Laniado, R. Samuel b. Abraham
Keli Yakar. *See* Ephraim Solomon b. Aaron of Luntshits, R.
Keller, Bill, 10n3
Kesef Mishneh. *See* Caro, R. Joseph
Ketav Sofer. *See* Sofer, R. Abraham Samuel Benjamin
Kimhi, R. David (*Radak*), 34n11, 180n3
Klepfish, R. Samuel Zanvil, 113n1
Koch, Edward, 62, 64–65
Kohath, 34, 129, 132–133, 196n2
Kook, R. Abraham Isaac, 58n22, 103, 114n1
Korach, 8, 167, 186–190, 191–192, 195–196, 198–199
Kotzker Rebbe. *See* Morgensztern, R. Menahem Mendel, of Kotzk
Kramer, Ralph M., 44n5
Krohn, R. Paysach J., 74n4, 134n8
Kurtz, Howard, 62n3

Labaton, Stephen, 150n1
Lady Potiphar, 86, 275

Lamm, R. Norman, 43n3, 148
Lane, Charles, 218n2
Laniado, R. Samuel b. Abraham, 50n15
Leoni, Eliezer, 247n10
Le-Or ha-Halakhah. *See* Zevin, R. Shlomo Yosef
Lessin, R. Jacob Moses ha-Kohen, 148n7
Levi, 196, 278, 279
Levi, R. Yaakov, 210n9
Levi Yitzhak of Berdichev, R. (*Berdichever Rav*), 281
Levine, R. Aaron, 26n9, 75n5, 86n7, 87n1, 111n17, 245n4, 280n8
Levine, R. Aharon (*Reisha Rav*), 210n11
Lipstadt, Deborah E., 104n11
Loew b. Bezalel, R. Hayyim, 246n9
Loew b. Bezalel, R. Judah (*Maharal*)
Derekh ha-Ḥayyim, 220n6
Gur Aryeh, 11n6, 12n12
Lutzker Rav. *See* Sorotzkin, R. Zalman

Ma'ayan Beit ha-Sho'evah. *See* Schwab, R. Shimon
Ma'ayanah shel Torah. *See* Friedman, R. Alexander Zusha
Magen Avraham. *See* Gombiner, R. Abraham Abele b. Hayyim ha-Levi
Magog, 168
Maharal. *See* Loew b. Bezalel, R. Judah
Maharam me-Rotenburg. *See* Meir b. Barukh of Rothenburg, R.
Maharik. *See* Colon b. Solomon Trabotto, R. Joseph
Maharil Diskin. *See* Diskin, R. Moses Joshua Judah Leib
Maharsha. *See* Edels, R. Samuel Eliezer b. Judah ha-Levi
Maharshal. *See* Luria, R. Solomon b. Jehiel
Mahseiyah, 92n1
Maimonides (*Rambam*)
Mishneh Torah, 11n6, 12n8, 37n4, 38n9, 39n14, 45nn11–13, 57n15, 57n20, 59n1, 60n2, 69n5, 71n13, 71n17, 75n5, 86n6, 93n2, 98n4, 109n5, 110n14, 110n16, 115n6, 116n9, 118n1, 127n6, 128, 129n16, 147n2, 148nn9–10, 149nn16–18, 152n11, 154n2, 160n1, 177n10, 181n1, 189n8, 227nn18–19, 228n22, 244n2, 245nn3–4, 257n7
Perush ha-Mishnayot, 109n8, 112n21, 164n2
Sefer ha-Mitzvot, 63n5, 69n5, 109n6
Malakhi, 92n1
Malbim. *See* Weisser, R. Meir Loeb b. Jehiel Michel
Malki Tzedek, 187n4
Malkiel, Burton G., 85n5
Mankiw, N. Gregory, 24n15
Marchant, R. Dovid, 114n1
Marineau, Robert J., 80n9
McKenzie, Linda P., 218n2
Medad, 168–169
Megaleh Amukot. *See* Shapira, R. Nosson Nota
Meir, R., 238
Meir b. Barukh of Rothenburg, R. (*Maharam me-Rotenburg*), 193n9
Meir Simhah ha-Kohen of Dvinsk, R. (*Or Same'aḥ* or *Meshekh Ḥokhmah*), 154n3
Melamed, M. Y., 26n7, 27n10
Menorat ha-Ma'or. *See* Al-Nakawa, R. Israel b. Joseph ibn
Merari, 129, 133
Meshekh Ḥokhmah. *See* Meir Simhah ha-Kohen of Dvinsk, R.
Metzudat David. *See* Altschuler, R. Jehiel Hillel b. David
Micah the Morashite, 92n1

Michal, 28, 34–35
Midrash Shoḥer Tov, 24n17, 55n4, 272n4
Midrash Tanḥuma, 169n11, 174n2, 205n15, 238n1, 266n14
Mikhahu b. Yimlah, 92n1
Mikhtav me-Eliyahu. *See* Dessler, R. Eliyahu Eliezer
Minḥat Shai. *See* Norzi, R. Jedidiah Solomon b. Abraham
Miriam, 93n1, 169, 175, 208–210
Mishael, 161, 162n9
Mishnah Berurah. *See* Kagan, R. Israel Meir ha-Kohen
Mishneh Torah. *See* Maimonides
Mizrahi, David Toufic, 209n6
Mizrahi, R. Elijah (*Re'em*), 11n6, 192n5
Mohilewer, R. Samuel, 113n1
Mordecai Bilshan, 92n1
Mordecai b. Hillel ha-Kohen, R. (*Mordekhai*), 88n3
Mordekhai. *See* Mordecai b. Hillel ha-Kohen, R.
Morgensztern, R. Menahem Mendel, of Kotzk, 37n1, 43n2, 189
Morin, Richard, 83n5
Moses, 8, 17–20, 21, 33, 92n1, 130n7, 133n6, 138, 139, 140, 161, 166, 167–171, 182–183, 187n4, 192, 195–196, 198, 199, 200, 202–204, 206, 234–236, 278–279
Muppim, 112n22

Naaman, 47–51
Naaman b. Benjamin, 112n22
Nadab, 17, 19, 32–33, 162, 199n9
Nahmanides (*Ramban*), 6n6, 12n12, 18n7, 18n10, 26, 30n8, 37, 56, 110n12, 116n8, 129, 132–133, 165n10, 169n8, 204n6, 205n11, 222n8, 235n1
Nahum, 92n1
Nathan, 92n1
Nebuchadnezzar, 229n24
Nefesh ha-Rav. *See* Schachter, R. Hershel
Nehemiah, R., 220n6
Neriah, 92n1
Netziv. *See* Berlin, R. Naphtali Tzvi Yehudah
Newman, Jon O., 150
Nix, Crystal, 267n17
Nixon, Richard, 23n14
Norzi, R. Jedidiah Solomon b. Abraham (*Minḥat Shai*), 171n16
Novello, David P., 80n9

Obadiah, 92n1
Obadiah b. Abraham of Bertinoro, R., 133
Obed-edom, 30
Oded the Prophet, 93n1
Olsvanger, Immanuel, 247n10
Onkelos, 71, 288n1
Or ha-Ḥayyim. *See* ibn Attar, R. Hayyim b. Moses
Or Same'aḥ. *See* Meir Simhah ha-Kohen of Dvinsk, R.
Oratz, R. Ephraim, 37n1
Oznayyim la-Torah. *See* Sorotzkin, R. Zalman

Palaggi, R. Hayyim, 153n16
Papo, R. Eliezer (*Pele Yo'etz*), 272n4
Pear, Robert, 11n3
Pele Yo'etz. *See* Papo, R. Eliezer
Perfet, R. Isaac b. Sheshet (*Rivash*), 71n18
Pharaoh, 95n11, 193n9, 209, 276
Pinhas, 92n1, 179–180
Pirkei de-Rabbi Eliezer, 71, 205n15
Porter, Michael E., 39n11

Potiphar, 86
Purdum, Todd S., 280n10

Ra'ah. *See* Aaron b. Joseph ha-Levi, R.
Rabbah, 259n17
Rabbeinu Beḥaye. *See* Bahya b. Asher, R.
Rabbeinu Ḥananel. *See* Hananel b. Hushi'el, R.
Rabinowitz, R. Zadok ha-Kohen, 187n6
Rachel, 112n22, 270n2
Radak. *See* Kimhi, R. David
Radbaz. *See* ibn Abi Zimra, R. David b. Solomon
Rahav, 179–180
Ramah. *See* Abulafia, R. Meir b. Todros ha-Levi
Rambam. *See* Maimonides
Ramban. *See* Nahmanides
Ran. *See* Gerondi, R. Nissim b. Reuben
Rashash. *See* Strashun, R. Samuel b. Joseph
Rashi. *See* Solomon b. Isaac, R.
Rav ha-Nazir. *See* Cohen, R. David
Raviv, Artur, 85n2
Reagan, Ronald, 146n1, 289
Re'em. *See* Mizrahi, R. Elijah
Reinitz, R. Yaakov Koppel, 193n9
Reisha Rav. *See* Levine, R. Aharon
Rema. *See* Isserles, R. Moses
Resisei Laylah. *See* Rabinowitz, R. Zadok ha-Kohen
Reuben, 183, 191
Ridvaz. *See* Willowski, R. Jacob David
Rif. *See* Alfasi, R. Isaac b. Jacob
Ritterband, Paul, 44n5
Ritva. *See* Ishbili, R. Yom Tov
Rivash. *See* Perfet, R. Isaac b. Sheshet
Roke'aḥ. *See* Eleazar b. Judah of Worms, R.
Rosh b. Benjamin, 112n22
Rosh. *See* Asher b. Jehiel, R.
Rothermund, Dietmar, 252n8
Rothschild, R. Mayer Amschel, 246–247

Salant, R. Samuel, 113n1
Samson, 142–145, 156
Samuel, 92n1
Samuel b. Nahman, R., 132
Sarah, 93n1
Schachter, R. Hershel, 170n13
Scharfstein, David, 85n4
Schiff, Gary S., 44n5
Schwab, R. Shimon, 198
Schwartz, Richard H., 37, 38n10
Sefat Emet. *See* Alter, R. Yehudah Aryeh Leib
Sefer Ḥafetz Hayyim. *See* Kagan, R. Israel Meir ha-Kohen
Sefer ha-Ḥinnukh. *See* Aaron b. Joseph ha-Levi, R.
Sefer ha-Mizraḥi. *See* Mizrahi, R. Elijah
Sefer Yere'im. *See* Eliezer b. Samuel of Metz, R.
Seigel, Reginald, 208n4
Sha'agat Aryeh. *See* Gunzberg, R. Aryeh Leib b. Asher
Shabbetai b. Meir ha-Kohen, R. (*Siftei Kohen* or *Shakh*), 88n3, 227n20
Shakh. *See* Shabbetai b. Meir ha-Kohen, R.
Shapira, R. Hayyim Meir Yehiel (*Sorof* of Moglenitz), 281n12
Shapira, R. Nosson Nota, 50n12, 171n16
Sharon, Ariel, 156
Shaynfeld, R. Yehoshua, 203n5
She'iltot de-Rav Ahai Gaon. *See* Ahai Gaon, R.
Shem mi-Shemuel. *See* Bornsztain, R. Shmuel

Shema Shelomoh. See Algazi, R. Nissim Solomon b. Abraham
Shemayah, 280
Shimoff, R. Ephraim, 113n1
Shimon b. Gamliel, R., 120
Shimon, R. *See* Shimon b. Gamliel, R.
Shiryah, 92n1
Shulḥan Arukh. See Caro, R. Joseph
Shurkin, R. Michel, 286n3
Siftei Ḥakhamim. See Bass, R. Shabbetai b. Joseph
Siftei Kohen. See Shabbetai b. Meir ha-Kohen, R.
Simeon, 205n14
Simeon the Righteous, 155n8
Sirkes, R. Joel (*Bah*), 88n3
Sofer, R. Abraham Samuel Benjamin (*Ketav Sofer*), 169, 194n12
Sofer, R. Moses (*Ḥatam Sofer*), 75n6, 111n18, 140n5, 199
Solomon, 92n1
Solomon b. Isaac, R. (*Rashi*)
  Deuteronomy, 22n6, 109n4, 129n14, 192n5, 205n11, 251nn2–4, 258n11, 260, 261n4, 262nn6–7, 266n14, 279n3
  Exodus, 6n6, 8n14, 31n12, 45n12, 95n13, 196n4, 204n9, 222nn4–6, 235n1, 236n6, 258n14
  Genesis, 18n6, 31n11, 154n2, 209n8, 252n6
  Kings, 48n4
  Leviticus, 11n5, 17n4, 20n16, 25n1, 223n15
  Numbers, 6n4, 127–128, 129n13, 131–132, 133n6, 155n7, 156n9, 167n1, 168nn2–3, 169nn6–7, 169n11, 174n2, 175n5, 176n7, 186n3, 188n7, 192n2, 192n5, 193n8, 195n1, 196n2, 199n9, 203, 204n7, 208n1, 210n12, 212n1, 227nn19–20, 228n21
  Psalms, 187n4
  Samuel, 7n12, 30n5, 34nn12–13
  Song of Songs, 56n8, 197n8
  Talmud, 7n10, 11n6, 21n2, 44n6, 71, 92n1, 139n3, 164n3, 204n10, 223n11, 238n1, 257n7, 258n11, 258n16, 273n7
Soloveichik, R. Ahron, 94
Soloveitchik, R. Joseph B., 30
Soloveitchik, R. Yosef Dov (*Beit ha-Levi*), 70
Sorof of Moglenitz. *See* Shapira, R. Hayyim Meir Yehiel
Sorotzkin, R. Zalman (*Lutzker Rav*), 246n9
Spektor, R. Isaac Elhanan, 113n1
Stern, Kenneth S., 104n11
Strashun, R. Samuel b. Joseph (*Rashash*), 99n8
Sussman, Barry, 126n3

Tarfon, R., 120n11
Targum Onkelos, 71, 288n1
Tiferet Ḥayyim. See Shapira, R. Hayyim Meir Yehiel
Torah Shelemah. See Kasher, R. Menachem Mendel
Torah Temimah. See Epstein, R. Baruch ha-Levi
Tosafot, 12n8, 45nn9–10, 93n5, 110n14, 119n7, 121n11, 135n1, 165n10, 230n24, 258n15, 259n17, 271n3
Trunk, R. Israel Joshua, of Kutno (*Yeshuot Malko*), 113n1
Tur. See Jacob b. Asher, R.
Turei Even. See Gunzberg, R. Aryeh Leib b. Asher

Tykocinski, R. Yehiel Michel, 114n1
Tzavvarei Shalal. *See* Azulai, R. Hayyim Joseph David

Uriah, 92n1
Uzzah, 29, 32, 34–35
Uzziel, 161, 196n2

van der Heide, Albert, 194n12
Vilna Gaon. *See* Elijah b. Solomon Zalman, R.

Wallace, George, 80
Wallfish, Asher, 44n7, 75n7
Weinraub, Bernard, 62n2
Weinstein, R. Yitzhak, 128n9
Weiss, R. Yitzhak Yeshayah, 128n9
Weisser, R. Meir Loeb b. Jehiel Michel (*Malbim*), 7n11, 34n15, 49n7, 144n12, 180n4
Weissman, R. Moshe, 49n10
Willowski, R. Jacob David (*Ridvaz*), 114n1

Yalkut Re'uveni. *See* Katz, R. Reuben Hoeshke b. Hoeshke
Yashar, R. Mosheh Meir, 140n5, 170n13
Yavetz, R. Joseph b. Hayyim (*He-Ḥasid Yavetz*), 43n3
Yedusun, 187n4
Yehoshafat, 47
Yehu b. Hanani, 92n1
Yeshuot Malko. *See* Trunk, R. Israel Joshua, of Kutno
Yishmael, R., 55n4, 86
Yose b. Zimra, R., 132n3
Yose ha-Gelili, R., 161n3

Zaks, Mordecai Judah Leib, 130n17
Zaretsky, David, 140n5
Zechariah, 92n1
Zedekiah b. Josiah, 229
Zephaniah, 92n1
Zevin, R. Shlomo Yosef, 114n1, 176, 177nn10–11
Zicherman, R. David, 128n9
Zohar, 18n11, 19n12, 220n8

Subject Index

Ahavat ḥinnam, 58
Akedah, 55n6, 272
American legal system, 84, 147
Anavah. *See* Humility
Anninut, 19
Ark, 28–30, 32, 34, 129, 131–132

Baseless hatred. See *sin'at ḥinnam*
Bein adam la-Makom, 69
Bein adam le-ḥavero, 9, 111
Berit milah, 257
Bikkurim, 153
Blessings
  Balaam, 212–216
  Grace after Meals, 241
  priestly, 17n2, 147
  R. Meir's dictum, 238–240
  on the Torah, 209n5
Breastplate of the High Priest, 6

Charity. See *Tzedakah*
Cherubim, 31
Coercion in Jewish law, 11n7, 12, 88
Covenant between the Parts, 17

Debtor, 12n8, 84–86

Eglah arufah, 250–252
Eivah, 111
Eldad and Medad, 168–169
Emunah, 145
Evil Inclination, 11, 220, 259n18
Exodus from Egypt, 37, 93, 95, 109, 111, 183, 205
Ezra's ordinances, 139

Fear of Heaven, 99, 133, 278–281, 288
Free will, 183
Friendship, 72, 74, 99–100, 109, 112, 163–164

Gog and Magog, 168
Gratitude. See *Hakkarat ha-tov*

Hakkarat ha-tov, 70, 79, 86, 89, 182
Hallel, 92–96, 197n9
Hashavat avedah, 257–258
High Priest, 5–9, 60–61, 64, 142, 154–157, 196n2
Ḥillul ha-Shem, 108, 111, 149, 203
Holocaust, 80, 95, 101–105, 266
Holy of Holies, 7, 12, 56, 189
Honor of the Torah, 32–35
Ḥukkim, 25
Humility, 50–51, 135, 136, 167–171, 236

Intermarriage, 111, 263
Iran-Contra Affair, 11, 163

Jewish destiny, 46, 168, 207, 208–209, 257, 271
Jewish education, 34, 206, 280n6, 285
Jewish identity, 137, 161, 222, 257, 262–263, 274
Jewish leadership, 33, 154, 198, 200, 203, 279
Jewish sovereignty, 28, 179
Jewish unity, 30, 190, 215, 262–263
Justice, 79, 203, 253

Kahane movement, 45
Kan tzippor. See *Shiluaḥ ha-ken*
Kashrut, 22–23, 26–27, 267
Ketoret, 8–9, 60, 64, 98, 197–199, 236
Kibbud av ve-em, 70–72, 86
Kiddush ha-Shem, 86
Kil'ayim, 260–262
Kofin principle, 11
Korach
  rebellion, 8, 167, 191–192, 195–196, 198–199
  sons of, 186–190
Korban pesaḥ. See Paschal offering
Korban tamid, 222
Kristallnacht, 102

Land of Israel, 28, 30, 95, 113–114, 165, 169, 175–176, 180, 182n5, 187, 203–205
Lashon ha-ra, 8, 54–56, 59–61, 64, 170, 183
Levites, 29, 43n4, 127–129, 131–134, 139, 164–165, 200, 223n11
Liberty Bell, 219–220
Lifnim mi-shurat ha-din, 79, 87–88
Lost objects. See *Hashavat avedah*
Love your fellow as yourself, 68, 73–76, 215

Manna, 37, 137, 175, 204
Marit ayin, 262
Marriage, 72
Mattan Torah, 97, 135, 138, 182–183, 222
Menorah, 7, 19n12
Messiah, 46, 96, 263
Middah ke-negged middah, 203
Miracles
  Exodus from Egypt, 37, 93, 95, 109, 111, 183, 205
  Splitting of the Sea of Reeds, 95n10, 179, 182, 183, 198, 205
  Staff of Aaron, 193, 197, 200
  Ten Plagues, 167, 182, 183
Mitzvot
  between man and God, 69
  between man and man, 9, 111
  hukkim, 25
Moral climate of society, 6, 9, 55, 59–61, 72, 200, 250, 275
Morning Prayer, 70n11, 179n2, 215, 281n13
Moses, 8, 21, 92n1, 130n17, 133n6, 138, 139, 140, 182–183, 187n4, 206
  Dathan and Abiram, 192
  Eldad and Medad, 168–169
  humility, 167–169
  Korah rebellion, 167, 195–196, 198, 199, 200
  leadership, 202–204

mishneh Torah, 278–279
Nadab and Abihu, 17, 33
Pesaḥ Sheni, 161, 166
prayer, 182
Tabernacle consecration, 18–20
Torah, receipt of, 234–236

Nadab and Abihu, 17, 32–33, 162, 199n9
Nazir, 143, 154–157

Ona'ah, 45, 111

Pardes, 193, 194n12
Paschal offering, 102n2, 160, 165, 221–222
Pesaḥ Sheni, 165
Pledge of Allegiance, 218–220
Polygraphs, 146–149
Prayer
afternoon (*Minhah*), 139
Anenu, 272
Hallel, 92–96, 197n9
Kaddish, 268, 288
morning (*Shaḥarit*), 70n11, 179n2, 215, 281n13
Shemoneh Esrei, 271
Prophecy, 17, 92–94, 167–169, 171

Redemption, 24, 182
Religious freedom, 82, 220, 274
Reproof, 179, 274–276, 278
Resurrection of the dead. See *Teḥiyyat ha-metim*
Retirement, 126–130, 131–134
Ribbit, 109

Sabbath, 39, 70, 85, 111, 114–115, 118, 139, 239, 256n1, 262n5
Sabbatical year. See *Shemittah*
Sacrificial offerings, 12n12, 164, 177
for error in judgment, 5–8
guilt offering, 151–152, 156
kofin principle, 11
Musaf, 102n2
paschal lamb, 102n2, 160, 165, 222
peace offering, 44n4, 176n8
Tabernacle dedication, 16n2, 19–20
temidim, 221–223
Sanhedrin, 6, 12, 93, 98n4, 120n11, 229n24
Secular professions, 275–276
Self-incrimination, 148
Separation of church and state, 218
Shaatnez, 262
Sheḥitah, 37
Shemittah, 113–116
Shiluaḥ ha-ken, 260n2, 261, 264–265, 267
Shirah, 94–96, 208
Sin of the Golden Calf, 181–183, 195, 235n1
Sin of the Spies, 181–183, 195
Sin'at ḥinnam, 58, 227, 229
Son of Sam Laws, 150
Song of the Sea of Reeds, 208
Song of the Well of Miriam, 208
Sotah, 147, 149
Splitting of the Sea of Reeds, 95n10, 179, 182, 183, 198, 205
Staff of Aaron, 193, 197, 200
State of Israel, 43, 44n7, 94–95, 137, 208
Symbolism
Altar, 12
Balaam's blessings, 213–214
charitable giving, 246
eglah arufah, 251
fig, 175
Menorah, 7
metzorah purification, 57
paschal lamb, 222
pomegranate, 175
robe of High Priest, 143
Staff of Aaron, 193
tzitzit, 262

Symbolism (*continued*)
  vineyard, 261–262
  water, 50n15

Tabernacle, 7, 16–19, 32–34, 128–129, 131, 171, 199n8, 221
Talmud Torah, 54–55, 222–223, 284–286, 289
Tefillah. *See* Prayer
Tefillin, 21n2, 257
Teḥiyyat ha-metim, 270, 271–272, 288–289
Temple, 43n4, 58, 59n1, 149, 221, 227, 262n5, 288
  consecrated property, 45n9, 45nn11–12
  destruction, 226–227, 270
  Levites, 127n7, 128, 133n6
  location, 12, 112
  Priests, 155, 189n8
  temidim, 222, 223n11
Ten Commandments, 196n4, 235
Ten Plagues, 167, 182, 183
Terrorism, 218, 265–266
Three Cardinal Sins, 54–55, 181n1, 226–227
Tithes, 43n4
Tzedakah, 11, 12n8, 75n6, 109, 110, 244–247
Tzitzit, 170, 260, 262

U.S. Supreme Court, 150–151, 153

Vegetarianism, 36–39
Vows, 226–230

Well of Miriam, 175, 208–210

Yom ha-Atzma'ut, 28–31, 92–96

The fonts used in this book are from the Arno family

Other Works by Rabbi Dr. Aaron Levine

Free Enterprise and Jewish Law: Aspects of Jewish Business Ethics (1980)

Economics and Jewish Law (1987)

Economic Public Policy and Jewish Law (1993)

Case Studies in Jewish Business Ethics (2000)

Moral Issues of the Marketplace in Jewish Law (2005)

The Oxford Handbook of Judaism and Economics (Editor) (2010)

Economic Morality and Jewish Law (2012)

Seasons of Nobility: Sermons on the Festivals (2019)

Maggid Books
The best of contemporary Jewish thought from
Koren Publishers Jerusalem Ltd.